To Pascale, Karl and Mathias

TABLE OF CONTENTS

ACKNOWLEDGEMENTS

Brett Stevens:
For the music, philosophy, discussions and counsel.

Dr A. Yazigy:
For the guidance, patience and generosity.

✝RADITIONALIS✝

FOREWORD

There is no doubt that humanity has been experiencing a major cultural shift since the period known as the Enlightenment, and whose effects can be clearly measured and observed today. The ruling political powers on the world stage are using all their resources for the purpose of controlling human behavior and also redefine what it means to be 'human'.

Some of the most basic notions (customs, family, sex, country, social ties, etc) are being 'deconstructed' in a bid to redefine what makes individuals who they are. Linguistic consensus is gradually being lost. Almost everything, every keyword is now politically charged in a way that gives it at least two meanings, depending on their user. For example, people on the left of the political spectrum view words like Nationalism and Populism in a way that is antipodal to what these same words mean, or stand for, to the opposite side. This linguistic and semantic divide mirrors a deeper chasm separating two entirely different worldviews differing on the means to solve the issues of the human condition, and their inexorable showdown.

This book is a collection of observations about the world in its current state and the author's personal insights on matters of Culture, Politics and Art. Those observations are mainly based on documented reality, but also on personal interpretation, because what are we if we have no ability to make our own opinion from personal experience? The following thoughts and insights focus on humanity's shift from a theocentric world (Man as part of a hierarchy), to an anthropocentric one (Humanism: The religion of Man).

This book is also about Lebanon, the author's country, a country whose political importance on the world stage is inversely proportional to its size.

Why tiny Lebanon?

Because Lebanon is a microcosm of events past present and future. It stands as an example of successes and failures, as an ongoing real-time thriller whose pages are still being written, keeping its worldwide audience on the edge of its seat: What is going to happen next, in this minuscule but strategic place? How will its people cheat death and annihilation yet again? Will they pull it off, this time?

Lebanon is a time capsule. Social experiments festering in the West happened in Lebanon and the Middle East first. Culture wars breaking out in the West, were already tried in Lebanon as well. Lebanon endures, despite everything, and not for the reasons that proponents of social engineering believe in.

-JH, November 2019

INTRODUCTION

We live in interesting times.

The ideas, concepts and common terms we used to know and universally agree on, are no more.We are witnessing an erosion of language and communication, and are losing consensus over the most basic things in the process. Some find it scary, and some welcome it with relish - the tearing down of the "old system"... Enter the "new system":

No identity.

No gender.

No parents.

No borders.

No race.

No nation.

No culture.

No heritage.

No God.

The 'beauty' of the "new system" is that words mean whatever one feels they mean, *in the now*; tomorrow, their meaning will change with one's mood

(and on Wikipedia), and the same goes for one's gender, race and identity[1]. We are 'free' from the

---

1   French health minister Agnès Buzyn: 'Un père peut etre une femme (a father can be a woman) - Youtube interview. - French president E. Macron: 'Votre problème, c'est que vous croyez qu'un père est forcément un mâle' (your problem is that you think a father must be a male)- Valeurs Actuelles article,

shackles of having 'fixed' concepts that invariably mean the same thing (what a boring concept, right?). We create meaning as we go. And the world better keep up!

Concepts like Diversity and Equality used to mean a diversity of races, ethnicities, cultures, systems of thought flourishing inside their own demarcated living space, and an equality of human dignity between different people under law. But now, Equality means women and men are completely interchangeable, ironically allowing transgender men to identify as females and win all olympic competitions reserved traditionally for women). Equality today means that an equal number of female CEOs needs to be enforced by law, not by competence, and that equally suitable quotas for black, latino and female astronauts have to be observed as well[2], but nevermind that no female or minority* quotas are being as aggressively pursued for 'ugly' jobs like infantry, plumbing or the sanitary sectors.

The equality quotas are strictly being pursued for positions with attached prestige. Anything else does not interest the Torquemadas of the Equality dogma.

Diversity, for example, is not about forcing Saudi Arabia, China, Indonesia or Israel to "integrate" floods of immigrants from different and often completely incompatible racial, ethnic or cultural backgrounds. It is actually only about flooding Europe and North America with the above mentioned migrants with a different cultural background, race and beliefs all while maintaining the usual trope of the non-existence of race, through media, academia and the "soft sciences" like anthropology, sociology and psychology, which happen to be gangrened with identity politics and political correctness zealots.

Those are but two terms from a long list of

29/01/2020.
2   See: 'Whitey on the Moon': Race, Politics, and the death of the U.S. Space Program, 1958 - 1972, by Paul Kersey

Minorities: Here, the term refers to black, latino and non-white people living in the West.

manipulated and twisted terminologies, a spit in the ocean of a vast and thorough operation to warp vocabulary and language beyond all recognition. If a communication breakdown happens, whoever caused it can control the directionless masses with considerable ease.

Who is doing this, is not the subject of this book.The question we care about, is Why: A society with a well defined culture, identity and lineage and whose constituents are sane people who are not confused about what bathroom they need to use[3], is a society that can make its own decisions.

And today's world is ruled by elites who do *not* want people to make their own decisions. These rulers are not kings nor emperors, nor even well known by name or face. They are corporations; anonymous entities with iconic brand logos. They appoint puppet governments, politicians, celebrity spokespersons and influencers who keep their profit margins up. These corporations don't want independent free people with independent minds because independent people are not predictable and thus, do not guarantee steady economic growth. They want a herd to *farm*. The Herd can be controlled through impulse, peer-pressure, panic or emotion. The only way to ensure steadily growing profit margins is predictability- a streamlining of corporate consumer base. Turning people into docile, but impulsive consumers, who do not think.

Zombies.

The zombie's Modus Operandi is very basic: See commercial of X product ---> "Consume.product.X".exe is launched ---> Consume X product. Repeat. No thinking involved, just impulse and raw appetite. Since zombies cannot think for themselves, a sprawling government is needed to cater to their every need as long as they can supply labor and give off heat obediently. Governments

3   Obama Decrees ALL Public Schools Must Allow Transgender Bathroom Use (Snopes.com - 2016)

are, therefore, inversely proportional sizewise, to the quality of the individual. The more mediocre an individual is, the more they tend to crave the safety net of Big Government due to their own inability to manage their own life. And Big Government is all-benevolent of course... It is here to help!

The enemy of this "new" system is not 'conservatives', nor 'communists' in checkered scarves meeting at Starbucks, flashing their iPhones and 'fighting evil capitalists' on their Apple laptops.

It's Traditionalism.

It is the system of those who think for themselves. Those who do not need the help of television, media and sex-tape celebrities to tell them how to run their life.

To Be A Traditionalist

Defining Traditionalism will require from most to shed all the preconceived abstractions which come with the aforementioned term. Visions of Amish-like people, living off the grid in wooden sheds, allergic to modern technology and closed off from the world, are to be banished. Traditionalism is not just "the past".

Traditionalism is not a stubborn donkey which refuses to budge. It is not allergy to the present nor fear of the future. To better understand Traditionalism as a concept, one should examine an old tree; its leaves will wither in the autumn, fall in winter and bloom again in spring. That tree will probably be alive long after its examiner is gone. And of course, let us keep in mind that this tree was alive for centuries; it came from a past where you and I, dear reader, did not exist. The old tree is the embodiment of the concept of traditionalism in its triune nature of being an earthly vessel for past, present and future. It is present in all three dimensions of time and is the living earthly organism that is closest to what a theocentric worldview would define as "the Eternal".

As traditionalists, our roots are our ancestors, their cumulative memory and that which they left for us to build upon. We are the present, and like our forefathers, we shall build a solid present for our children to inherit, and so on... Our past was our ancestors' present, our present is our ancestors' future and at the same time our own future will be our children's present. This solid link between the generations serves to transmit knowledge that morphs with each generation's input, but does so imperceptibly. We can only notice it if we take time leaps of several generations, or even several centuries.

The Amish community is not a valid example of traditionalist living, because it merely conserves what it inherited; Its knowledge remains the same. It is frozen in time, unchanging over generations, a moving still shot like those described in Harry Potter stories.

Traditionalists can of course, be someone who lives off the grid, in a wooden shed, but can all the same, choose to be surrounded by the latest high-tech and living the suburban life; either way, they are individuals who have extensive technological and survivalist knowledge, as well as **Curiosity**, a necessary ingredient for creativity-curiosity for the past and for what lies ahead.

This Curiosity makes the traditionalist thrilled by challenges which makes others afraid. While linked to their heritage/past, they are not mired into it, and their behavior is considered odd by their peers, who either live in the present, are stuck in the past or are living in a bubble of dreams about the future. To be a traditionalist, is to be in all three time dimensions at once, at all times. The closest thing to a tree, but minus the tree's lifespan, which means quick thinking and pragmatism are the highly prized qualities of the one who knows that time is irreplaceably and inexorably running out.

To be a traditionalist, is to always keep reality in focus and have constant awareness of one's own size within the cosmic hierarchy: We are born of Nature and Nature is born of something much bigger than our understanding. As beings who know how to use nature and its resources to our advantage, we are set high on the natural cosmic hierarchy, and are therefore, an easy prey to arrogance. We are not everything, on the contrary of what Leftism, Humanism, Liberalism and Rationalism claim. Humanity is not the center of the universe, but rather an important part of it, in the sense that it has great power, and with it comes great responsibility to avoid the destruction of its own habitat and consequently, itself. Man is weak, fallible, vulnerable, finite. By putting Man first, Leftist ideologies with great utopian visions are achieving the exact opposite of what they want. Crusading against poverty created more poverty (and more inequality). Fighting addiction created more of it. Fighting for a liberated world has created a society enslaved to economic 'growth'. Programs to liberate speech have created more censorship, and so on... And that is due to an ideology that measures the universe with an imperfect ruler: The human individual.

Traditionalists value time, and their enemies are set to rob them of that most precious commodity. The enemy's weapon is confusion and doubt. Confusion about identity, sexual preference, family values and historical background, redefining age-old concepts and countless more traps carefully camuflaged as 'philosophies' and 'schools of thought'.

By recognizing our size on the Cosmic scale, and reconnecting with our metaphysical nature (everything which falls outside the bounds of Rationalism, Materialism and the realm of the five senses), we will re-achieve and perhaps even exceed the great heights of the ancients.

Instead of erasing Poverty, welfare created more dependance because egalitarianism is inherently a race to the bottom. Co-founder of Move-On-Up.org Christopher Arps (left), says "The War on Poverty has arguably destroyed the black nuclear family,... Roughly 75 percent of black children were born to a married two-parent family when the 'war (on Poverty)' began in 1964. By 2008, the percentage of black babies born out of wedlock numbered over 72 percent" - *Source: 08 Jan 2014 LBJ's "War on Poverty" Hurt Black Americans (https://nationalcenter.org)*

TRADITIONALISM & TECHNOLOGY

Whenever we hear the word 'Traditionalism', we usually visualize a bunch of primitive people driving ox-pulled chariots, tilling the field and living in some modest cabin. This is the image cultivated by leftist mainstream media and academia alike, because the official narrative is to make tradition appear as backwards and obsolete (and therefore, useless) as possible. Mocking our elders in movies and sitcoms has become so mainstream that we don't notice it anymore; but let us take a minute and really think: Are our elders really as dumb as the media wants us to believe? Any historian with integrity would beg to differ.

Traditionalism is difficult for most people to depict because it's a crucible of complex cultural factors, which, when they come together, need a special type of cement to give us the fruit of any real tradition:

Continuity

It's thanks to continuity that individual car makers (for example) have grown to become household names and cultural icons. Without continuity, their vehicles would have remained at the stage of sketches or a one-off experiment. It is due to this continuity, that the early designs of vehicles were taken by like-minded engineers and designers, becoming an evolving phenomenon representating a specific people, how they think and see engineering and transportation. The Mercedes of today is the sum total of the unbroken continuities that took the original Benz/Daimler/Maybach vision, the seed of that vision, and nurtured it into the world class vehicle with a rich tradition behind it. Other examples from around the world abound, but the process is the same: Jewels of technology and innovation were started by an initial burst of creative energy, and that seed was subsequently nurtured by people who recognized its greatness and its cultural, economical, and political potential. These people saw the future, just like the first person who had the original seed-idea; they saw the immense cultural and national impact that would collectively benefit them as a nation and with their innovation gaining wider approval, came the necessary drive to grow. This initial vision, nurtured by its subsequent success, provided the drive necessary for the required continuity of the vision, turned national, then world symbol.

Billion dollar brands that have impacted our way of life in every practical way (in transportation, clothing, media, technology, warfare, food, medicine, etc...) are shining examples of traditionalism in theory and practice. They are the result of decades of building up on one original idea, discarding that which does not work, improving the good, slowly but surely, up till the latest evolution which we witness in the present.

Only a generations-long time leap through documented history can make us realize the magnitude of the slow evolution of a tradition (through any of its many cultural branches, be they technological, culinary or philosophical). Ordinary people need this documented history to appraise and 'see' the evolutionary leap. Visionaries like Da Vinci, Benz, Von Braun or the Wright brothers already could see the future while standing in their own present.

As a nation/culture/people grows and evolves, so does its technology. The technological fruit of generations of thought and genius, is not the product of the present, or what in our arrogance we call 'the modern times', but a cumulative result of past knowledge passed on through generations and through DNA. Forests do not sprout in an instant. As a nation stops its cultural growth by breaking with its traditions, it becomes a political entity kept alive by consuming/adopting another culture's output. Though its people are biologically alive, they are a stagnating political unit on life support because their own cultural output is null and therefore their collective memory is dead.

EQUALITY & INEQUALITY

I believe in Equality and I firmly strive towards it.

Why would a traditionalist, a staunch proponent of hierarchy, be in support of Equality!

It's actually very simple; I see what I consider to be an inspiring ideal, then I strive to follow their example, because wanting is only a small portion of the road. The measuring stick is inspiration, and excellence, not resentment. It makes us look "up", and reach "up", not to tear down those who are already up there. My concept of Equality is joining those who are "up there", not mob them and tear them down so that they, become 'equal' to me. In 1793, during the Reign of Terror, aristocrats were made "equal", by being summarily guillotined with their wives and children. The Equality of the Leftist seeks to tear down the strong and the successful, by fueling its own ranks with a sense of resentment and inferiority, then by spamming and overpowering the successful people with sheer numbers. the equality of the Leftist is a *negative* one.

It's weaponized jealousy.

Leftist equality is always assuming that successful people got their success through 'undemocratic' or 'unfair' ways. But what about those successful people who deserve their success? The Leftist believes those do not exist. Leftists' insanity goes further yet and they are seen calling for the abolition of inheritance, or hilariously enough, slap a 100% tax rate on it. This madness is not an imaginary scenario; it has been duly documented in the pages of The Guardian[1].

Every social justice crusade we have embarked on, for the last couple of centuries, has achieved the exact

---

1   'Why not fund the welfare state with a 100% inheritance tax?' - By Abi Wilkinson, The Guardian, July 2017.

opposite results of what was initially intended. Why, we ask, and rightly so. We had the best intentions at heart... Everyone knows that famous saying about the road to hell and good intentions. We're missing something crucial along the way. Mainly that now, the measure of all things is not a perfect, unchanging Good anymore, because we have killed that concept a long time ago and enthroned the individual in its place in our humanistic lust. The measure of all things is now us. But we are fallible, we are irrational, we are weak and imperfect. We are also Different. And because we are different and therefore have differing opinions and standards, we cannot be the measure of all things 'good'. No two human individuals are the same, not even identical twins. And so our wars to end famine, drugs, poverty and inequality, monitored through our 'own' moral prism, will achieve the opposite result everytime we wage them, because we've thrown the skipper and the compass overboard.

Why is it, that in our war to 'end inequality', we find that the most 'equal' socio-economic strata -the middle class- is being thoroughly erased and faces the imminent risk of disappearance? This specific strata is traditionally the backbone of national and social stability and the largest tax-paying category, without which, the economical and financial health of the nation quickly deteriorates. But wait, it's not just a money issue; the middle class is a cultural repository of society, providing a well learned, well behaved and well educated crop of future leaders, managers, teachers, business owners and entrepreneurs; people who understood the hardships of their parents and the responsibilities lying ahead of them. And yet, it is that particular economic/cultural/political slice of society which is suffering the most from the War to End Inequality and its dumb sibling, the War on Poverty.

Some people have discovered a way to make a living in our endtimes society; they call themselves activists and their job is to make a loud noise about some group being a victim and another being the oppressor. Usually they declare 'war' on abstract and/or ambiguous concepts like 'inequality', 'terrorism', 'drugs', or 'poverty'. It's part of the game never to clearly define those terms so that funds keep getting raised in the name of a 'feel-good'-sounding cause, which is severely lacking in details and that no one bothers to measure because more and more 'activists' are joining the game and don't want anyone to discover their scam. Their 'activism' is so deeply ingrained in our collective psyche, that exposing an NGO who 'raises awareness' about say, breast cancer or domestic violence or also animal rights, is viewed as a declaration of war *against the cause* these NGOs supposedly represent: The 'attacker', becomes a hater of women, a lover of domestic violence, a proponent of poverty, etc. They become a social pariah if they expose anybody profiting from the actual misery of other people.

In the end, everything good becomes ultimately perverted, and so, noble causes become money-making games in which every scoundrel who knows how to trick the system, ultimately joins the fun, bringing the actual cause down, decredibilizing the very few, actually honest people who are genuinely working for that cause, and finally achieving the opposite of the intended target. Instead of one moral compass, we now have a multitude.

The Equality of the traditionalist strives upwards and seeks to emulate that which inspires by its success, strength, talent and excellence. It's fueled by inspiration. It is *positive* Equality. This Equality is sadly less popular than Leftist equality because it requires constant work, self-improvement and *will*. It requires standards and, most of all, realism. But when "journalists" tell women that they can be 'healthy and beautiful at every size' and that toy makers should make a plain Barbie so as not to trigger plain-looking girls, we see a small example of the no-standards culture of the liberal left, on feminism. Another example is school curricula devoid of grades so that no pupil feels 'inferior' to the other. Everybody *feels* like a winner and mere presence wins you a trophy. This kind of negative equality seeks to punish the outstanding and cuddle the mediocre. And that "race to the bottom" kind of Equality is not the one we should be pursuing.

FEAR OF INEQUALITY
IS HUMANITY CHASING ITS OWN TAIL

-Edited by Brett Stevens for www.amerika.org-

"The system is unequal," One keeps hearing. Everybody needs a fair chance. And I agree. Everybody needs the chance to prove themselves. Every person must have access to the basic social, cultural and economic footholds needed to make it in society today. This is a non-debatable issue that most systems agree upon. Children deserve to live their childhood, get a solid education and be culturally enabled to take on the world by the time they graduate. This is the starting point that exists everywhere, and where all people kick off from zero, from equal standing. So what seems to be the real demand of the equality jihadist?

What the equality jihadist fails to tell us is that they also want equality *of outcomes*. What if, by some foul nasty trick, someone again gets ahead of the rest? What if by some cheat code, inequality rears up its ugly head again and be a cause of injustice and misery for humanity? We hear a lot about equality and fairness but this is all a scrambling tactic hiding the real motive behind the calling for equality: The obliteration of any end results beyond the generic and the mediocre- the removal of all standards.

Leftist activists confuse their readership and the public at large by creating the narrative that they want equality of chances — a noble ideal — for people starting up in life, so that they are able to succeed. Such an impassioned demand is guaranteed to captivate all audiences. The equality jihadist wins the attention of the public. People are entranced by so much altruism and nobility of the heart. Leftists are Jedis of posturing and they manage to cling to the proverbial high ground from which they now dispense their moralizing and virtue signaling. They then claim that only *they* want equality of chances and that other political opponents are sadists. Massive applause ensues.

But as soon as they get to develop their idea, those who are not yet fully entranced by the equality jihadist start replaying their own life. They clearly remember that back in class, there were the poor and the rich students, bright and mediocre ones, lazy and studious ones, and smart and slow ones. Sometimes, there were poorer students who did better in class than richer ones, and vice versa. In sports class, there were those who made it to the school football team, those who climbed a rope in seconds, those who had superior muscular strength, and those who collapsed after running thirty meters. There were those who were gifted in painting, or handy in bushcraft and making campfires. There were those who were the most at ease in the chemistry lab and awed the rest of the class with their chemical mixes. They remember their own childhood and how each one of them had different preferences and ability for different activities, hobbies, food, music or clothing.

Clearly each of those children and each of those siblings had their equal chance to start, and each used their time differently and in varying degrees of efficiency and outcome… creating a colorful diversity. It is that same diversity which the equality jihadist is now calling "inequality" because they have translated this diversity into economic values, which are the only criteria that matter to them!

People start to wake up and realize what the Leftists are saying. They realize they are trying to make not all opportunities uniform — because they already are! — but all ends too. Horror replaces trance as the true intentions of the equality jihadist start taking shape, but it is probably too late because everybody already cast their vote for the equality jihadist. The equality jihadist is in fact, frothing at the fact of seeing some people earning more and achieving higher social and economic success than others. Such getting ahead is deemed unfair by this false priest of equality and so, many of *their own* supporters are brought under the blade for failing to be 'equal'. Could 'Animal Farm' be a documentary?

Equality is an attractive concept, because in our times, it has become loaded with notions of fairness and nobody getting left behind. This is what makes it popular to the masses and by consequence, to the voters, regardless of how distinguished their diplomas are. It only shows its actual meaning once the voting and partying daze are over and reality knocks on the door.Let us consider the reality of inequality, which is that not only is it inherent, but that we benefit from it as revealed in a short parable:

"For the kingdom of heaven is like a man traveling to a far country, who called his own servants and delivered his goods to them. And to one he gave five talents, to another two, and to another one, to each according to his own ability; and immediately he went on a journey. Then he who had received the five talents went and traded with them, and made another five talents. And likewise he who had received two gained two more also. But he who had received one went and dug in the ground, and hid his lord's money. After a long time the lord of those servants came and settled accounts with them.

He who had received five talents came and brought five other talents, saying, "Lord, you delivered to me five talents; look, I have gained five more talents besides them." His lord said to him, "Well done, good and faithful servant; you were faithful over a few things, I will make you ruler over many things. Enter into the joy of your lord." He also who had received two talents came and said," Lord, you delivered to me two talents; look, I have gained two more talents besides them."

His lord said to him, "Well done, good and faithful servant; you have been faithful over a few things, I will make you ruler over many things. Enter into the joy of your lord.'Then he who had received the one talent came and said, "Lord, I knew you to be a hard man, reaping where you have not sown, and gathering where you have not scattered seed. And I was afraid, and went and hid your talent in the ground. Look, there you have what is yours." But his lord answered and said to him, "You wicked and lazy servant, you knew that I reap where I have not sown, and gather where I have not scattered seed. So you ought to have deposited my money with the bankers, and at my coming I would have received back my own with interest. Therefore take the talent from him, and give it to him who has ten talents.

For to everyone who has, more will be given, and he will have abundance; but from him who does not have, even what he has will be taken away. And cast the unprofitable servant into the outer darkness. There will be weeping and gnashing of teeth."

-Matthew 25:14-30, the New Testament.

The equality jihadist is here not to help one have a better life, but to rob them of choices, of dreams, of aspirations. In an equal world, where all outcomes are state-managed to remain equal, the equality jihadists suffer no complaint from those who voted for their program. A complaint means someone is an obstacle to the equality Utopia. The equality jihadist finds your lack of faith disturbing...

THE 'Z' AXIS

The Left and its liberal thought paradigm have won the culture war, and contrary to the prevailing mainstream thought, there is no more such a thing as "The Right". Only fifty shades of Leftism. The Left/Right 'debates' seen on the news are a diversion. There are actually two leftist adversaries (one slightly more or less leftist than the other) playing with each other for viewers' entertainment. That is why the liberal paradigm has now entered a neurotic phase, not unlike the years that followed the 1789 French Revolution. We're now in the ideological reign of terror; the enemy (Aristocracy and with it, the true right) has been guillotined, and now the victor is turning on its own, and it is seeing enemies everywhere. Liberalism, having defeated its opponent, is in the process of eating itself. Already more and more people are beginning to see the tyrannical behavior of the "party of tolerance"; it suffers not even its adherents to deviate one iota from the Sacred Liberal Dogma. It's an age of absolute politics where total and utter humiliation and annihilation await the defeated side (and those who don't condemn it hard enough), as Francis Parker Yockey announced in his prescient work 'Imperium'[2].

How do we fight an idea? Well, with another idea of course, says Roman Tribune Missala in the movie Ben Hur (The 1959 original, not the effeminate remake). And this 'other idea', does not even have to be 'new'; Traditionalism eschews the tired and failed paradigm of the Left/Right dichotomy and its frivolous palette of two-dimensional issues proper to each side: Gun control/Gun rights, Free Speech, Pro-Life*, Pro-Choice*, Environmentalism, Fossil Fuels, Sexual Liberation, Multiculturalism, Open Borders, etc...

Conservatism failed to understand eternal truths in their essense and dwelled on their outer husk,

---

2   "Imperium", F.P. Yockey (Iron Sky Edition) p. 749-60.
Pro-life/Pro-choice: In the West, defining people who are anti-abortion and pro-abortion, respectively.

Pharisee-style, without understanding anymore how to make them evolve, and leftism thoroughly bombed every bridge linking it to the past, condemning itself to repeat avoidable mistakes.

Traditionalism is at both ends of the spectrum; firmly anchored in, and aware of the present, but reaching towards both past and future, towards left and right, seeing through the filter of hard reality and the causality laws which govern the universe. Its movement is tranquil, thoughtful, and strong, like Tolkien's mighty and ageless Ents. It takes what works and throws away that which is flawed, then perfects what works and improves it further. It is not afraid of ancient tradition, remembering it well, and at the same time it embraces the future with equal interest. Its curiosity has no ideological bounds. It realises that reason is but one of the many keys to decipher the world and is one of many tools available to the human intellect.

Traditionalism is not afraid nor distrustful of religious sentiment, the metaphysical realm and what liberalism calls "irrational". Traditionalism embraces the world and reality in all their dimensions; it recognizes hierarchy and the fact that humanity outside nature is bound to die. It sees through the sterile, boring, utilitarian and materialistic discourse of modernity and reminds us of the power of mythology (metaphorical and motivational) and its capacity to give us wings and to strive *upwards*.

Traditionalism nourishes the spirit, whereas modernity has forsaken it, not recognizing its existence, too busy focusing on the material and the "scientifically measurable". Modernity, the neurotic daughter of Liberalism, has left a terrible trail of misery in its wake. It left a world devoid of spirit, song, humor, and purpose. It focused strictly on what the five senses could feel and made the individual the center of the universe. By enshrining the individual above all else, it achieved the opposite, and ended up enslaving that individual in the service of an economical and industrial beast, dedicated to an impossible target; continuous material growth within a finite world.

Traditionalism puts back the individual in its place in the cosmic hierarchy, as part of a greater whole, which must be preserved and respected.

Clear reality, free from the shackles of political baggage and outdated social/economical imperatives[3], is the only requisite to a traditionalist mindset, the mindset that will replace the dead Liberal/leftist view, ushering the paradigm of the Eternal and an age of new beginnings.

---

3   "Nous voulons défendre une civilisation et non un marché !" (we want to defend a civilization, not markets)- Marion-Maréchal Le Pen

A New Kind of Warfare

'One who despises himself is nearest to a proud man'-Spinoza

We have been conditioned by history books, literature, the media, and all kinds of social interaction to view War as a military endeavor. At the mention of the term, the mental image that forms in our minds is that of a pitched battle between two well defined opponents. War has changed a lot since two enemy armies met on a field and tested the strategic and tactical abilities of their respective generals and soldiers. Today, wars are rarely military and more about deterrence through technology. This deterrence is made more effective when coupled with economic sanctions and media disinformation and propaganda.

But there is another more interesting kind of war unfolding today, namely in the West: It is a war of open immigration and open borders. A pure trojan horse re-en-actment, but with a twist: Those bringing the wooden horse inside, are the sold-out and cowardly collaborators already within the gates. These collaborators in the highest political, academic, religious and media spheres are playing the long game, shaping the collective western mind, relaxing border laws, revising history and culture, and preparing the west for an unstoppable 'camp of the saints' influx of foreigners that would secure a permanent foreign-backed voting base to secure the definitive and final upending of western Christian culture. No military and no economic means would have been used here. Nothing that would suggest any kind of hostility, except a long, patient eroding of social, cultural and historical tenets of the west from the inside. What makes this warfare interesting is that it is not being deployed anywhere other than in the western world (Europe and North America).

Those who would recognize this assault being waged are already being shut down with accusations of xenophobia, hate speech, job firings, social media de-platforming, and online demonetization; ostracized from society and branded as pariahs.

No one resists such a punishment for long without a comfortable financial situation and redemption is not possible for the pariah. The only satisfying outcome is the physical death of the offender (usually self-inflicted in desperation due to all doors being shut in front of them).

War is on several fronts; its targets are the traditional family, cultural, racial and sexual identity, human ability for critical thinking, and the human soul itself. One would think the targets are nations with borders, the concept of nationalism and patriotism. They are as well, but what are nations without their people? Nations and borders are strong when the people who believe in them are strong.

The weapons of this warfare are historical/cultural revisionism, Modernity as a past-negating ideology, time-wasting technological gizmos as social media that nurture individual narcissism, as well as rampant consumerism.

Finally, laws[1] are put in place to silence the dissent of anyone who still manages to keep their wits through the tsunami of consumeristic pleasures unleashed upon their society.

'Hate-speech' laws, a fancy term used to silence dissenting opinions, like the Avia law in France, have effectively enshrined a totalitarian system into countries previously known for their freedoms and civil liberties. A "Brave New World" and "1984" mash-up.

---

1   "Memes 'will be banned' under new EU copyright law, warn campaigners" - www.news.sky.com, 2018 (imagine banning internet memes!)

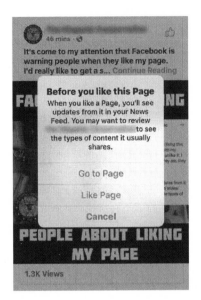

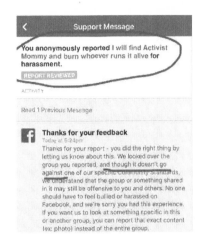

Facebook would like to warn you, an adult, of what to read and what not to read, so it gives you a 'warning' on some pages you might want to access. We dont want you to commit WrongThink, comrade. It's for your own good.

'Activist Mommy' & blogger Elizabeth Johnston found her facebook account suspended for three years after she has cited the Bible on Homosexuality (www.sermonaudio.com)but a facebook group which stated its intent to 'find and burn the Activist Mommy alive' was found to 'meet facebook community standards' when attempts to report it were made (https://true-pundit.com).

THE LIBERAL LEXICON
DIVERSITY AND OTHER STORIES

Conservatism is dead so that traditionalism resurrects. After its resounding cultural win over conservatism, Liberalism/Leftism devised an intricate vocabulary of positive-sounding terms in a covert bid to keep control of its own narrative, with a carefully designed, but heavily distortable lexicon. Everything now has a double meaning and will have its signification distorted to the Left's needs. The terms are either brand new for the purpose of disinformation, or older ones whose meaning has been warped.

The following list is by no means exhaustive. Here are some terms and concepts that immediately betray their liberal nature.

Populism

In the ruling democratic paradigm, any democratic result that clashes with the will of the chief decision-makers of the world is decried as 'populism'. The masses will be made sure to view that term as negatively as possible while reading their daily news. The term used to mean the political power derived from popular leaders. But today, this same term has been perverted in such a way as to induce feelings of nausea and disgust among the public, so that their knee-jerk reaction is summarized by 'populism=bad', in sheer zombie-like fashion.

Creative Destruction

Sourced from Marxist theory, this concept is chiefly applied to economics, but more and more so, in architecture. Budding modern 'urbanists' who really want to please the developers hiring them, have the perfect excuse: Let's tabula raza that Roman hippodrome or this intricate network of heated public baths because really, who uses clay to heat their water anymore? Modern arrogance applied to architecture is why most of today's 'architecture' is bleak, uninspiring and depressive, not to mention energy-hungry and with an extremely high maintenance cost. It's all filed under "creative destruction", though, causing humanity to lose precious knowledge of ancient architecture, building know-how and vernacular thought-process, solely due to arrogance and enslavement of architects-for-hire, to building deadlines.

What the 'creative destruction' advocates fail to notice is that what they label as creative destruction, is an unforseeable phenomenon in which an established idea gets organically replaced by a newer, more practical idea, like mail being replaced by e-mail, telephone replacing the telegram, or The Telex and fax going extinct with the advent of the Internet. Consider the cherished tradition (at least in my home country Lebanon) of participating in "rally-papers", a few decades ago, before high-speed internet; people relied on knowledge they amassed from reading books, and the photographic memory and research prowess of the few, to help their team win by answering tough cultural questions delivered to motorized youngsters at specific points and areas. With Google, anyone with a smartphone could answer nowadays any rally-paper challenge and so the rally-paper tradition died out. Digital cameras killed the 35mm film industry the same way- not in a conscious way, not on purpose.

Creative destruction is how online courses and free tutorials have made expensive universities obsolete. It's how automation has wiped out many jobs which traditionally required human manpower. On the other hand, The Creative Destruction advocates see historical treasures, and they *intentionally* want to turn them into rubble, and **that** is different. They call their vandal urge "creative destruction" but we all know what it really is. It's resentment and jealousy, and an inability to understand, learn from and improve on the past let alone emulate it, so they want it "creatively dismantled" and replaced by generic energy-hungry cubicles where people get by with daily doses of Prozac... Modern bridges are falling after barely decades of service, while Roman ones still stand. Many modernist architects are aware of that and this literally sickens them. These vestiges of Antiquity remind them of a knowledge they still lack, and that the ancients mastered a wisdom and a know-how we may never reach again, and this fuels their hatred towards the past even more...

Progress

Anything which adheres to the world-thought of the last three centuries -known as The Enlightenment- is categorized by the current mainstream, as 'Progress'. This implies that Anything Else, is *not* progress. This effectively forces the masses to stay indoctrinated and to actually make sure, mainly through peer-pressure, that the pro-gressist status quo is maintained. The Idea of calling one's own time period "Enlightenment" arrogantly implies that anything outside that time bracket was Un-enlightened, and actually leading quite the barbaric and backwards existence. Such a claim is amply disproven by historical evidence; our ancestors were smarter, wiser and consid-erably humbler. They actually never called themselves 'modern', 'enlightened' or 'avant-garde'. We are the only cultural time-bracket to flatter itself with such vain pomp-ousness. The excessive self-referencial and self-flattering mentality of the "Enlightenment/post-Enlightenment" par-adigm should be the chief evidence of its own intellectual and cultural inferiority. This also explains why The people of this paradigm have such disdain for preserving or studying any vestige of culture that predates them.

Cultural Appropriation

A recent contraption of the fertile liberal mind, the cultural appropriation fad, is the latest trend on hip and overpriced university campuses. Bands of liberal Grand Inquisitors chase anyone -actually only white people- wearing, displaying or enjoying a cultural aspect that is not 'theirs': White guy wearing a sombrero, White girl with dreadlocks, Young white guy listening to Rap music, another white guy eating a taco, some white guy with a man-bun, etc... The circus gets really hilarious with 'oppressed' minorities waging war on those white "cultural-appropriators" while using things like smartphones, the internet, cameras, printers, fridges, microwaves, cars, airplanes, modern medicine, television, radio, air-conditioning, or some other European-made invention that makes their daily existence more bearable and longer-lasting. Cultural Appropriation is just another proof of how cheerless, boring and close-minded the Liberal Left Cancel Culture actually is.

Microaggression

In the fascinating times we're in, new additions to language are being made daily – Mansplaining, Stare-rape, Trigger warning, Manspreading, Slut-shaming or also Microaggression are, recent vocabulary entries the modern man must get acquainted with. Let's say you are in an auditorium and in your introduction, you say 'ladies and gents'. Congratulations, you have committed a microaggression by omitting non-binary kin, transsexuals, minorities and people with disabilities. On the other hand, a gay pride parading with naked men on leashes in front of your kids, is NOT a microaggression. And it should be encouraged, because, you know, tolerance, or whatever.

source: sherdog forum

source: sherdog forum

500 Mom Stronger

Jakub Baryla, a 15-year-old Catholic boy in Poland, commits a major microaggression by standing with a large crucifix and rosary to block an LGBT Pride march, August 12 2019 - Source: www.churchmilitant.com

Body Positive

The 80/90s aren't so far back, and for all their craziness and excesses, they were a healthier time when People used to hang posters of chiselled men and women and exercise like mad, in an attempt to look like their idols. There was also that thing called 'Consensus', where people in general agreed that fit was beautiful. Not so anymore[1], because today, fit is whatever you feel it is, even when you look more like a beached whale than an actual human being. This is the "Body-Positive" mindset, comrade. Third-wave feminism brings you the good news: You are healthy at every size[2], so time to change those

[1]   "Are you beach body ready? Controversial weight loss ad sparks varied reactions", by Rose Hackman - The Guardian, 2015

[2]   See the 2019 Calvin klein campaign "I speak my truth in my Calvins" (such campaigns are being described as 'woke' a term used by anti-globalists to deride politically correct companies).

'unrealistic' beauty and fitness pageant rules and include cetacean beauty criteria because fitness is non-inclusive (more on that exciting new term later) and therefore, oppressive.

Affirmative Action

In a world where equality reigns, we have to ensure that things are, well... Equal! Which means we have to give precedence to racial minorities and women so that they get 'equal' opportunities and overcome the oppressive and clearly evil patriarchal system devised by evil men whose joy is to sadistically bask in the suffering of the "disenfranchised". Did affirmative action reach the desired results? Are women happier today? Have all racial tensions become a thing of the past? Is the racial gap closed? Fifty years ago, life was simpler and better, because simply, people performed their roles and through their role, they achieved purpose. Harvard now racially segregates its graduation ceremonies:

"Black graduates at Harvard University are holding a separately organized Black Commencement ceremony." www.snopes.com

By pursuing an all-inclusiveness ideology, the exact opposite has been achieved and reality has been ditched in all its subtle nuances, for blockheaded political correctness. Well done, academia...

The US Space program was dead and buried (before president Trump recently relaunched it anew) because NASA has shifted its priorities from Space exploration to gender and race quotas. If US astronauts want to ever get back into space, they use Russian rockets, ever since president Obama cut funding for NASA in 2011:

"After analyzing the sanctions against our space industry, I suggest to the USA to bring their astronauts to the International Space Station using a trampoline."-Russian Deputy Prime Minister

Dmitry Rogozin, who is head of Russia's space program, after he was personally targeted by US sanctions.

Racial violence in America and Europe is at an all-time high. Men and Women are more miserable than ever and their relationships are dominated by distrust. Anti-depressant use is at its peak:

"The rate of antidepressant use in the United States increased nearly 400 percent over the last two decades, according to a report [by the Centers for Disease Control and Prevention's National Center for Health Statistics] released Oct. 19", cites Janice Wood, an associate news editor at Psychcentral, with anti-depressant intake starting at the astonishingly low age of twelve[3]. We are still not equal.

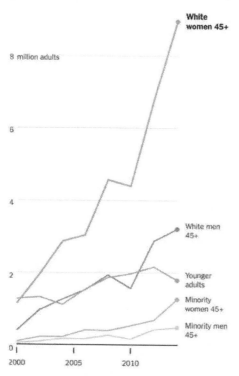

"Older white women account for 58% of adults who have used antidepressants for at least five years", says a Demographics of Long-term antidepressants graph, published by the New York Times.
Source: The National Health and Nutrition Examination Survey.

It's a scientific fact. Equality exists nowhere in nature.But inequality today is worse than ever before! The

---

3   "Antidepressant Use Up 400 Percent in US": https://psychcentral.com/news/2011/10/25/antidepressant-use-up-400-percent-in-us/30677.html

rich are becoming richer and the poor, poorer. College degrees are getting more expensive while at the same time becoming more common and therefore, worthless. In their pursuit of equality, feminists caused women to ape men by adopting masculine attitudes in everyday life and the workplace, as well as masculine clothing, losing their essence in the process. And are we still wondering why women are more miserable today than ever before? Their very identity, their feminity, is being sacrificed for equality.

Consistent IQ and test scores keep shattering the equality myth. Women and men have different aptitudes and excel in different capacities. So do the different races. So let's celebrate the Diversity which already exists instead of inventing a new 'diversity' where everybody is equal to everybody else in looks, performance, preferences, aspirations, aptitudes and earnings.

Affirmative action is then, a scheme devised by reality-challenged idealists, living in segregated neighborhoods, to punish the successful and reward the under-peforming, all under a fake appearance of "meritocracy" and "fairness".

Diversity

The diversity advocates operate chiefly in Europe, North America and anywhere with posh universities teaching liberal Cultural Marxist brainwash. In Lebanon for example, It's not unusual to see graduates of very expensive private universities extolling the 'virtues' of Communism and Marxism. Of course, being the bratty kids of well-off families, these deluded college-goers can *afford* to act communist. Listen to them hiss and foam over the very system that helped their parents afford the obscene tuition of their ungrateful offspring. But that's besides the point. These pampered and idle brats want diversity (with a small 'd').

What is diversity again? diversity is a morbid infatuation with an *incompatible* (and generally worse-off) *other*. This fuels the pity instinct of the liberal because he/she/xe* wants to feel good by helping the 'disadvantaged', coupled with an undying hatred for one's own ancestry. Only a liberal can buy into such a concept enough to switch off their own survival instincts by wishing for their own demise. As mentioned earlier, diversity advocates operate mainly in the West, and any other foothold they can infest, so they are mainly (but not exclusively) white. These whites never miss an opportunity to tweet about their inherited and undeserved 'privilege', and how bad they feel about being white.

And what is the cure for their malaise? diversity.

You won't see a liberal clamouring for diversity in Saudi Arabia, Israel, China or Indonesia, despite the strongly homogeneous populations of those countries (and therefore, a glaring lack of 'diversity').

Most interestingly, the diversity advocates only profess it in theory: The Pope, the Bush family, the Clintons, Macron, Merkel, Tony Blair, Jean-Claude Juncker, Bill Kristol, Justin Trudeau or the Clooneys only want diversity for others, all while being safe and secure behind their gated, and heavily guarded places of residence.

The Greater Good

We keep hearing about it- The Greater Good- where we have to somehow achieve happiness for the greatest number of people possible, even when people have radically different views of what makes them happy. How to reconcile this utopian ideology with the fact that every group or social/political unit advances their own interests and works for their own goals, which are most of the times in conflict with those of the 'other' group? What is the 'smaller good', then? Selfishness? Impossible! Those advocating the Greater Good are proverbial in their own

Xe: *One of the many newly coined 'non binary' gender pronouns designed to 'break' the masculine/feminine binary. Any such pronouns here are purely used in sarcasm.*

selfishness [But we will get to define what actually is the smaller good, in a bit]. Their crusades have been blatantly obvious since 1968: Hedonism and the worship of the self has been their consistent creed.

Ask any of the proponents of the Greater Good to define it. They won't be able to. It's one of those ambiguous concepts that loosely unite mobs and could whip them into a stempeding frenzy if the right mob conductor is available: Freedom, democracy, equality, human rights, the Greater Good, etc... hazy and blurry concepts that are used to hide the good which actually matters: caring for one's own family, community and culture. Isn't it strange that those advertising for the Greater Good, Modernists, are those who are most guilty of erasing cultures, destroying families, degrading eco-systems, and crushing the souls of the youth?

It is evident, even to the most hopeless cases of denial, that humanity is formed of different groups, and these different groups have different interests. In this materialistic world, most interests happen to be material, and since our world's resources are finite, many group interests will end up encroaching on other group interests; may the best win, in such scenarios. Diplomatic solutions are devised to ensure that rivaling political entities (groups) can as civilly as possible split the earth's resources, delaying as much as possible the inevitability of armed conflict, military solutions and bloodshed.

In such a world then, how can one in their right mind speak of a "greater" or "common good"? If, for the sake of argument, this unicorn is ever to be found, and God forbid that we ever find it, we would have reached in that case, the equally unicorn-like state of "world peace"; standing idle, looking awkward and asking ourselves "is that it? What do we do now?" No. Instead of the ever-elusive "common good", we need to look at the very present, real and palpable **"Common Group Good"** or **"Group Interest Good"** (GIG!).

The GIG can easily be defined according to each individual political group: If a certain group agrees that women do the hunting, men do the child-rearing and cooking, priests organize rituals and seasonal feasts and the elderly are used as human shields in case of hostile invasion, then whether we like it or not, this is the GIG which this particular group has unanimously agreed upon. Don't like it? There are other groups with a different GIG which might suit you more. Every group thus formed around a commonly agreed-upon system is automatically a political unit with a sense of culture, a purpose, a sense of direction, and its set of beliefs is the basis for its collective soul. Those are its invisible borders. Outsiders will be fought off. Which calls for the need to build a house, with a protective fence. This house becomes a village, the village becomes a city and the city becomes a nation, then an empire, then the cycle repeats itself with varying intensities and timelines.

Outside of that context - ie, in the globalist context- notions of 'greater good' or 'common good' are baseless myths and only work as catchy slogans for the gullible. What matters, is the *smaller good*, the GIG!

Liberalism, internationalism, feminism, LGBT, marxism/ communism/socialism, positivism, humanism, progressivism, globalism, intersectionality, relativism, pluralism, multiculturalism, rationalism... This growing -like a tumor- list of 'isms', constitutes the Leftism worldview and those are part of the Leftist ideology which promotes hatred of one's traditions and origins and group dilution via multiculturalism and cosmopolitanism.

Reproductive Rights

A fancy term used in 'enlightened' western societies, used as camouflage for an ugly reality; the 'right' of a 'mother' to end her pregnancy at any time without any valid scientific reason. A sad way for western liberal women to abuse their own freedoms and avoid responsibility as mature adults and grown-up mothers, citing 'reproductive rights'[4] or even 'reproductive justice'.

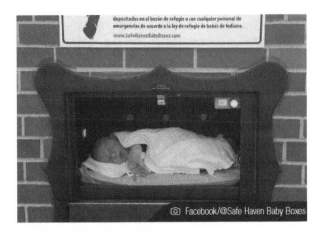

Facebook/@Safe Haven Baby Boxes

While a welcome alternative to abortion, baby deposit safe boxes, installed at fire departments or also orphanages, allow people to offset their parenting responsibilities over to someone else. Would the child-trafficking or organ-trafficking industry welcome such a solution? Very likely.

All-Inclusiveness

"Including everyone" is another utopian wet dream which looks good on paper, but reveals its pointlessness as soon as it's applied: If everyone is included, then no one is included. This concept carries the seed of its own demise in the event that should it succeed, it would have failed at the same time. By seeking to get everyone into the club, we have beaten the purpose of having a club. we have killed the exclusivity of belonging *anywhere*. Imagine a school where everyone gets an A, regardless of output or even attendance. Imagine a world where good law-abiding people are trying to raise their children next to a neighborhood infested with drug dealers, sexual predators and delinquants. It's truly a 'diverse' street, to be sure. The above examples are quite banal since they already exist and even are the norm in many places. All-inclusiveness obliviously leaves out the tiny fact that each group pulls the blanket towards itself, leaving the blanket tattered and ripped and everybody deprived of its benefit.

---

4   see: "SICK: Feminists Perform Bloody Fake Abortion On Woman Dressed As Virgin Mary" (www.dailywire.com) March 2017.

Minorities

In western circles, a 'minority' means the non-white living in White territory. It used to have a purely quantitative connotation to it, but soon began to mean 'disenfranchised' people or people whose lot in life has obviously been less than *others* (read: Whites). And somehow, Whites are to blame because of *Imperialism*. These non-white minorities are majorities (racially speaking) on the world scale, but somehow, liberal/globalist whites still insist those are minorities to whom he/she/xe must grovel, apologize and vilify themselves. Ironically, any minority person who rejects the victim/oppressor narrative peddled by the globalist left, is attacked by the offended left and its media, like black or latino republican politicians or prominent African-American rapper Kanye West for example.

Multiculturalism

Much has been said about this concept, where several cultures are socially engineered to 'coexist' (by force of law) in the same place (mainly in Europe and North America where generous social programs still exist - for now). This is all-inclusiveness but repackaged under a different brand name. Polite and civilized people are forced to share the same roof with considerably less polite[5], less civilized people, with differing values, beliefs and concepts of family, life and culture in general.
What could possibly go wrong?

Liberalism

In short, Liberalism is the ideological umbrella under which concepts like gender or racial equality, democracy, internationalism, human rights, freedom of press (read: Propaganda) or freedom of religion warmly nestle, except that this is only so in theory. In practice, anyone found to

---

5   See: "Ungrateful Migrant complains That Tax Funded Meals Are 'Not Nice' "(www.youtube.com)

be lightly disagreeing with any tenet[6] of the liberal dogma is promptly found guilty of hate crimes, thought crimes, xenophobia and bigotry, and just as promptly fired from their job and made a social pariah. Ample evidence[7] of the 'tolerant' practices[8] of liberalism abound, that one can safely confirm that this concept is just another '-ism' where anything lying outside of it will not be tolerated and will be actively fought until it's thoroughly obliterated.

Feminism

This particular '-ism' claims repeatedly and in ever more shrill a voice that it stands for equality. Real life evidence of wrecked households, miserable women living alone in their forties, miserable men who keep opting out of marriage, SlutWalk marches and dyed armpit rebelliousness actually disprove that claim entirely. Feminism is an impostor who committed regicide against Feminity. It is a hate and terror movement based exclusively on material resentment, turning women into manlike creatures, were-women, who have stopped being women and would never be men. Feminism's rabid materialism is only directed towards positions of economic power and comfort. Feminism is obsessed in putting female CEOs everywhere even where no CEO is needed, but is never concerned in evening army gender quotas or quotas where jobs are almost 100% male, like sanitary or plumbing. Feminism only cares about cushy jobs with well air-conditioned offices. It does not want equality but dominance[9]. By declaring war on men[10], feminism ends up achieving the opposite goal: hurting women by making them lose

---

6   See: "Denver Post Columnist Says He Was Fired for Saying There Are Two Sexes" (www.westernjournal.com)
7   See: "Catholic College Employee Investigated By Police For Saying There Are Only Two Genders" (www.avemariaradio.net)
8   See: "College student kicked out of class for telling professor there are only two genders" (www.foxnews.com)
9   See: "Baltimore Museum of Art goes all women in 2020" (gulftoday.ae) 2020
10   See: "7-year-old whose mom tried to 'transition' him chooses to attend school as a boy" (www.educationviews.org) or google the Georgulas case or the James Younger case.

their identity; feminity. As a result, 'proud' feminists today 'celebrate' their abortions and brag about it online. Another field where feminism support has entirely backfired on women: Supporting transgenderism. The tragicomical result is transgender men beating biological women in every sport and olympic discipline[11].

Socialism

This ideology aims to equalize society by eradicating all economic classes so that everyone becomes finally everybody else's economic replica. Socialism only thinks in economic and materialistic terms. Anything else, like personal aspirations, natural talent, personal abilities, IQ, strategic thinking, common sense, intuition, or even luck and how people have a different ability in either earning or squandering it, is something outside the ideological bounds of Socialism. It wants to streamline quantifiable and exclusively materialistic parameters and make humanity fit that one-size-fits-all mold in its quest to achieve Equalitopia.

Everything is economics for the communist and the socialist, to which, Amerika.org's writer Jonathan Parker Wilkinson gives this kind reminder: *"Anyone who thinks the health of a nation can be summed up in GDP is an idiot"*. Needless to say, Socialism and its chief ideological and executive tools, Equality and Bureaucracy respectively, is the first level of Communism, where people become completely interchangeable and equal cogs deprived of dreams, aspirations or any chance of advancement. Did you think, dear reader, that Socialism wants equality of opportunities? Fat chance! As an egalitarian ideology, what it actually seeks is equality of outcomes, which explains why these days the mediocre is elevated and the

---

11   See: "transgender man crushes womans skull" (youtube) and "Transgender weightlifter smashes women's world records, sparking backlash from Olympians" (www.aol.com), or also "Transgender female weightlifter smashes multiple women's world records in single day — and female Olympic medal winners cry foul" (www.theblaze.com)

outstanding is punished. This is how socialistic thought proceeds to 'equalize' society, using a technocratic caste of soulless bureaucrats. By choosing man as the measure of all things, ideologies like Socialism who claim to seek freedom, and liberty for all, end up achieving the opposite: the enslavement of humanity. And since Socialism innately knows that the world's resources are finite and that not everybody can be a king, then all shall be equally poor and miserable under socialism. Equality is achieved indeed!

Post-Racial

Ironically, the same forces pushing for diversity are also pushing for a 'Post-Racial' world, assuming that Racism is at the origin of much of the hate going on in the world. So, removing the diversity of races already existing by mixing them all together into one generic racial mush, we will finally achieve diversity. Take a brief moment to savor leftist logic. In the meantime, leftist scientists for hire proudly declare that 'race is a social construct and therefore, doesn't exist'! The world is dealing with people who want to remove all races, but at the same time, say that race is a myth! Another anti-scientific blunder by the 'party of science'.

Gender-fluid / Non-binary/ Pansexual

The historical period known as the Enlightenment, starting in 17th century Europe, spurred by the Renaissance and peaking with the French Revolution, produced the philosophers, thinkers and ideologues who shaped modern thought- the measure of all things would now be Man, the Individual. God, clergy, and aristocracy were declared obsolete and killed, replaced by individualism and egalitarianism. Every man has kingly abilities, every man can be a leader and every man is God. This set the course of what would become today's reality: By deriving all morality from himself, Man's values, moral choices and principles change with his moods, and since man is the new god, whatever man decides is 'good'. If today I feel like I belong to the other sex, then that is absolutely fine! I can even feel trans-species if I so desire. Nothing is fixed anymore; my feelings, my heart and my self-centered mental condition dictate my own ever-changing reality. Anything outside of 'Me' does not concern me, on the opposite, it must conform to me because I am the new god. And the world shall revolve around Me!

The problem is that everyone else is encouraged to create their own reality by following this anti-logic, resulting into not one reality we must adapt to, but to billions of realities, and with the impossibility to adapt to all of them, we shut ourselves in! No wonder why people with gender confusion have the highest suicide rates[12].

Pro-choice

Like Reproductive Rights, choice is todays word for abortion on demand or euthanasia for the elderly or for organ-harvesting purposes[13].

Humanism

'Humanism' is yet another attempt to place ourselves above the environment in which we exist. The unit of measure is us, as we become the center of attention and the element by which all other elements derive their meaning. As we change, evolve, age and regress, so does the definition of the world around us. Humanism is an ideology that puts Man -a fallible creature- on the highest pedestal, and is currently Liberalism's religion. It is popular because it has no standards other than one's own -ever changing- human nature.

---

12   See: The suicide rate for transgender people is nearly 10 times the national rate. A center is changing that (www.wcpo.com)
13   See: "Canada Conjoins Euthanasia and Organ Harvesting" (www.spectator.org), 2019.

Open Marriage

In Pagan times, polygamy was the norm. Then Christianity, and to a lesser extent, Islam established equality between man and woman, husband and wife (Islam allowed up to four wives for those who could afford it). That husband-wife equation stabilized the family, and gave focus to both man and woman; their aim became the welfare of their own children and their own family life and no one else may enter that equation. The man would be working for his own children and the woman would know her man is hers alone and that the fruit of their union comes from them. Today, such a model is seen as 'oppressive' by the mass media and the Left -yes, the same group who militates for equality. They are pushing for 'Open Marriage', spearheaded by none other than the American Psychiatric Association (APA), in an effort to give 'scientific' coating to their agenda[14]. Such a model will remove that serenity of knowing that the children you have are your own, and of knowing you are working to give a better life to your own family. It plants permanent doubt in a couple's life. This is another result of removing God from the equation. *We now, decide what is good.* Until we decide it's not good anymore, or something else is better, and so on... The consistent and eternal is replaced by the fickle and ephemereal.

Social Media (SoMe)

Popularized by Facebook since 2006, the social media ecosystem grew to contain several other platforms like Youtube, Instagram, Twitter, Reddit, Tinder and Whatsapp. These platforms then started consolidating into a central entity owning whatever information and content you could have ever posted. The irony with SoMe is that, like all of Modernity's lingo, the name lends itself a beneficial aura, bringing users 'closer' to everyone else, all while

14   See: "APA Promoting Open Relationships" (www.caffeinatedthoughts. com) - July 2019. and also from the New York Times (www.nytimes.com): "Is an Open Marriage a Happier Marriage?" - 2017.

actually disconnecting them from the outside world and what *really* is happening around them. One day I thought I was being creative by taking my 10 year-old nephew for some horse-riding. It was to be his first time ever to see and ride an actual horse. He answered me "Why do we need to go anywhere to see horses? I could see them anytime I wanted on my iPad". Eventually, he did discover the difference between a horse on Youtube and one in real life, but his retort earlier that day stayed in my mind.

Social Justice

As in every principle based on good intentions and on concepts of fairness, Social Justice is unsurprisingly now, yet another positive sounding ideology with bad intent. One would be excused if they thought that Social Justice warriors were out to right the wrongs in societies riddled with actual injustice. Instead, the Social Justice Warrior (SJW) exclusively operates from behind a screen, from the comfort of their own prosperous, industrialized milieu. The SJW is highly emotional, has degrees in humanities, is economically well-off, and generally still depends on their parents. Their 'causes' are targeting mostly inoffensive people to accuse them of racism, sexism, cultural appropriation, manspreading or a similarly nonsensical 'aggravation'... You will not find them mobilizing against sectarian genocides, female genital mutilation, child bride cultures, under-age grooming or sexual slavery.

Safe space

As the political correctness virus started spreading in western society, humanity started discovering a new breed of people, who could actually be harmed by *words* and *ideas*. And just like a bomb shelter used to protect our parents and ancestors from actual bodily harm and physical death, these people devised a place where they could be safe from 'harmful' ideas and words, usually of a right-wing nature. College Campuses started having

---

* also look up 'Mansplaining' and 'Manspreading' as increasingly popular forms of feminist misandry.

their safe spaces[15]. Academic insitutions where the thinking elite was supposed to be enjoying healthy intellectual debates became refuges for triggered 'liberals' hiding from 'unpopular' concepts like race, politics, religion, IQ or heritage (unless it was about someone else's heritage, preferably an 'oppressed minority').

Love Wins

The Marriage For All (Mariage Pour Tous) is a 2013 French law stipulating that Marriage is a 'human right', not an actual institution through which a man and a woman publically declare their intention and commitment to create a family and so, own a stake in the future of society. The wording of the term 'Mariage Pour Tous' again in typical liberal bad faith, plays the discrimination game; heterosexual couples were simply being too 'exclusive', too 'privileged' in that marriage club of theirs and it was now time to let everybody else in. The whole concept is not about allowing gay people to marry as much as to make heterosexuals feel guilt for simply existing and being able to reproduce naturally.

And so, as the Marriage for All is enshrined into law, gay people and their lobby revive a sensational slogan for their cause: Love Wins. The tagline further plays on antagonizing heterosexuality by implying that this was a battle between love and hate and that love (ie, the LGBT lobby) won. This has never been about equality or inclusiveness; this is war and the 'adversary' is clearly designated by the LGBT lobby as the heterosexual 'model' and the traditional nuclear family.

Tolerance

Leftism claims tolerance as one of its most sacred cows. As most of its slogans call for Tolerance (for

---

15   See: "Safe Spaces On College Campuses Are Creating Intolerant Students" (www.huffpost.com) -2017: Another example of ideological pursuits achieving the contrary of their desired effect.

pedophiles, murderers, social misfits, junkies or terrorists), the reality is that leftism actively seeks the eradication of differing opinions (and those who say them) through any means necessary. Sharing private information of an opponent -doxing- is now a common procedure of AntiFa and the one-way tolerance hordes. In his major work 'Imperium', Francis Parker Yockey warns of the incoming 'Age of Absolute Politics' where the winner will not be content with having the popular majority, but will seek physical, economical and social humiliation and total ruin of their opponent. Leftists, however, are aware of the glaring loophole in their ideology and have addressed the issue by labeling anything they disagree with, as 'Hate'. And of course, nobody should tolerate hate... Right?

The Wage-gap / The Glass ceiling

A favorite dead horse of the Left is bewailing the oppression of women by an evil patriarchy which proceeds to pay females a magical 33% less than men for the same amount of work. Nevermind this economic impossibility (no company would hire a man if a woman would cost the company 33% less to do the same job), Leftists also forget that one gets the salary they manage to negotiate during their job interview. This specific point is addressed by Canadian psychologist and thinker Jordan Peterson, where he highlights that women in general, tend to be more agreeable and therefore, accept an offered salary with less haggling than men.

And while wage-gap discussion goes on, a very important point tends to be completely overlooked: The (very real) Gender Tax Gap: According to a Gender Tax Gap study conducted in New Zealand, men pay twice the tax amount that women pay. The study is reproduced on the 'New Modern Man' blog, putting the spotlight on an angle never before explored by the equality pundits[16]. Another sacred cow of the Left is the famed Glass Ceiling,

---

16   "The Gender Tax Gap: Men Pay 200% of the Taxes Women Do" www. relampagofurioso.com - 2018

where women are magically left out of higher posts like CEO's or scientists, another myth disproven by the existence of female scientists like Margaret Hamilton, Hedy Lamarr or Marie Curie. All three are women -to just name a few- who owed their achievements to their own brilliant intellect, not to the victimhood culture of feminism and the emancipation movements.

Yet another point that Leftism and Feminism tend to overlook, is that women and men tend to have different preferences and career choices, and equalizing both sexes through social engineering and robbing them of free choice will only result in misery.

Free Speech

Let us remember that the current paradigm belongs to the Left and that whatever apparent Left v/s Right debate you might see happening, is actually between two different nuances of Left. In this context, free speech is of course 'tolerated' in the sense that whatever you say that falls inside the cultural/social/political limits set by the mainstream political specturm is deemed as 'safe', making you in internet slang, a *normie*. Anything else would of course, be labeled as 'hate'. If your employer discovers 'hateful' content on your social media, you might as well fire yourself. Such is the state of Free Speech today that many are establishing an 'Alt-tech' - independent platforms that welcome civilized debate and which are slowly being populated by people who have left the Facebook/Google ship.

Political Correctness (PC)

PC, another tool of Leftism, claimed that communication in the upcoming utopia must enjoy the widest consensus, and in an increasingly diverse society, it was becoming more and more difficult to achieve that task organically. Social engineering and legislating PC was the solution. The zeal of the PC people nowadays is such that people no longer want to talk or exchange their ideas publically from fear of the PC police dashing their career opportunities. In a growing culture of victimhood, professional victims and attention whores are also joining the PC police in its crackdown in the service of **Social Justice**. Everything from jokes to factual opinions to using the 'wrong' gender pronoun is now offensive -and punishable.

Sensitivity Training

In the age of PC fragility, companies and governments are diverting considerable financial resources towards training their staff and people in how to be nice. 'Being nice' -as in, 'being as bland, uninteresting and shallow so as nobody notices you even said anything- is now an enforced requirement by the social engineering gestapo in any western country. Dumb blonde jokes? Sexist! 'N' word? Racist! Wrong pronoun? Transphobic! Random Jewish reference? Antisemite!.. The aim is to neuter the current population and any future one into total submission through dumbing down its language to the point of making it accepted by all, ie, rendering it tasteless and meaningless. Ironically, this is all happening in the reign of the culture that claims Tolerance as its chief virtue.

Safe Schools

In the progressive modernistic West, where all terms are inverted and mean the exact opposite of their outward appearence, 'Safe Schools' is a term referring to schools which implement the LGBT curriculum. One would think that by 'Safe Schools', it is meant 'a school which is safe from drugs, rapists, bullies, or deranged shooters thanks to a well thought out, secure teaching apparatus. But no; it is a codeword for schools where people making up barely 2% of the total population, can parade their peculiar lifestyle upon the remaining 98%, disrupting the academic nature of the school as a learning institution, turning it instead into a social engineering lab where certain lifestyles are forced upon an unsuspecting majority. The trick is indirectly making the majority feel guilty for the high rates of suicide and the overall mental mess that LGBT people are in -due to their own sexual choices and self-imposed sexual 'identities'- wrecking schools and academic insitutions -and generations of healthy kids who come to school to get an education- for the sake of a vengeful LGBT ideology.

Universalism, Globalism

When materialism is the ruling worldview, everything is defined from a profit/loss perspective. Concepts like Universalism or even Globalism, that had philosophical and cultural connotations, should now be understood, whenever they are encountered in a text as facades for the hegemony of corporations and their ideological tool, Modernity.

Think-tank

Always in the same relentless tradition of inverting everything, Modernity leads us to believe that a think-tank is a group of people putting their intellectual capacities in the service of society and its betterment. What actually is closer to the truth is that Think Tanks are the corporate-funded lobbies behind every social engineering scheme happening in the world. Their traditional covers are NGOs and academia (learning institutions, scientific research hubs), allowing them to undertake long-term socio-political subversion plans, in any desired field, undetected.

Empowerment

This term will almost always be followed by the word

'women' or 'minorities', and is an all-time favorite in Leftist and Feminist circles. 'Empowering' women or minorities always suggests that another demographic is to blame for 'oppressing' whoever the Leftist/Feminist seeks to 'empower'. The Leftist who wants to be seen as some promethean figure enabling a 'weaker' person to have access to 'power'. The level of condescension enclosed in this term speaks volumes on Leftism's petty messianism.

Pluralism

In sociological terms, Pluralism is "a conviction that various religious, ethnic, racial, and political groups should be allowed to thrive in a single society". The term 'should', in the previous quotation, contains all the essence of Leftism. In Leftism, the world is never seen as it 'is', but as it 'should be'. While the outlook is commendable in its potentially inherent creativity, its unchecked emotionality always leads it to disastrous results. Re-reading the quotation, we notice that the Leftist overlooks the next logical step of pluralism, meaning, *after* it has happened; state-enforced equality laws, PC laws, militarized police, increased distrust, segregation among racial, ethnic and other cultural lines, lowest common denominator standards, higher crime, no-go zones, etc... Leftism day-dreaming resembles those fairie tales which end with 'and they lived happily ever after'. It always chooses to ignore a historical constant: The primacy of group interest. A pluralistic society is a society in constant internal war.

Cisgendered

A term that means a human being has both their biological sexual identity and their mental one *aligned*. the opposite of the above term is 'transgendered', meaning that there is a disruption between the biological and the mental sexual identity. The term is less than 30 years old and has gained traction in LGBT circles, where the term 'Cis' has come to designate straight persons. To the casual straight person who's unaware of the war the LGBT lobby is waging on heterosexuality and the traditional family, the word cisgendered sound and looks vaguely as the medical diagnosis for some obscure illness. And perhaps this was the intention behind the term: To invert the values as usual and make the straight people look odd, in a bid to better control and manipulate them through guilt and confusion.

Privilege

The 'Check Your Privilege' phrase, originating from a 1988 women's studies paper, became a worldwide meme for targeting straight white males for being the apparent repository of an unfairly earned privilege -according to the feminist who wrote the paper.
According to her, straight white males who lead whether in academic excellence or in financial status, owe their success to 'Privilege', meaning that someone else should be enjoying such success but isn't, due to not being a straight white male. Typically, emotions like resentment and victimhood are the ideological weapons of any under achiever, not just leftists, to try to trationalize their own mediocrity.

Positive Discrimination

The 'positive discrimination' concept started gaining popularity among the constituents of the victimhood culture, raising the banner of 'Inequality' and addressing that existential scourge in the name of 'social justice': Since the mediocre largely outnumber their betters, it makes sense that in a paradigm of democracy and equality, the mediocre gets the greater political representation. Consequently, insane societies start rationalizing concepts like Positive Discrimination, where less deserving postulants get to be in positions of power, at the expense of better candidates, simply due to racial and gender-based quotas. Fairness and 'equality' on display!

Gender Pronouns / Identity Politics

When you hear someone say 'the science is settled', brace yourself internally for a deluge of pro-LGBT propaganda washing your way. Biology and genetics have by now been successfully brushed aside by the American Psychological Association (APA) after the APA istelf, was bullied in the early 70s into normalizing homosexuality[17]. And today, the APA normalizes transgenderism by removing it from its list of mental illnesses -but hilariously enough, keeps ADHD. Soon, the APA's very existence would need to be questioned at the pace in which, everything is being normalized. But in the meantime, we will need to practice memorizing a cancerously developing list of 'gender pronouns' like 'zer', 'zhe' or 'xey'.

Multitasking

The modern corporate structure, after succeeding in doubling its workforce by adding women into its meat grinder, has just as successfully convinced women that they're the best at being 'single' moms, as shown in many global advertisements, accomplished chefs, social leaders and career achievers all at once. It is the single most powerful ego boost a modern woman could get- the world telling her that *she can do everything all at once*. In contrast, men are almost always portrayed in every media as complete idiots who cannot even succeed in completing a single and very simple task. Pointing that out, is considered *fragile masculinity*!* In the end, we have yet another seemingly innocuous term that is being used to further divide the sexes by massaging the female ego via painting women as 'self-sufficient' and men as obsolete.

---

17   "Homosexuality and American Psychiatry: The Politics of Diagnosis" by Ronald Bayer, p. 3-4-5-105-6-89.

Islamophobia

Initially coined by Iranian fundamentalists[18], the term 'Islamophobia' gained significant popularity with western liberals to shut down any civilized discussion about open border policies disrupting the demographic and cultural balance of western societies. While proponents of civic nationalism* have made it clear that an immigrant should adapt to the host country's laws and not the opposite, questioning this immigrant's inability/unwillingness to do so, is considered Islamophobia by the Leftist/globalist elite currently ruling Europe and America.

Antisemitism

Traditionally, the term 'Antisemitism' would lead one to think it defines the act of baselessly hating on Jews but actually it is among the most abusively overused terms in modern vocabulary. Whether asking honest questions about jewish overrepresentation in media and politics, jewish absence of reliable demographic statistics, the actual number of jewish WWII victims, the relation of jewish elites to bolshevism, the Young Turks and the Armenian Genocide, Jewish control of world banking or the USS Liberty incident, one is automatically labeled an antisemite. Yet, it is Jews who are (to borrow some leftist terminology) culturally appropriating a term that no longer racially and ethnically defines most of their current population[19].

Racism

Terms appropriated by the Left soon lose their universal meaning and become ideologically distorted slogans. Racism is no exception as it is now the sole propriety of the Left and cannot be used by anybody with nationalist or hard conservative views, especially if that anybody

---

18 "The Invention Of Islamophobia" (www.newrepublic.com), by Martin Peretz, 2011.

19 "Most Jews Are Not Semites" by Marek Glogoczowski - www.rense.com

Fragile Masculinity: *A feminist term used to attack males; feminists contradict themselves yet again - How can an oppressor also be fragile?*

happens to be white. Leftist madness goes so far as to claim that only whites can be racist- a racial propaganda that is pushed by western big government and posh academia alike (for whom, the concept of race 'does not exist'!)[20].

Sexism

As Sexism is, according to its wikipedia definition, a condition that could affect anyone, the Left has appropriated that term to antagonize men. Like Racism, sexism is now a term that nurtures a victim culture growing mostly in feminist circles. Preventing women from actually asserting themselves, the sexism excuse provides them with an excuse to rationalize any social failure by blaming it on men. The victimhood culture relies on many people to stay comfortable with their under-achiever status because somehow, someone else has caused them to fail!

Climate Change/Global Warming

One should not deny man-made ecocide, but the Climate Change/Global Warming circus has a weird take on the subject. Instead of addressing the hard issue of overpopulation, it seeks to implement silly non-solutions like Earth Hour, 'carbon taxes' and technologies which look 'clean' (hybrid, electric cars, wind turbines, solar power) but have an even heavier toll on nature in terms of recycling and dangers to wildlife. They also have a comparatively much weaker output with a much higher production cost. Carbon taxes and posh climate summits have not reduced nor addressed man-made environmental degradation and people are still consuming insane amounts of plastics. The best and most efficient ways to produce energy remain nuclear[21], and when possible, hydraulic power.

---

20 "There Is No Such Thing as Race" (www.newsweek.com), Wald Sussman , 2014.
21 Thorium-based nuclear power: www.slideshare.net/preetam92/seminar-51360700

Civic Nationalism: The notion that ethnic foreigners or immigrants from different cultural backgrounds can become full citizens as long as they adhere to their host country's laws.

Comparatively, the impact of electric car battery waste, discarded wind turbines/solar panels and oil-spills far outsizes Chernobyl[22]. The dangers of nuclear energy remain very real however, but the success story of nuclear powered military ships and submarines is proof that harnessing nuclear energy is not an impossibility. Should we abandon wind and solar-powered energy sources? Doing so, would be uneducated (not to mention contrary to scientific curiosity), and so is discarding nuclear power.

Hate group/Hate Speech

This term used to define any group of people guilty of irrational ideological attacks on other groups and demographics but today, they encompass everything the globalist Left does not like- nationalists, whites, comedians who make fun of the globalist Left, christians, straight people, family advocacy groups, anti-abortion groups and people who don't need the media to tell them what and how to think. This includes successful women and minorities who do not adhere to the leftist victimhood culture).

The War on Terror

In the name of man-centered humanism, the industrialized world has declared war on terror, through its 'right-winged' branch of global Leftism. The result was even more terror groups and consequently, even more 'war on terror'. The term doesn't fool anyone now and is a pathetic cover for trade route control, opiates 'regulation', arm trade and resource control.

Social Construct

Leftist lunacy has its sights on scientifically established notions like race and gender or also species. The biological and genetical facts we thought

---

22   "There's No Argument Against Nuclear Power" - www.futurism.com - 2017

were confirmed verities do not hold in the face of this ideological onslaught. Race does not exist, but beware white supremacy (let that sink in)! There are an infinity of genders but gender reassignment surgeries only have male and female options...

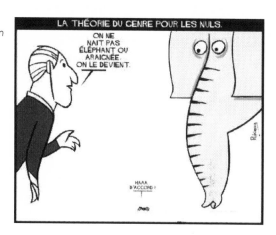

Gender theory for dummies: "One is not born a spider or an elephant. One becomes it!" -illustration by: Rakman

Welfare Reform

The 'right-wing' branch of global Leftism is, in the US, more known as 'republicans'/'neo-cons' or in Europe, as the CDU, the Tories or the 'Droite Républicaine'. They are all, however, part of a rebranded Leftism which submits to man-centered humanism and modernity. They want 'welfare reform', which is another way to say that they want to keep the welfare system unchanged in order to maintain their voting base of para- sites and leeches who are the reason hard working people pay half of their income in tax and get nothing in return.

Open-mindedness

One would think that whoever manages to test their own ideas and manages to adopt better ones as a result, is open-minded. Unfortunately, the liberal age has rendered such an antiquated concept totally obsolete.

Today, anyone who is not a liberal/leftist, is not open-minded and therefore, narrow-minded. Just ask any liberal.

Self-Love

Another name for masturbation, as a Canadian 'sex-education' company, Shaftesbury, actively normalizes pedophilia by warping kids' minds through its online youtube videos, 'Every Body Curious'. An 'enlightening' experience for parents lauding the Canadian education system.

Other Stories

Cultural Marxism (in short)

Cultural Marxism is notion of egalitarian thought which is a direct result of the 'Frankfurt School', a group of modernist marxists (themselves influenced by the communist Antonio Gramsci) who fled Nazi Germany to the United States. Among the leaders of this movement was Herbert Marcuse, a marxist who thought that through the Frankfurt School's Critical Theory, a new society would emerge that would question, tear down and deconstruct the old order of hierarchy -God, nation, family and even gender- and usher in a new age of sexual freedom, anarchy and moral relativism. The unanimous adoption of the Frankfurt School of thought by western academia in the 1950s and 1960s, and up till now, resulted in the current mood of political correctness, gender studies, transgenderism, black studies, latino studies, white privilege studies, feminism, the LGBT lobby, the normalization of homosexuality, the ongoing normalization of paedophilia, the Social

Justice Warrior (SJW)mentality, and many other ills tearing down today's society under the grotesque banner of 'progress'. One can even notice a total inversion of values where heterosexuality, chastity, faith, or

studiousness are mocked and ridiculed, where one's love for one's own nation, culture or race are demonized, while pick-up artists, druglords, pedophiles, serial divorcees or sexually confused people are revered and idolized as 'brave', 'courageous' and of course, 'stunning'.

(Excessive) Abstraction

We have, as a modern society, reached a terminal phase of semantic ambiguity; there is an abyss between reality and the words we use to define it. Terms like 'Marriage', 'Freedom', 'Justice', 'Evolution', 'Nature', 'Peace','Revolution', 'Race', 'Gender', 'State', etc are growing fuzzier as we gradually lose universal consensus over them. Art, for example, is now just an ephemereal consumable. National Independence loses its meaning as we lose all contact with violence, which is delegated to armies, police forces and other law inforcement services. The more we become domesticated and self centered, the more ambiguous some terms are bound to become to us.

Already, words like 'Love' or 'Family' (terms that are much more intimate to us than patriotism or territorial independence) are becoming more and more materialistic concepts completely removed from their initial nature, which used to enclose sacrifice, commitment, trust or also selflessness, and were devoid of any financial or materialistic baggage. On a positive note, art forms like for example, cartoons, use excessive abstraction to their advantage, as say, showing a mouse living in a gruyere house, and everyone finding the depiction lovely.

In addition to its attacks on language, Liberalism with its socio-economic hydra (Globalism) 'deconstructs' humanity through a series of world-renowned entities which also betray an egalitarian and marxist agenda with hidden duplicitous motives camouflaged under benevolent and feel-good names. Here are a few examples:

The Southern Poverty Law Center [SPLC]

Originally founded for the noble cause of defending the civil rights of the disadvantaged, the SPLC grew later to label almost everybody it politically or ideologically disagrees with, as a hate group. Using the "hate group" bogey man allows the SPLC to raise obscene amounts of money that were stashed fraudulently in places like the Cayman Islands[23]. This modern-day inquisition has now lost all of its original goodwill and credibility, but none of its political influence, which it may have had in its formative years. Its name still stirs feelings of humanism, sympathy and pity, which are powerful leftist tools that suppress reason and bring emotions to a boil.

The Anti Defamation League [ADL]

Same as the SPLC, the ADL hides its exclusively Jewish interests behind a benevolent name falsely evoking universalistic sympathy for all, but actually labelling every group with differing political opinions as a "hate group". Those "hate groups" almost always happen to be exclusively white, traditional Catholics.

Amnesty International

Continuously "at odds" with Israel and international jewry due to its heavily publicized pro-BDS*, pro-Palestine and "anti-Israel" stances. Founded by Jewish Londoner

---

23   "Will the IRS investigate the SPLC on taxes?"-www.washingtontimes.com- 2017.

***BDS:** Boycott, Divestment, Sanctions (BDS) is a Palestinian-led movement for freedom, justice and equality.*

Peter James Henry Solomon (known for his more europe-
anized name 'Benenson'), there is every reason to believe
that Amnesty Int'l is controlled opposition. Watching the
controlled opposition circus is always good entertainment,
as long as one keeps its deceiving nature in mind.

Planned Parenthood [PP]**

PP is another benevolent-sounding name hiding
a ghastly reality. PP's scandalous video leaks of doctors
discussing the price of harvested baby parts and joking
about dead foetuses over wine, definitely has nothing parental in mind. This is yet another evil liberal scheme hiding
its depravity (Spirit Cooking comes to mind!) with innocent
words evoking feel-good images of people helping their
brothers and sisters in humanity, in the making of a family. It is a tricky name that alludes to helping someone to
better plan their life as a parent, while the reality is helping
people avoid parenthood. The trick is to always choose a
positive-sounding name because naming your organization something like "the anti-parenthood league" would
not draw as much fund-raising enthusiasm or PR.

The Population Council [TPC]

This Rockefeller-founded organization sounds like
something good for the people in general and hints at
being an entity in the service of helping communities grow
in numbers. Again, the cunningly chosen name was probably devised by people with good advertising/market-
ing flair, because of course, calling it the "de-population
council" would be a tough fundraising and PR challenge.
But This is what the Population Council actively pursues:
The de-population of places through various contraception methods, and these places where contraception is
heavily promoted, are predominantly Christian Catholic
areas. On the Population Council's website, in 2018, One
of the organization's projects consists of testing a Male
Contraception gel in "Chile, Italy, Kenya, Scotland,

**The International branch of Planned Parenthood (IPPF) is behind the World Health Organ-
ization's **Standards in Sexuality Education in Europe**. These rules put enormous emphasis
on 'Consent' (childhood manipulation by adults) as a way to sexualize children from their
earliest age, therefore planning for the normalization of pedophilia.
The Standards PDF can be downloaded from: www.bzga-whocc.de

Sweden, United Kingdom, United States", which are countries whose vast majority is of Christian denomination.
You will never see the Population Council operating their birth-control schemes in Israel, China or in Saudi Arabia.

The Scientific-Humanitarian Committee

Founded in Berlin on May 1897 by Jewish homosexual sexologist and physician Magnus Hirschfeld, the Scientific-humanitarian Committee was the first LGBT rights organization in history. While the actual cause may be commendable to some, one wonders why it was not simply named something like the 'Gay and Transgender Protection League', which is a more straightforward definition of the organization's aims.

Those are some of the more popular terms and entities which ensure global Leftism's control on today's society, its socializing habits, and behaviours via inversion and manipulation of traditional values. In short, a cultural deconstruction of the human mind is under way and those were but a fraction of its array of methods and semantic distortions.

LEGALIZING UNFAIRNESS: 5 REASONS WHY QUOTAS ARE DESTRUCTIVE AND SHOULD BE AVOIDED

Another egalitarian idea makes its way to the forefront of modern politics, which are now nothing more than a social justice competition: Quotas.

Politicians (read: Demagogues) who seek extra popularity points, play the SJW card by demanding quotas- for women, for minorities, for handicapped people, etc... Of course, the idea appeals to the general public because it carries an aura of 'fairness'; everybody would be represented! How can one be against such a just concept? But like many sales pitches, Quotas look good from a distance, but once we actually put the idea under the microscope, its underlying evils become obvious:

1-   Quotas do not respect actual demographic representation: To take the example of Lebanon, where females outnumber males due to the excessive migration of young male graduates (and to heavy male casualties during the 1975-1990 war), political quotas are increasingly on the demand list of the civil society. A popular opinion is to have at least 25% of parliament and cabinet be composed of women. First, on a purely demographic basis, the 25% quota would still be unjust and an inaccurate representation of Lebanese demographics. Second, on an individual basis, the idea itself insults women by suggesting their inability to reach the upper political echelons without relying on the State.

2-   Quotas do not reflect individual aspirations: Sociological studies have proven time and again that each sex has its own distinct career choices and preferences, and political engagement is no exception. For egalitarian ideologues, every field showing a choice or interest difference between men and women is a glaring inequality that needs to be addressed. That problematic (a favorite term with modernist ideologues) gender gap is a sign that things are NOT ok (for women) and that such oppression must end! Quotas enforced anywhere (not just politics) highlight a social justice over-zealousness to 'rectify' a social 'wrong' regardless of individual preferences. Ironically, no such quotas are enforced in lower army posts (like infantry) and no feminist SJW group is seen clamoring for equal women representation in plumbing, sanitation or mining. The Bell curve shows there are more men that are clustered at the bell's extremes (meaning the highest percentage of geniuses *and* losers or mentally deficient is male), while women are hovering more around the middle of the curve (meaning we are more likely to find women with stable cognitive abilities than men). Such a scientifically proven core biological difference can never be effectively reflected through equality quotas.

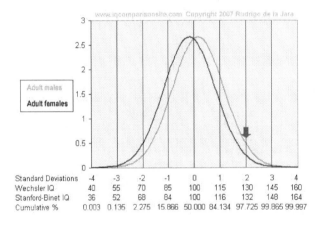

Adult Sex Differences on the Raven Progressive Matrices:

The male-to-female ratio increases (for males) the further we are on the Bell curve's extremes - Source: www.iqcomparisonsite.com

3-   Quotas create discrimination by choosing a less eligible candidate over a more eligible one, purely on a 'social justice' basis: When reviewing a number of eligible candidates for a limited number of posts, quotas can get in the way of the more capable ones who are unlucky enough to belong to the 'wrong' demographic. Those will be culled by the quota's unfeeling and uncaring social justice razor and less deserving ones will be hired.

4-   Quotas enshrine an egalitarian ideology that goes opposite to the inherent inequality in people:
People are equal only to their creator, not amongst themselves, but in a godless world, modernity has substituted God with Man. Since Man is modernity's measure of all things, modern ideologies are hard at work to equalize humanity despite the fact that we are different.

Enter a classroom and observe; every student has different abilities, is suitable to different tasks and has their own distinct individuality. Egalitarian dogma seeks to nullify one's humanity in the name of social justice and consequently, denies the individuality and uniqueness of individuals.

5-   Quotas create a false narrative of victimhood and enforce it by legislation: When Quotas are introduced, there is an immediate -though subconscious- indication that a certain group or demographic is the underdog. This creates a victim/oppressor narrative that degrades the so-called 'victim' and antagonizes/demonizes the 'oppressor'. In the case of sexes, women are made to feel like victims and men are made to feel like rapists. In the case of race, whites (because racial quotas are only applied in white-majority countries) are made to feel guilty and bad, while blacks are made to feel inferior. Such an ideology is bound not to solve social differences but worsen them in the long run.

How can African-Americans, who only make an estimated 13.4% of the population[24] be credited with twice electing Barack Obama to the US presidency? Were they alone in electing him? Have the 'racist' whites (roughly 65% of the American population) nothing to do with such an election?

        This brings us to a sixth underlying layer : Division. A divided society is a doomed one. When division happens along racial or religious lines, civil war and secession are inevitable but when it occurs along gender lines, when men and women are enemies, the

---

24   "Race and ethnicity in the United States" - (Source: Wikipedia.org)

only outcome of such a diabolical scenario is death; the death of all. Egalitarianism and its tools (Quotas being one of them) appeal to our inner couch potato but when applied, will dehumanize society, invariably achieving the opposite result. Reject quotas and every other egalitarian trend. They claim to empower but weaken instead.

SEPARATION OF CHURCH & STATE [SCS]

Liberalism and Leftist politics have been dominating the cultural landscape for the past three hundred years. We can clearly see the result in political discourse today, especially when hearing so-called conservatives and right-wingers argue *for* separation of Church and State, a concept that both the commoner and the aristocrat from three centuries ago would have considered as a total travesty.

What is separation of Church and State [SCS] and how did such a concept manage to make everybody want to proudly wear it as their political slogan? One would think SCS is asking for people to give precedence to nation over personal beliefs to minimize religious interference in daily political and social life. Right? Well, not exactly! SCS is a nebulous concept that is interpreted in various ways depending on whoever is using it. It doesn't specifically say the individual has to give precedence to their nation over personal belief, but in practice, it basically wants the following: The *division*, within the individual, between both that individual's spiritual nature and their national belonging respectively; meaning that said individual is required to build an inner wall, so to speak, separating their soul -the Church- from their body -the State. Now, why would a community who shares the same beliefs and has formed its own culture and nation, switch to this famous SCS concept[1]?

Quite simply to accommodate for Diversity!

And what is Diversity again?
It is (according to global Leftism) the mixing of all people, all races, all religions with all other people, races, religions and political backgrounds into one utopian post-racial, post-spiritual, post-cultural, positivistic and rationalistic

---

1   "The True Meaning of Separation of Church and State" by Bill Flax, 2011 (www.forbes.com)

Liberal paradise, comrade.

SCS is quite simply the removal of the spiritual side of man because in the current materialistic world, there is no more need for it, so why offend our brothers and sisters in consumerism with our silly superstitions of old? Just give up your church -ie: your beliefs, your spirituality, your soul, and therefore, your purpose- and enjoy a 'full' life where everything is a consumable, including modern Marriage, under the protection of the new god: The State. Now, what is the State, once its institutions are all privatized and its culture erased? Merely an ensemble of corporations who own the citizen and can dispense with it. The end-game of SCS is the complete removal of the moral code that society has inherited from the old system and a return to the Jungle, but this jungle will be an industrialized one -like the one we see in the Matrix movies- not the romantic and enchanting Jungle of Rudyard Kipling.

SCS is a prelude to a soulless, corporation-controlled world where humanity unlearns and surrenders its soul for the sake of "coexistence" in a borderless, multi-cultural, pluralistic and cosmopolitan 'utopia' where no one could offend anyone with their cultural identity. SCS clashes with cultural identity and only one can survive at the expense of the other. People who believe in having both, are disconnected from reality. If a country imple-ments SCS, it will have to enforce it with laws, as it would never happen organically.

What is historically proven to happen organically, is homogeneous populations with a shared set of behaviors, religion, ethnic and racial traits, language and cultural ancestry, agreeing together to form a political unit. This political unit can become a nation, and can grow into an empire and civilization, if its drive is strong enough, at which point, its people would have forgotten the hard-ships and sacrifices of their ancestors and start to think in 'humanistic' terms; talk of welcoming migrants, abolishing borders, installing multiculturalism and diversity, worshipping the self, etc... would quickly become the norm. And of course, when these concepts end up democratically voted upon and implemented, SCS will de facto become the new religion and people will find themselves as automatons serving a large economic machine and not much else, as is the case in the West, right now.

Fortunately, we can make an empirical comparison between the people who bought into this idea, and those who still didn't: The Islamic world, Israel and the Far East and Russia, as well as a few eastern European countries. These places largely do not subscribe to the SCS ideology because obviously they see it as a failing destructive trend. Europe, Australia and North America are its main proponents, and are culturally in full decline (I'll explain): What we are seeing today in the West, is a dying culture, cruising on the successes of its past, heavily recycling old technologies and failing to create new ones bold enough to induce cultural paradigmatic shifts, the way the airplane, the telephone or television did. The West is currently stagnating, at a standstill, too busy with tech gadgets to be aware of its own decline. The rest of the world is not so unaware; while the 'rest of the world' definitely enjoys western-invented gadgets, it is carefully and systematically taking advantage of western ideological "progressiveness" to flood it with waves of immigration, most of which has already clearly stated its intent of subduing the decadent West *coughs in Islam*.

Those bent on overthrowing the West don't have its military firepower, but they don't have western end-stage SCS either, are unified by religion and identity, and currently have the demographic upperhand. Who could fault any demographic for wanting to replace another demographic that indulges in self-loathing and is in civilizational free-fall? Nature abhorrs a vacuum, as they say.

Existing western technology, after being offshored (because corporate profit margins are more important than cultural pride in one's technology) is heavily recycled into new gadgety shapes; bulky TVs, phones and radios are now much slimmer and lighter, computers are faster, yet completely NEW technology is still lacking. This stagnation of the West is also best illustrated in its inability to repeat technological feats done fifty years ago, like the Moon landing. This digression was necessary in order to emphasize that the West not only is stagnating, but is regressing, at roughly the same time when it made several catastrophic decisions: Open Borders, Contraception, Separation of Church and State, Affirmative Action, and Sexual Liberation/Gender fluidity. Recently, the regression has accelerated with historical revisionism illustrated by mass vandalism of traditional landmarks and statue removals happening all over Europe and North America. Western University professors clamoring for the removal of "triggering" words, Safe-Space creation on campuses, race - segregated gradutations and many other examples are proof of the sorry cultural state of a West in the deathgrip of Cancel Culture*.

This state of things shouldn't make opponents of the West and its competitors on the world (culture) stage feel happy. On the contrary, they should be worried, because once the West crashes and burns, the entire system it created, and which we all are benefiting from, will be no more.

If anything, cultures competing with the West should pick up some speed in finding technological and cultural alternatives to those rapidly fading western ones, to ensure the continuity of the human race in terms of technological and cultural advancement. We should also learn from the mistakes made by the West, namely its adoption of a cultural direction that negated and antagonized tradition.

*Cancel culture: *The popular practice of withdrawing support for (canceling) public figures and companies after they have done or said something considered objectionable or offensive - Source: www.dictionary.com*

When the church is separated from the state, this means the two elements which have always coexisted in us since the dawn of time, are now being forced out of each other. (And) since the State is the ruler of our material existence, the Church has to go. The Church -the religious, spiritual and cultural side of Man- will be not just relegated into the background, but thoroughly obliterated, as 'secular' laws are devised to make sure such obliteration is enforced and the State be declared the new god of the multicultural 'utopia' and Diversity its official religion. Can a body live without a soul (rationalists would laugh, albeit nervously, at such question)? Can a people survive without their church? After The World Health Organization report on suicide and atheism was mysteriously removed, I will mention a statistical research made by the American Journal of Psychiatry[2], which demonstrates that atheism is linked to much higher suicide rates, as "subjects with no religious affiliation perceived fewer reasons for living, particularly fewer moral objections to suicide". Loss of purpose destroys life. And purpose is never found in materialistic or ideological pursuits[3].

The demand for SCS increases with diversity. A homogeneous society would never feel the need to introduce this type of social engineering unless it's suicidal (as in the case of modern Europe and North America). In Lebanon, a country where Islam and Christianity have been coexisting as early as the 8th century AD, the need for SCS has been growing steadily, voiced by Lebanese civil movement activists since the 90s. SCS, they believe, would help usher in a modern, more just Lebanon, indirectly blaming the country's woes on its religious diversity. That is another irony, where Lebanese civil movement activists celebrate Lebanon's diversity but want to

---

2   "Religious Affiliation and Suicide Attempt" -Source: https://ajp. psychiatryonline.org

3   "Europe is the most suicidal region in the world, while the Eastern Mediterranean is the least" - List of countries by suicide rate (Wikipedia)- Sourced from: https://www.who.int/gho/mental_health/suicide_rates_crude/en/

legislate its religious diversity out of its daily life). They tend to forget that the Muslim majority in Lebanon that outnumbers its christian population 2 to 1, has been very open minded towards its Christian compatriots by allowing a 50/50 sharing of the Lebanese parliament. On a one-man, one-vote basis, there would not be a Christian president in Lebanon as it is the case now and the Lebanese Christian demographic (between 30 and 40% of its population, (not counting Lebanese diaspora) would be marginalized.

Thus, blaming Lebanon's problems squarely on religion is an easily disproven myth. SCS in lebanon as a Legislation, would seek to nullify an important part of the Lebanese identity- its religious components- and would seek to socially engineer what is purely an organically evolving identitarian socio-cultural trait. Instead of pushing for SCS, a simple decentralization of Lebanese administrations would bring in a healthy competitive spirit between the different lebanese regions with clear religious majorities. Currently, the centralized system allows many to slack and depend on the efforts of others, while in a decentralized Lebanon, everyone would be motivated to stay ahead of their neighbor which would push the nation forward and keep the religious sentiments from degenerating into petty sectarian squabbling. A centralized Lebanon used to work back when one clear majority, Christian maronites called the shots. Today, Lebanon is divided roughly into three demographics (Sunni, Shiaa and Christian) each pulling the political blanket towards itself, which is causing the rapid degradation of the country as a people and as a land, as no common vision is reached. As a result of such demographic shifts, centralized administration is no longer valid and the need for economic and social decentralization is more urgent than ever.

While most SCS advocates in Lebanon are leftists, many of its proponents are ironically from the Christian communities, while Muslims are unconvinced, just like they are having none of it in Europe, where sharia courts are sprouting everywhere a muslim community firmly establishes itself despite the host countries' "laicity" (read: Anti-christian sentiment promoted by non other than the host states themselves). And what is the response of liberalized Christian "humanists"? Separation of Church and State! The **only** part in Lebanon that *could* benefit from SCS would be the judiciary, and nothing else. Lebanon could benefit from a centralized legal authority that is independent from religious authority. Complete SCS can only work if all the citizens of a community are atheists, therefore rendering the whole notion of SCS useless, since there would be nothing to separate from the State to begin with.

In Europe and the USA, talk of SCS has never abated, as liberal christians who still make the demographic majority, are still enamored with this utopian concept without any evidence of its successful implementation. It is a theory, an idea, but with huge popular traction among the "educated" (read: The brainwashed idealists) and gullible alike, due to its apparent positive nature; it has an appealing simplicity to it, like most Leftist concepts but most importantly, it is *human-centered*. Its partisans have given in to the liberal mindset, abolished their borders, ditched God for state laws and materialism, legalized abortion and euthanasia and actively pursued contraception; they are for the first time, about to become a minority as the migrant waves they welcomed, have never bought into the any of the contraception, abortion or SCS shams.

SCS is a relatively novel idea in the context of human history. As history shows, great civilizations, like the Greeks, the Romans, the Persians, The Aztecs, the Egyptians or the Phoenicians, to name a few, reached their apex with a homogeneous population where 'Church' (culture and spirit) and State (as an organic political mass) coalesced into one driving cultural pulse. European Christianity was at the height of its political power in a time where there existed no such thing as today's quite modern concept of SCS.

The above cultures eventually became diluted, degraded and decadent as weaker, more humanistic leaders surfed on the past successes of the civilization they inherited. They magnanimously opened their borders, slackened their laws and gave free reign to the pathological altruism that caused their ultimate demise. SCS, like Socialism, Atheism or Sexual Liberation, is not a new idea; it's a part of a recurring cycle of rise and fall, which has been happening for as long as civilizations existed. Those are signs of decline, masquerading as tolerance and progressive thinking; they are glaring holes in a ship that is taking water, because under their innocuous appearance, they are demanding a radical shift in one's identity and therefore, one's being and consequently, one's purpose and reason to exist.

Back to Lebanon, SCS would cause only the Christian population to surrender what makes it christian (due to its noxious exposure to Western Liberalism), while the Muslim population still clings to its religious identity, and who could fault them in doing so? Preserving and defending that which gives them drive and purpose-their spiritual identity! To what did the Christians owe their drive to civilize and unite Europe and the New world, defeat Islamic and Nordic invasions, form homogeneous (yet culturally distinct!) European nations at the forefront of technology and learning, build monasteries and schools in the farthest confines of the earth and keep hand-written and printed documentation of history about much of what we know today ? Separation of Church and State? Pathological altruism? Diversity? Equality? Humanism and Positivism? None of these ideas of course. They owe it to the faith that molded their culture and gave them a purpose. To the **union** of Church and State. Their drive cannot be quantified by science and is, therefore, spiritual and so is every real cultural drive. The cultural drive (the power which gives us purpose) can never be human-centered (ie: ideo-logical) because we are not the center of the universe but *part of it*. It comes from *somewhere else*. Negating that reality has a name: Hubris. The Ancient Greeks recognized this emanation of human arrogance as a clear sign of decline.

The Church is the soul and the Soul is the Church*. Separating it from its human mass, replacing it with man-centered ideologies and 'civil' laws only results in a zombified human clutter which will 'live' on for a short period of time before collapsing from lack of purpose.

---

*the Church: *Any religious institution (not necessarily the Christian Church).*

The Strongman

"Kingship, like serfdom, slavery, peace, misery, love or freedom, is an eternal concept. Many mistake it for a mere temporal political status" - John Stormcrow

The common thread between communist Soviet Russia, the 3rd Reich, Napoleon's France, Ancient Rome, Genghis Khan's Mongol empire, or any political entity with a distinct cultural identity, is the presence of the 'Strongman' leader, with a clear vision and purpose. When this vision and purpose radiate with so much focus and intensity, they gain a godly aura and are therefore, removed from the bounds of common human morality - i.e., beyond Good and Evil. Historians and people later calling the leader 'good' or 'evil', is an opinionated perception, rather than the full story. It's the luxury of those who cuss from the comfort of their sofa at the football player who fails to score a goal; they're completely disconnected from something that has happened in real time and yet, still want to pass judgement upon it.

It is that power, which drives a mass of people into becoming a culture.

Without it, people lose purpose and direction because there is no inspiring figure, no 'strongman' (you will need to rid the term of all its negative modern connotations, though it is hard to do so) to harness their collective identity into a focused cultural pulse. Be it on the left or on the right of the (outdated and simplistic) political spectrum, a strongman with a vision, makes achievers out of their people. Rome offered humanity architecture, law, warfare and political strategy; Napoleon brought military, legal, political and religious reforms; The 3rd Reich's achievements were mainly industrial and technological (the Highway being one of them) but perhaps some would be surprised that Nazi Germany pioneered animal rights and animal conservation legislation. The Mongols under Genghis Khan left no significant culture to speak of (except dried milk and hand grenades!) but without his fearsomely inspiring guidance, the many divided mongol tribes would never have united under one ruler, before challenging the entire western civilization's existence. Stalinist Russia sent the first animal, then the first man into space. And by the time the democratic West sent a man on the Moon, the West as a culture, was already dead and cruising on the industrial and technological prowess of a defunct paradigm. Ever since the double-blow of both world wars and the triumph of the rule of the masses against the old system, the world has been steadily declining in terms of culture, technology and humanity. It has been shown how easily small groups of ideologically driven leaders could disrupt and even topple much larger political entities and systems where people have grown complacent and disconnected from their common cultural purpose.

In the absence of culture, ideology is a substitute, a whole lot of drama masquerading as purpose or 'cause'. The bottom line is that a small quantity of culturally or ideologically united people can easily overcome much more numerous quantities of atomized individualistic 'free-thinking' moderns and have their bureaucratic technocratic representatives promptly replaced. As mentioned earlier, an inspiring figure or a strongman, is of course not enough; this figure needs an intense vision to achieve through their people so that those people gain a cultural aspect.

Countries with visionless tyrants abound, and those are cesspits of corruption and misery; an abyss separates them from actual culture. Democratic and bureaucratic systems are separated from culture just as much, but what prevent that from being noticed, are the many layers of good manners, protocols and civility inherited from the old system, giving off a semblance of morality. This keeps a lid over the decay and cultural rot happening underneath. Under a bunch of 'democratically elected' technocrats, life is materialistically oriented and existence becomes like farm life, where the individual is milked for their capacities before being sent to retirement -or likely euthanized to have their organs harvested- after an uneventful and purposeless life. This is probably why we get to hear about some random average joe who blows up a hotel or a crammed train station after living a life of compliance and tedium under the rule of an anonymous and unaccountable mass of bureaucratic nobodies who were marketed and parachuted by corporations. This is the sham of Democracy revealing itself to more and more people every day. Despite material abundance, people are on antidepressants and increasingly miserable. They have been voting for centuries and yet things are not getting better -quite the contrary.

Under Democracy and individualism, real leaders with outstanding vision have been smothered, replaced by docile and compliant technocratic monkeys. There is a risk linked to leaders with a purpose, as history has showed us. In a world of corporations, risk cannot be tolerated and profit margins cannot be disrupted.

POLITICS AND EMOTIONS

The aim of politics is to create the widest social concensus achievable within a given political group. This allows for the possibility of achieving long-term goals benefiting said group. Most people mistake a political alliance for a personal one (the two party leaders shaking hands and smiling on TV) because they see things from their own perspective as individuals. Many cannot understand that a political alliance is aimed at uniting the respective popular bases of the leaders they see on television, towards common goals and most importantly, a common history.

As humanity sinks deeper into idiocracy, and its language further eroding, loss of consensus over several vital cultural concepts reaches a critical stage; politics get increasingly associated with emotions. Political terms become emotionally charged so that they achieve maximum election campaign effect. Important, but complicated issues like keeping the population's culture healthy, intact and at sustainable levels, demand too much cognitive process and are therefore unpopular in democratic sales pitches. The aim is to appeal to the widest audience, and we all know that this specific audience is not known for its bright intellect. The same is with the students in a highschool class; 5 or 10% of every class are highly intelligent. Geniuses are even more rare.

The problem with Democracy, is that it doesn't care about those able to read past emotional smokescreens and political campaign trigger words. It seeks the voice of the majority, and this majority processes the world through the prism of emotion.

In a nutshell, the majority of society is not the brightest sample of humanity, and yet, their vote equals that of brighter minds, in a democratic system whose main pillar is absolute Equality. Predictably, and since no one is a loser in egalitarian systems, modernity decided to bestow a prize on the majority so it can keep feeling special: Emotional Intelligence (EI). For lack of raw cognitive power, the majority can feel relevant nonetheless, by proudly wearing its EI badge.

The Story of EI started with a journalist, Daniel Goleman, who coined the term in one of his articles. He's not a scientist, but who cares in today's emotionally-driven times? The term grew immensely popular, gaining dogmatic status. Today, every educational panel uses and abuses the term EI to sell its egalitarian schemes, camouflaged in pseudoscientific terminology. In a 2010 research about EI, Alabama University scholar Peter David Harms concluded the following:

"Our searches of the literature revealed only six articles in which the authors either explicitly examined the incremental validity of EI scores over measures of both cognitive ability and Big Five personality traits in predicting either academic or work performance, or presented data in a manner that allowed examination of this issue.

Not one of these six articles (Barchard,2003; Newsome, Day, & Catano, 2000;O'Connor & Little, 2003; Rode, Arthaud-Day, Mooney, Near, & Baldwin, 2008;Rode et al., 2007; Rossen & Kranzler,2009) showed a significant contribution for EI in the prediction of performance after controlling for both cognitive ability and the Big Five... For correlations involving the overall EI construct, EI explained almost no incremental variance in performance ([change in prediction] = .00. Findings were identical when considering only cases involving an ability-based measure of IE...."[**Remaining Issues in Emotional Intelligence Research: Construct Overlap, Method Artifacts, and Lack of Incremental Validity**]

Unlike Cognitive intelligence, Emotional intelligence -a fancy name for conscientiousness, tells us clinical psychologist Jordan Peterson- is not a 'psychometrically valid concept'. Peterson then points out that cognitive abilities (IQ) are different from the big five personality traits (openness, conscientiousness, extraversion, agreeableness and neuroticism) in that those five traits can in no way be measured as indicators of cognitive ability, which invalidates the concept of an emotional intellect: *"IQ (Peterson states) is a different story. It is the most well-validated concept in the social sciences, bar none. It is an excellent predictor of academic performance, creativity, ability to abstract, processing speed, learning ability and general life success".*

So EQ/EI is a fad, a marketing ploy, a plain lie masquerading as scientific truth. And this lie lives on as a testament to human nature: We prefer convenient lies to hard truths and the former has always proved itself much more popular than the latter -which explains why books that lie to us, would still sell like hot cakes. Emotional Intelligence is the measuring stick in today's politics, which explains why the 'emotional politician with emotional media' cocktail is so explosive. The majority of the public will always choose to believe -and be manipulated by- the EQ/EI consolation prize, massaging their hurt egos, while buried deep in their subconscious, is the hurtful truth: We are not equal.

GLOBALISM ATTRACTS THE ZOMBIE

Proponents of globalism solely reason in economic, materialistic terms. Their logic exclusively revolves around money, just like the rhetoric of their ancestor and idol, Marx -what are globalists, other than rebranded closet marxists/socialists?. Their 'revolutions' focus entirely on economics, and essential facets of humanity are, in typical Marxist fashion, discarded. Traditions, family values, identitarian values which are behind the formation of communities everywhere, are first mocked, then decried as oppressive and in the forseeable last stage, outlawed.

A gay pride in the streets of formerly catholic Paris, is welcomed by Parisians, but a Nativity Scene makes them literally hiss and spit, reminding us of that famous possessed girl scene in 'The Exorcist'. Even better, it shows us that the so-called Tolerant Left isn't so tolerant after all.

For the Neo-Marxist and the Globalist, not only religion, but Identity is the new opium of the masses which needs to be eradicated.

Identity, is now the new target of Globalism, after the successful dechristianization of the West. Today, Christianity is being fought by ideologies that comply with Globalism (Marxism, Feminism, Atheism,...). One would ask that if Globalism is anti-religious, why does it promote and pander to Islam? Simply because Globalism views Islam as a rising market, not a religion, and it's therefore necessary to be friends with it in order to better exploit it. So Identity is the new target, but identity, while sounding abstract, is a gathering of tangible and measurable factors that constitute the basis of every concrete community with a shared language, borders and values:

-Traditions (spiritual and habitual) and beliefs.

-Arts, architecture and craftsmanship.

-Culinary and agricultural knowledge.

-Folk-lore and mythology (a massive source of inspiration), stories of a common ancestry.

-Race and ethnicity, dress code.

-Familial/tribal organization and structure/behavior.

-Military/defense/tactical knowledge.

The above are usually the products of the geographic environment that makes possible the existence of a people. The above factors, according to Globalism, are remnants of an older system, outdated and irrelevant, as we keep hearing in the media. These factors are existential threats to Globalism. With Globalist open borders policy, and the mocking of traditional values, the dismantling of the traditional family, gender roles, the wrecking of childhood by confusing our kids with the theory of gender fluidity, and by creating a generic architecture and meaningless art, Globalism is erasing the identitarian tenets of the old system, one by one, leaving only the one thing that really matters to it: Markets, the consumer-zombie's ideal habitat/ecosystem. Humans are now farmed like cattle, to consume and keep the economies growing.

Growing... for what exactly?

Globalism, a not-so-hidden facet of leftism, accuses its opponents of being 'un-scientific', while globalism itself and its cronies are guilty of doing exactly that- ignoring, sidelining, downplaying and downright attacking a universal science; biology and genetics. Because biology, like every real science, is rooted in observable reality, Globalism is currently fighting it to advance its own destructive 'equalizing' gender and race fluidity agenda. Proponents of unfettered Globalism/Marxism/Socialism are either knowingly or unknowingly supporting an anti-science agenda while claiming to be the party of scientific knowledge.

Today more than any other day, we find out that Globalists and assorted Leftists have always been pursuing a centuries-old agenda of linking religion to backwardness and anti-scientific progress in a bid to destroy the traditionalist paradigm. The most laughable attempts of the Global cabal to deny biology are hiding behind a pseudo-scientific association, the APA and claim that homosexuality and transgenderism are not psychological disorders while maintaining mild conditions like ADHD or OCD as mental disorders in order to keep the kids' drug industry going.

The notion of backwards religiosity has become so ingrained in the minds of the masses that nothing is easier than getting those masses to chant 'religion is poison' in perfect unison while feeling enlightened and rebellious. A visit to an ancient temple or church, and a below-the-surface research, can however, easily disprove that notion of religious backwardness that is pursued by Globalism and cronies. Architectural, artistic and scientific breakthroughs were never hindered by religion, on the contrary, much of those was achieved by the same religious figures the Party of Love, Equality and Tolerance passionately hates.

It appears that Religious Sentiment is not a hindrance to the creative genius of Humanity, but rather an enhancer of that creativity and a spiritual tool of discovery in the pursuit of knowledge. Even as the Quran forbade visual artistic creation, 8th century Islamic artists found a way to 'circumvent' that rule by becoming pioneers of pictorial calligraphy. Religion being like a spiritual 'operating system'[1], can be corrupted and turned into a weapon of destruction. Religion distorted into ideology has proven itself to be a most disastrous combination. Scientists with a religious background are, rather than ignoring the spiritual facet of their own humanity, embracing the Eternal

---

1   See: "The Barbarian Bible" by Ianto Watt.

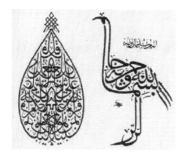

Photo: In the muthanna or "doubled" style of calligraphy shown on the left each half of the design is a mirror image of the other. The basmalah in the thuluth script on the right has been written in the shape of an ostrich. (www.islamicity.org)

Photo: The angular kufic script is here used to put a well known religious expression into the form of a mosque with four minarets. (www.islamicity.org)

and are thus finding renewed purpose in their scientific pursuits. Isaac Newton, Michael Faraday or Louis Pasteur are but a couple of examples of a long list of religious scientists. Atheist Nobel laureates make less than 10% of the total number of Nobel Prize Laureates[2]. This is not to say that atheist scientists find no purpose in their scientific practices, but they surely are suppressing the metaphysical side of their humanity and are strictly confining themselves to the domain of Materialism, as a field and an ideology. This voluntary suppression of an angle of research that is still largely unexplored demonstrates a lack of curiosity -or is it fear?- that is peculiar, because people of science are generally children of curiosity.

The aim of the above digression was to show that Leftism and Globalism are the real obscurantism. Leftism and globalism are the real party of empty slogans and anti science. They are the side of pure materialism and everything else is decried as 'backwards', 'oppressive', 'insert-adjective-of-your-choice-phobic', 'bigoted', 'hateful' and 'non-inclusive' and is to be dismissed as supersitions borne of evil obsolete minds. Thus the Party that labels itself the party of Tolerance, Love and Inclusiveness, is itself

2   "Religion of Nobel Prize Winners" (upload.wikimedia.org)

hateful, intolerant, bigoted and exclusive to anything that is not compliant with its own agenda of the annihilation of borders, standards, morals, values, history, culture and heritage. And because globalism and its political arms (marxism, socialism, communism, feminism...) seek the tearing down of all standards (they call it 'deconstructivism'), it appeals most to the largest majority of people, whose standards are dubious at best and non existing, at worst. And because globalism has a powerful ideology rooted in abstract and ambiguous concepts such as Freedom or Equality, it enslaves highly educated minds whose idealism disconnects them from reality and that's what makes Globalism the greatest danger of our times.

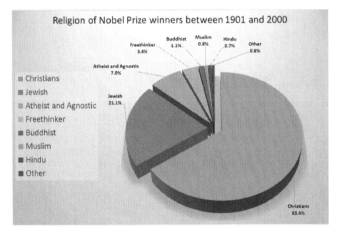

Zombiefied globalists and assorted ideologues like to bash religions and depict them as backwards, but numbers don't lie. Source: wikimedia.org

Today's battle -let us keep that in mind- is not between Left and Right; this paradigm has officially died with the XXth century, as we noticed how Leftist and Rightist parties who hate each other on TV, would gladly gang up on anyone who would challenge their existence and future. They both share the same emotionally charged rhetoric that only the lowest common denominator is receptive to. Throughout the modern world, the Left v/s Right circus is on its last legs as the battle reveals itself as a showdown between the traditionalist paradigm and the globalist one, which has been trying to assert itself for the last 200 years. Both Left and Right have fallen, to reveal an even more sinister enemy. The real enemy of humanity. This enemy wants to turn male into female, black into white, the unequal into equal, the good into the bad, the artful into the trashy, the innocent into the sordid. Everything turned upon its own head.

This great annihilator has deceived many into its ranks, with flashy high-tech, convenience, pretense (the *illusion* of doing something v/s *actually doing* something) and pseudo science. This is classic Tolkien, as Mordor's armies seem invincible and all hope seems so lost that desertions are to be expected. But hope in humanity remains and like that unforgettable tale of Middle Earth, evil can -and will- be defeated by the most unlikely heroes, no matter how small and puny they might seem.

NARCISSISM DESTROYS SOCIETIES

Each new generation receives less from the previous one, to the point where nowadays, we witness new generations inheriting debt and problems, rather than a cushion of stability to build on.

A parent bequeathes a land, a house, or some form of asset to their progeny; now there are 2 ways this newly inherited asset will go:

1-squandered by the prodigal sons, or
2-preserved, and ideally, multiplied.

In self-centered times like ours, each generation chooses not to care about what it leaves behind, due to focusing solely on the Self. Modernist 'philosophies' relentlessly glorify the 'Me' and the 'I'. Self gratification is paramount and for that end, people not only squander their own resources, but go into more and more debt for the sake of immediate satisfaction, offsetting the result of their narcissism to unborn generations.

In older times, people who came from even the most modest families inherited lands and sizeable assets, enough to live comfortably off and pursue cultural interests. People went to universities and studied new skills without the stress of failure, and as a result, those were better and simpler times, where the scholar learned for the sake of learning and, as a result, learned happily. Artistic output, architecture, craftsmanship and the overall quality of literature were also better. How do we know that? Modernity is actively distorting classical literature and art with its modern/postmodern 'artists' out of
sheer resentment.

The 'pillars' of Modern 'art' are:
Shock, Irony and Price tag.

This banana duct-taped to a wall, and 'presented ' at the Miami's Art Basel sold for 120000 USD. (2019) - Shock, Irony and price tag are the new 'criteria' of modern 'art'and are the reason why nobody today, takes modern art (and modern artists) seriously anymore. *Source: CBS News: "Performance artist eats banana duct-taped to wall that sold for $120,000*

Art and craft were not tainted by the pursuit of material gain made from their sale or the number of outraged reacts they received on social media; they were a product of a long labor and a desire to transcend one's own creative boundaries. A desire to be remembered, not for days or weeks, but for *posterity*, outside the boundaries of time. In contrast, today's 'art' is very much confined within very short time boundaries, at the antipodes of the Eternal.

Fast forward to the present: For an exorbitant fee, a university will 'teach' you a major that will enable you to successfully shackle yourself for 10-12 hours at a desk, pretending that "you've made it". People today rush into university without even pondering whether this major is truly what they want to be doing for the rest of their life, or if they should even **be** at a university.

Quickly and without thinking, they are ushered into college because pausing for a minute will give others a headstart! And that cannot be allowed... A Lifetime's decision is made in a split second; the chains are on, and off to the rowing deck, dear graduate.

Now why would the young graduate think about the future if they inherited nothing from their own past but debt, apathy and no guidance? Upon finding a job, they will rent a small place, and blow their salary money over trips and parties. It sure is a highly entertaining way of life, to be honest, but such memories will later be remembered alone, because as life passes us by, we were traveling, partying and paying the rent, oblivious to the future, with whom to spend it or how to spend it. This is the terminal stage of a dying society, killed by the self-centered lifestyle of its own people.

In the case of a person who is not a narcissist, such a person will understand that any inherited assets were hard-earned, and that the same is expected of the heir of their own progeny. They will learn new skills, languages, arts and culture while knowing that if the mechanistic rhythm of modern society is disrupted, as it will ultimately be, and should things go horribly wrong, they have a place to fall back on. The skills they're learning, are not for the self-gratification provided by a meager wage. They're here for a bigger purpose: To give the descendent generation more power to achieve and a wider array of choices than the previous generation had. It is a continuous struggle *upwards*.

We need to buy as many assets as we can, and teach our children the worth of those assets and the need to multiply them so that when their children want to pursue a scholarly path, they'd be able to do it in happiness and serenity. This is how families grow strong and influencial, but in an age where the whole concept of family is eroded, the smallest societal molecule is undermined and is in danger. To destroy societies and reduce them to consuming cattle, all that's required is to atomize the extended family, then the nuclear family, and make each of its components only think about itself.

Cloggers

If traffic jams can teach us anything, it's the dangers of Equality. Equality sounds positive in theory, but in practice, nothing comes close in terms of 'passive-oppressive' potential. A non-moving traffic is a tyrannical, time-wasting, nerve-grating, life-shortening beast. It is also *equal*.

In traffic, the sputtering hatchback is equal to the roaring and rumbling hypercar stuck on its left. It's equal to the giant truck idling on its right. In traffic we're all equal because we're hardly moving. We're all moving at the same speed, which is no speed at all. The racecar has the potential to go from point A to point B in five minutes but due to the equalizing process of traffic, it now needs an hour. Just like the clunker idling next to it.

So what's the use of having a powerful, fast and performing engine if one cannot use it due to cloggers? Why go through the hassle of having or building such a technological masterpiece if it will not be allowed the use of its full potential, because cloggers are in the way?

Only when the clogger is removed, will we be able to witness a smoother commute. The clogger is everyone who wants to have a car so they can park it at work for twelve hours instead of simply taking the bus or carpool. The clogger is anyone who thinks owning a car is a human right. The clogger is anyone who doesn't know how to drive, but gets a car anyway. The clogger is the spirit of Equality and entitlement coupled with a lack of common sense. Equality is the stalling of the better, faster, more powerful, and more capable, preventing it from being itself, annulling it in the process.

Excessive individualism leads to an atomized society where no one wants to interact with anyone else, isolated in their own car with their earbuds on, and although they're in the middle of a mechanized human sea, it's a sea of bleak misanthropy. they're alone.

Equality sounds attractive, but so is the Sirens Song. When asking for equality, let's ask ourselves: *What equality?* Equality of what or whom in terms of which criteria or context? The word by itself is ambiguity incarnate. It can be interpreted in a million ways, each more perfidious than the next. Only when well put into context, can equality become productive, otherwise it will slowly clog our life and eventually smother us.

FREE WILL V/S NO WILL

The mere act of thinking is an act of will, yet modernist thinkers and philosophers still reduce existence to its mechanistic and chemical biological constituents, mistaking life for its organic manifestations.

Without free will, humanity succumbs to the mechanistic nature of their biological existence and behave the same way, submitting to strictly bodily urges. Reality teaches us otherwise; not all people are equal (since no two people make the exact same life choices) and not all people attain a goal in the same way. That is not to say that there can **either** be free will **or** the absence of it. Both conditions coexist in the same world. The more a person acts on their bodily urges -live to consume- the more they embody the absence of free will and the more they resemble the zombie, a creature that is only moved by its urge to consume. And the more a person applies their will, the more they become a living example of will fighting entropy. That is how we get authors, artists, inventors, athletes and geniuses. Christianity is arguably the clearest illustration of Free Will; a god who chose a people, who in turn, rejected him. The Gospel highlights another example of free will with the 'Faith of the Canaanite Woman' passage- A Gentile who recognizes the godhood of Christ and acknowledges him as the Lord*. There is no morality without free will and the possibility to recognize between the different nuances between Good and Evil. The animal kingdom, governed by the five senses and instinct, has no such compass.

Since both levels of existence -will and the lack of it- are found all around us, the world with its thinkers is dividing itself in two factions, each advocating and pushing for their own vision of humanity: an existence where people exercise their mental power transcendentally to shape their life and that of others, if possible, and a nihilistic one where humanity recognizes its own futility and succumbs to its strict organic urges in the name of 'freedom' and 'experimentation', because 'nothing matters'! The lines are drawn. Let each of us pick a side.

---

* The Faith Of A Canaanite Woman (Matthew 15:21-28): Many misinterpret Jesus' irony towards the 'ethnically chosen' (the Jews) as racism towards the Canaanite woman, interpreting scripture with a politically-correct mentality of the Modern.

THE PERNICIOUSNESS OF THE EQUALITY AGENDA

Let us look at a homogeneous community- same race, same beliefs, same behaviors, same cuisine, same values, same laws... We can say those people are an example of equality. In fact, stating that they are equal, makes it redundant. And stupid.

Because, what is the point? Clearly those people in that community share so many things in common and their social equality is so obvious that we don't ever need to mention it. It's like coming from the same parents.

Do brothers keep wasting their own time affirming their brotherhood to each other? So, in instances of equality, or of things affirming themselves by their mere nature, feeling a constant need to highlight them, is a sign that something is wrong. That something is actually, not *equal*. When a group keeps drumming the rest of us with talks of equality, some awareness is in order. This talk of equality might be hiding something.

When a people's cultural behavior resembles each other, they are equal, and because they are equal, there's no use mentioning it anymore. It's a self-affirming reality. If all people are rich, then there are no rich people. If all are insane then there are no insane people. You get the drill. So when we keep insisting that everyone be equal, this means we're trying to deny something; a diversity -not the one advertised in the medias- in humanity, among other things. This diversity already exists through the myriad of races, ethnicities, cultures, religions and customs that live on this planet. We're also trying to equalize noble human traits with base ones, refined human behaviour with the boorish, functional human beings with neurotic wrecks, responsible human behavior with the reckless, and intelligent human behavior with the retarded and self destructive.

Equality does not exist anywhere in nature. Man's stubbornness in pursuing the white whale of equality is the surest manifestation that Man has divorced oneself from Nature and wants to shape the world to one's own image, as does a god. The more we withdraw from nature and go inward, we seek to create an alternate reality- a 'new' reality where sweet Equality exists!

With equality as a Man-centered ideology, we're legitimizing the degenerate and nullifying the evolved, more civilized, and overall better human. But most ironically, we are demanding that which already exists, but which we do not want to see: Equality within, diversity without. The Liberal agenda wants merely to invert humanity, thinking it is adding to it; 'diversity' within and 'equality' without, ending up with neither.

(Follow) ⌄

Silicon Valley's reaction to the #NPC meme is only reinforcing it's original concept, whatdya know

RunProgram{IndividualResponse.Outrage}

MULTICULTURALISM

It is hard to view Multiculturalism as a modern ideology designed with the best of intentions. It is a revolutionary kind of warfare designed to weaken those who adopt it, and has never been implemented by the people who championed it[1]. It has instead, been marketed towards other people for their exclusive use[2]. What is omitted on the package is the social engineering required to install and run "multiculturalism.exe" successfully.

Israel Zangwill's oft celebrated 'melting pot' concept is not the prevalent system in the Israeli ethnnostate but it is the enforced system in the western world and many other countries who simply seek to ape the West. Multiculturalism bombards its adherents with an array of different values, that are most of the times completely paradoxal and contradictory, in a way that removes the focus necessary to move forward, let alone to process the quantity of diverging values and their cultural ramifications, all 'coexisting' in the same place.

With Multiculturalism, it soon becomes impossible to assimilate reality, process it and move along to something else. When things go wrong, as they always do, the ideologically-blinded zealot has a ready-made explanation: The multicultural religion has not been implemented in the 'correct' way or frequency.

The best way to get people to adopt an idea is to market it positively: All-inclusiveness, Global village, Open borders policy, Only one race (the human race!), 'Overcoming' the gender-binary, Affirmative Action, etc... all positive-sounding taglines that make anyone who hears

---

1   *"Jews took a new religion as a substitute for Judaism. And that was secular ideologies- you name it. Feminism, environmentalism, Marxism, socialism, and for some even communism." -Dennis Prager, Jewish American and founder of Prager University, 2020.*

2   *See: "Jewish Involvement in Shaping U.S. Immigration Policy" by Dr Kevin Mac Donald (The Culture of Critique, Ch. 7).*

Top picture: The mental image which forms in the average brain when one mentions the word 'multiculturalism' (Photo source: Anonymous).

Below: An internet meme showing jewish support for a multicultural, open-borders Europe while enforcing airtight borders at home...

Next page: Grateful Migrant spits on a European woman.
Source: Anonymous (many place the incident in Sweden but others place it in Vienna, Austria but the context is multicultural Europe).

them all warm and fuzzy inside. They definitely don't want to be missing out on such a 'vibrant', 'colorful' and 'progressive' utopia in the 'global community' -whatever that means.

As a virus attacks a living organism, ideologies like Multiculturalism are virii which attack one's mind and spirit. The twist is that it acts like a drug and its host becomes addicted to it, never aware of its finality until it's far too late. Even then, the mind is too corrupted, the soul too decomposed to even realize the mortal situation- Even in death, a mind possessed by Multiculturalism will still be zealously rationalizing and justifying its own killer.

As a result, and due to continuous media conditioning, anyone who questions the good name of Multiculturalism is committing suicide by social ostracism, loss of friends and livelihood.

Questioning Multiculturalism is akin to being guilty of heresy in front of an Inquisition Tribunal. Multiculturalism, a sub-god of Leftism, is still a god nonetheless, and has its zealots and Saudi-style inforcers (mutaweh) in the atheist West and everywhere this new religion manages to take hold.

MATRIARCHY/PATRIARCHY

There is no matriarchy or patriarchy except in the heads of whoever invented those labels for the purpose of antagonizing men and women. Inventing such wordings pits man and woman against each other in some kind of competition for power, in the hopes of the emergeance of a 'winner'. The reality is, in this modern battle of the sexes, both man and woman end up losers in this game, and the trust and companionship that are essential to the bonding of the couple into a functional unit are severely eroded. Millenia of complementary lifestyle are thus destroyed in a couple of generations.

We can already observe the five stages of societal rise/collapse by looking at Western society:

1- A society reaches great height in culture, trade and military organization. Its power allows it to subdue/conquer other cultures, spreading its paradigm and world-view over the rest of the world.

2- Centuries spent in opulence bring up a generation of people who take their culture for granted. In their complacency, they mask their own condescension with talk of equality and compassion. They demand open borders and an end to an 'oppressive system' that has created 'inequality'.

3- Self-loathing reaches new lows as it rots the minds of the majority, who seize power democratically and end the old system through 'progressive' laws.

4- The new society knows a few decades of booming economy due to lower labor costs made possible with the waves of welcomed immigrants and slackened border laws. Everybody thinks all is going well because they're measuring everything in financial or economic or material terms.

5- A decade later, the self-loathing society has forgotten voluntarily all of its knowledge and heritage and has now disconnected itself from any culture it has inherited from its ancestors. Cultural inertia is reached and the society's twitching corpse is eaten by the new immigrants turned settlers.

This is how centuries or even millenia of culture can be undone in only a few generations of social rot, where society becomes so divided that each sex starts blaming the other for the collapse (hence, the 'Smash the Patriarchy' slogans brandished by Feminism and the subsequent 'Men Going Their Own Way' -the MGTOW movement)!

There are only examples of societies where man and woman complement each other in their respective roles, and examples of societies where they *don't*.

In India and Africa, we find mostly what is being defined today as "matriarchal societies". The truth is, in these societies, lazy men have decided to take a back seat and leave everything to women, from child-raising, to home care, to business. Ironically, it's in these 'matriarchies' that rape and child slavery are most prevalent and it's in 'patriarchies' that rape is severely condemned and child labor outlawed. It is from so-called 'oppressive, patriarchal' Europe that the whole world upholds the sacred notion of 'Women and Children first', and the code of chivalry with the importance it puts in defending a woman's honor, not because she's weak, but because of her importance!

In their attack on 'Patriarchy', the Leftists are amusingly not attacking any Arab or Islamic country (known for their pronounced male culture), but European traditional societies *exclusively*. In truth, those European societies unjustly dubbed as 'patriarchal' are simply societies where men and women *cooperate*. They are Both, patriarchal **and** matriarchal. But end-stage Liberalism and Leftism still sees them as 'oppressive', not because they are, but because it is a system that is totally antithetical to market-driven liberalism and globalism.

Liberalism (one of the most misleading terms ever created!) sees the European cultural paradigm as an existential threat and that's understandable; this cultural paradigm and worldview has Christian roots and identity, and Christianity recognizes equality *only* from God's perspective, while Liberalism views it from Man's perspective. Christianity is the antithesis of Liberalism, Leftism and market-driven globalism precisely because it is hierarchical in nature*.

Liberalism rests on Egalitarianism as an absolute, but Traditionalism rests on reality and reality is an extremely organic concept, that reflects the progression (or regression/stagnation) of the organisms living within its contextual framework.

*Leftism and Humanism in Christianity are well documented attempts to infiltrate and subvert this religion for the purpose of diluting it from within. See "Aa-1025: The Memoirs of a Communist's infiltration in to the Church" (M. Carré) and "The Catholic Church and the Cultural Revolution" by Michael E. Jones.

DEMOCRACY

These are times of uncertainty for democracy and that's a wonderful thing. Why, you say? Well because we have just empirically discovered that democracy needs homogeneity to succeed; yet, those who want democracy also want diversity, and multiculturalism when combined with democracy, creates tribal and group alliances working against each other in the same host country, killing the country in the process by taking it towards civil strife. Every group works in self-interest, and in a pluralistic society, democracy is a recipe for disaster. But in a homogeneous society -same race, same religion, same level of education, and more or less same social level- we have a real chance of having democracy succeed.

Democracy is a tool that works in an organically orderly society, otherwise, it's doomed to fail, with too many groups lumped together, with differing interests. The strong shall get the weak eventually, through birthrate, economic means, violence, cunning or a combination of those four. In a heterogeneous society, let us just forget about democracy but let us look at a new system which is making an entrance in today's politics:
Proportional representation.

In Lebanon for example, where proportional representation has been implemented for the first time, feudal and tribal political forces are bracing themselves to see if that new law they have voted over will spell their doom or on the opposite, reinforce them and prove their resilience and resourcefulness in an increasingly modern political game. Proportional representation is one last ditch to salvage the sinking ship of democracy but it might work in organically multicultural* societies like Lebanon.

*(Unlike the socially engineered diversity being pursued in western countries) "Lebanon encompasses a great mix of cultures and ethnic groups which have been building up for more than 6000 years. Most of the Lebanese are descendants of the Phoenicians/Canaanites and/or West Aramaic (50-70%). The second largest ethnic group in Lebanon descends from Arabs (20-30%). Armenians, Greeks, Assyrians, Hebrews, Kurds, Persians and others form about (10-20%)- Source: Lebanon Profile - http://www.lgic.org

In the meantime, Modernity and Globalism keep hammering us through their various medias about the backwardness of tribalism, despite the whole world and its resources being concentrated in the hands of a handful of tribes. Family, tribe and clan are still the ruling models despite what your local 'academic' might say. The world is controlled by only a few families.

Modernism, despite painting itself as a liberal, inclusive and tolerant paradigm, is intolerant of any alternative to Democracy as a political system. How tolerant is that? Ask any 'enlightened' modern about monarchy and see them recoil in horror. They have been conditioned to view hierarchy, nobility, aristocracy and caste, as defacto tyrannical, and yet these same moderns are glued on series glorifying kings, queens, emperors, counts, barons and princes. They crave aristocracy and the media market obliges! But God forbid we want monarchy in real life!

The most glaring aspect of social schizophrenia is observed among modern liberalized, Leftist 'christians' (post-Vatican II[1] Catholics and Protestants alike): They worship Christ as king but are revulsed by the earthly concept of kingship. For them, kingship is a metaphysical title and cannot be conceivably a viable option on Earth despite ample evidence of its past successes and cultural legacies we still admire and write stories about, to this day.

---

1   *The Second Ecumenical Council of the Vatican (1962-65) through its ambiguous implementation, diluted much of the Catholic faith in a liberal effort to 'reach out' to Protestantism and Judaism. It called for a 'renewal' of the Church without specifying how, causing diverging modernist interpretations of this specific point. See "The Catholic Church and the Cultural Revolution" by Michael E. Jones.*

LIBERALISM IS NARCISSISM

A well known trend among liberal Hollywood celebrities is to adopt outside of their own ethnicity and cultural background. People coming from liberal 'elites' and families are often found traveling to poor war-torn places and hives of misery 'helping the poor', 'feeding the needy' and 'contributing to the betterment' of helpless societies. They also make sure it's in the press.

Closer at home, they make sure any socio-economically lower classes enjoy government subsidized welfare and special quotas to keep the victimhood culture alive. Removing this victim culture would rob those liberal elites of their opium: feeling good about themselves while basking in the illusion of appearing helpful and chivalrous. This is why anyone coming from a 'disadventaged' background, be they a third worlder or a woman, and succeeding on their own without the use of quotas and assorted liberal schemes, is viewed with a mix of suspiscion and disgust by Liberals.

How to recognize a Liberal?

Open your social media page and you see this dashing new civil society candidate for the upcoming parliamentary elections: She's speaking passionately about human rights, elder people, children, education, reform programs, baby dolphins and of course, Equality. She sounds so genuine and driven. You're intrigued, charmed by so much positive energy. But then, after some digging you find out she's divorced and her children are high school dropouts and live miserably, shuttling every week between their mother and their father; a dysfunctional family.

Liberals love to make trips to forlorn third world regions to help the dwellers of some forgotten village in the deep-end of Indonesia or Kwazulu Natal to help the poor children learn the alphabet or eat with a fork and spoon. They install mosquito traps in the Indian jungle and the villagers hail them like gods.

It provides the liberal with the ego-massage they crave. Meanwhile at home, their life has gone to hell, parents divorced, and siblings do not talk to each other, not to mention other dysfunctional relatives with some degenerate or self-destructive lifestyle. Nobody knows anyone in the same building and neighbors avoid each other. The Liberal, rather than fixing the wrongs they have at home, prefer to gain bonus ego points for benevolence and altruism in some far away place, then come back and virtue-signal about it to the whole neighborhood. They want to fix society but they won't start with themselves.

It's never really about helping the others, or anybody other than the Self. Run away from your own problems at home, find an underprivileged third world hellhole whose people are living in the mud at the mercy of nature and warlords, and feel good 'helping them' by teaching them how to use toilet paper, charge an iPod or apply mosquito-bite cream. Come back and brag about your important role in advancing civilization. Even better, write some moving article about it and about the need to help the underprivileged by sending them more iPods. Feel superior on your social media page but hide behind flowery rants about equality and global village kumbaya because false humility always gets you bonus equality points.

God forbid the Liberal actually tackles a real problem that requires real heroism, like delinquents in their own neighborhood, environmental irresponsibility in their forests, the lack of creative occupation for growing youths, or solving a family problem. If universal Equality ever happens, whom will the Liberal be condescending to?

Liberalism as a paradigm ushered itself with the Enlightenment, a period of great industrial and philosophical upheaval, mainly characterized with people removing God and the nobility -by 'law' and by violence- and by calling themselves 'moderns'.

Never in any other time period did we encounter people so narcissistic as to flatter themselves with an adjective. The Romans were romans, the Goths were goths, the Arabs were arabs, and the Mayans were mayans. Only in an age of no morality (God is dead), no hierarchy (killing off the aristocracy and now the middle class), no tradition, no ancestry, no borders, no family, no gender and no identity do we find an urgent need to define ourselves by something.

Despite all our efforts to shun traditional identity, it keeps coming back -in the form of pale trendy substitutes like identity politics.

But since we've suppressed and smothered all actual tenets of identity, we've gone inwards, resorting to the worship of the only thing which remains: The Self. The Self is declared king, god instead of God, and so it must be flattered. We laud ourselves with adjectives: We are the Moderns. We are liberals. We are diverse. We are humanistic... The ending arc of every civilization happens with Liberalism. When the Romans, the Greeks or the Arabs were building their empires, Reality was their sole focus. Harsh, amoral reality. An empire must be built. Therefore, blood -some of it innocent- must be shed, mouths need to stay closed, social justice and morality takes a back seat. An empire is born and like every birth, it comes in blood, pain and suffering.

The people of that empire live for generations in prosperity and greatness, gradually forgetting the blood toll of their ancestors. They begin to get soft, to have pity on their neighbors. They want to let them in. They want to give the outsider the opportunity to be like them.

To become 'better'... They want to atone for years, nay, centuries of 'colonial injustice'. Their liberal hearts profusely bleeding; they want to hold their conquered neighbors and kiss them... Perhaps, kneel and beg forgiveness?*.. This

*Update: White liberals are now kneeling and kissing the feet of Black Lives Matter protestors, in the wake of the George Floyd riots (June 2020) - "White people kneel, ask forgiveness from the black community in Third Ward" -Source: Youtube.

display of fake pity emanates from a subconscious feeling of superiority, and is not lost upon the recipient of this pity. Unlike the condescending liberal, the conquered neighbor has not forgotten. He knows the liberal has taken a steamy dump upon the sacrifices of his own fathers and is now ripe for the raping since his ungratefulness is now obvious, his tenets with his own past completely broken. He will not be making an effort to protect a world and a society he has himself unearned for too long. Time to punish him for his insolent pandering and for being a traitor to the memory of his own people, who were once great and powerful. He's but a cuckolded shadow of his former self, and trampling him into dust is but the most poetic justice!

Special treatment turns the recipient into a baby. Author Jason Riley exposes Liberal condescension hiding behind welfare programs and affirmative action policies in his book 'Please Stop Helping Us' - *Source: www.amazon.com*

The Left has, for the last six decades, successfully mastered the art of bending language to fit its own narrative.

Decades of headstart on the bewildered silent majority gave the Left the decisive edge over its opponents; Its semantic and linguistic acrobatics took the public by surprise, charming it with an apparently researched and learned vocabulary. By the time the opponent processed the linguistic distortion, the Left has already gone out to distort another aspect of reality through language and semantics.

As a result, we have entire generations of people who went through college, graduated with high grades, achieved several post-graduate degrees, but still do not question the Left's distortion of language. Their brains have been successfully conditioned by a Leftist mindset, where words and signals now have a heavily politicized extra Ballast. These people are not questioning the mindset which shaped their thought, but encourage everybody else- usually of Traditionalist background- to doubt their own values. These 'college-educated' people whose critical thinking skills are poor at best, still think themselves as being 'revolutionaries', 'vanguardists', 'open-minded' and most hilariously, 'anti-establishment'. These people just do not realize yet that they have been part of the establishment that has been ruling in thought, behavior and politics for the last sixty years at least.

The Left has now come full circle after its linguistic acrobatics has forced it to consider everything to be a social construct (best way to explain everything with minimal effort).

As a result, this social construct admission invalidates everything the Left shouts out against, namely:

- This person is racist!
- This person is misogynistic!
- This person is sexist!
- This person is Hitler!
- This person is a xenophobe!
- This person is a homophobe!

Let us debunk the above temper tantrums the 'moderate, centrist' (who is a rebranded leftist) spews:

This person is racist

This is a favorite. When the moderate Left (including Centrists) sees someone they do not like, shattering media poll lies, this is where they pull out the Racist Card. Let us remind them that the Left itself does not believe in Race, and that according to the Left, Race does not biologically exist, and is a social construct. Therefore, the Centrist, Communist, Marxist and their assorted Leftist flavors cannot use the Race Card anymore. You cannot be racist if Race does not exist. Notorious Leftist Rachel Dolezal added yet another dimension to the Race question, telling everybody that she's race-fluid, and that despite her white caucasian descent, she identifies as black. So dear Leftists, next time you hate on a white person, think twice, because this person might be of the Race-fluid species and actually identifies as a Red Indian... Like democrat senator Elisabeth Warren.

This person is a misogynist

Once again, the Left has also successfully torn down the oppressive artificial gender constructs on which society based itself for hundreds of thousands of years, therefore, words like misogyny and misandry are irrelevant and if used by the Left, will now ring hollow, after the Left stripped them of their meaning. Anything can be a gender now, and if the Left is fighting misogyny, why is it silent to genital mutilation of women, their stoning to death, their forced marriages, and crimes of honor involving women, and instead, is focusing on non-issues like 'mansplaining' and 'man spreading'?

It is good to remind the Left that before attacking someone and accusing them of the impardonable crime of mansplaining or man-spreading, they should first ask them what gender they are. Maybe this dark haired man sitting in front of you actually identifies as a blonde female top model. You don't want to be misgendering someone by mistake!

This person is sexist

If the Left wants to avoid accusations of sexism, now is its chance, and they should grab it by voting Frauke Petry into Office. After all, it's the Left who confirmed that they vote based on gender, when they tried to rationalize why Hillary Clinton lost to Trump. Sexism, the Left must be reminded, is a two-way street, and failure to help the women who lead the AFD or the Rassemblement National from reaching office, will result into yet another term the Left won't be able to use to attack their opponents for sexism.

This person is Hitler

Everyone I don't agree with is Hitler; even the act of questioning that, will make you a Nazi and you don't want that, do you? Especially when in Western society, which will lead to immediate ostracism, loss of livelihood and total abandonment by friends and relatives. When the Hitler card is used, you're basically in a minefield. This card remains the most efficient civil conversation shutter used by the party of Tolerance. Just remind them that they're either for tolerance or not, and that the NSDAP was democratically elected, so the Leftist you're debating, Must either respect the democracy xe worships (gender-neutral pronouns are always fun to use) or be the closet Hitler everybody will now suspect them to be.

This person is a xenophobe

Remind your leftist friend why, then, they live in a gated community that is racially and culturally homogeneous. And why do they not send their kids to a vibrant multicultural public school/college where all cultural backgrounds can freely mix? Also next time your Leftist friend cries their heart out for refugees, tell them you work at an NGO that cares for refugees and that your refugee homing program includes the volunteer housing of refugees in private homes; force your friend to accept at least one refugee family in their home to clothe, feed and look out for. Xenophobia must be fought at all costs and with all means necessary!

PS: Make sure as many friends and acquaintances are present, with their smartphones ready, to witness the ensuing meltdown.

This person is homophobic

The Left itself is homophobic. It ostracizes gay people who shatter its narrative on a daily basis.
Notorious anti-establishment gay names are authors Jack Donovan, Philippe Verdier and Milo Yannopoulos. Donovan promotes a Traditionalist lifestyle and a return to tribalism where manliness, honor, courage and mastery retake center stage. He is reviled by the Left for not conforming to the effete gay 'victim' stereotype the Left rabidly pursues. Philippe Verdier is a French journalist who successfully debunked the global warming industry scam, which resulted in his firing from France Television and his marginalizing by the media. Milo Yannopoulos was instrumental In dismantling the Leftist attacks on the Trump campaign and is arguably, single-handedly responsible for the online Leftist meltdown that resulted from the Left's own inability

to successfully exploit any weak spot in the Trump campaign. So the Left attacked Yannopoulos on the grounds of an interview where he expressed thoughts that were interpreted as Pedophiliac in content. While this resulted in a massive blow to Yannopoulos, it also annihilated the Left itself, which actually has championed every degenerate lifestyle under the sun (under the pretext of love/openness), *including* pedophilia. While Yannopoulos recovered from that PR blow, the Left's hypocrisy is now irreversibly exposed after it criticized pedophilia while encouraging it elsewhere. The Left has demonstrated its double standards by showing no qualms in attacking homosexual personalities who happened to be politically outside the Left's narrative. It has also been forced to take a hilariously puritan stance on pedophilia while actually being known for encouraging it through organizations like NAMBLA, and the whitewashing of several Hollywood celebrities guilty of the crime itself.

Judge not

Judging is actually good. The Left does it all the time but forbids everybody else from doing it. Anyone having opinions differing from the leftist globalist mainstream, will be judged. So it is time to make judging great again. Always laugh when a leftist 'judges' you. It means you've hit them where it hurts. Remind them that they have just judged you -bonus points if you ask them with which moral standard they are judging you-, but you'll forgive them for contradicting themselves this one time!

The above highlights the implosion of the Leftist narrative due to the excessive semantic, linguistic and mental masturbation the Left subjected itself to, for the last six-to-seven decades. Now the Frankfurt School bag of tricks lies empty, and all cards have been used. The Left has shown itself to be an empty drum; it took humanity many years to absorb the Leftist shock, but the pendulum is swinging back, and with it, the swiping away of the Leftist house of cards.

HARD TO SWALLOW PILLS

Advocates of rationalism and heralds of the age of reason alone are ironically the biggest consumers of hallucinogenics and drugs which -even more ironically- helps their consumers to "get spiritual" and escape reason altogether. A Study by professor Peter Schweizer, published into a 2008 book, "Makers and Takers", announces that liberals were five times more likely than conservatives to do drugs. Schweizer, a research fellow at Stanford University's Hoover Institution, quotes A study published in the American Journal of Drug and Alcohol Abuse, where "the ratio of Democrats to Republicans was more than 8-to-1.":

" A research team led by Gerhard Gmel from Lausanne University Hospital has shown in the journal Substance Use & Misuse that, in Switzerland, fewer religious young men consume addictive substances than men of their age group who are agnostics or atheists." - Science Daily, 2013*

Morality and moral codes go hand in hand with religious sentiment. An anti-religious individual is forced to adopt the moral code of the religion he/she rejects or have no moral code at all.The consequence of having no moral code is a higher propensity for social transgression, and one example is higher drug use.

Atheists give the impression that they have no taboos and hold nothing sacred. Until someone mentions their ideologies (a substitute to religion), lifestyle choices and appetites unfavorably. They are the most virulent of fanatics when their own taboos are exposed and trampled!

* *"Religion Is Good, Belief Is Better: Religion, Religiosity, and Substance Use Among Young Swiss Men"-(Gmel, Mohler-Kuo, Dermota, Gaume, Bertholet, Daeppen, Studer)Source: https://www.tandfonline.com/doi/full/10.3109/10826084.2013.799017*

Capitalism and Communism have both lured women out of the household and away from their children. This was bound to result in dramatic salary depreciation, due to the doubling of the workforce when women joined men into the cubicles. A way to address this situation is not to send back women to the kitchens, but to motivate households to, once again, rely on a single bread-winner, be it man or woman. Couples who still insist on both going to work, would be taxed heavier, while the single-worker household would enjoy more tax cuts, allowing the household's children to have a parent with them available at all times, saving costs on daycare, nannies and surveillance equipment. Having our culture focus exclusively on money, has produced generations of children out of touch with their workaholic parents, parents out of touch with each other, higher incidence of divorce and of wrecked childhoods, consequently wrecking society as a whole.

Family - not currency, not the individual- must once again become the smallest functional molecule of a society. When a family is dislocated, a society is dislocated. The economy be damned. It's here to serve humanity, not the opposite. Family first (if we still want healthy functional societies, that is)! The cure for Globalism starts with cutting the world's workforce in half. Also, gender roles are OK. They actually *work*!

Women suffrage: We hear a lot in the Alt-Right* and New Right circles that the fall of the West is largely due to women suffrage; had women not been allowed to vote, the western world would never have veered so catastrophically to the Left. The anti-women suffrage people forget that nearly all the western politicians who devised, wrote and implemented the Left-leaning bills which opened the gates of hell on the XXth century West, were male. Both the Eastern and Western hemispheres, mostly adopt democracy. Yet the manifest effeminacy

*The Alt-Right: The Alternative Right is a recent right-wing movement aiming to break with the heavily liberalized western conservative parties of the last century.

of the *modern* West virtually does not exist in the eastern hemisphere[1] (although Japan has been displaying some worrying trends lately), and women in the Eastern hemisphere do vote, just like men. So there must be a stronger reason (then just more women voting) for the veering of the west towards the political Left (and towards effeminacy which any self-respecting woman hates and rejects). Despite the statistical fact that most women tend to vote Leftist, one can still notice a stronger moral strength in the eastern hemisphere and this is due to moral codes only religion could impart to their populations. One can also notice that Eastern hemisphere women are more realistic, i.e. more in touch with the laws of causality which govern the real world. They are also more intuitive since their moral and religious sense are still largely intact, which gives them the edge over women who are exclusively "rational" and are in general "more educated" (i.e. more thoroughly brainwashed by years of indoctrination in the academic and ideological concentration camps known as universities).

Republicans are not conservatives.

Leftism is ungrateful- Today's Left and Liberal parties who clamor all day long for White Genocide, keep forgetting that the fathers of their movement, The Frankfurt School, Marx, Kinsey, Habermas, Hirschfeld etc... were all white males!

In an Equality utopia, what would we have left

---

1   When the East was effeminate, it was in its period of decline and decadence, which should ring a few alarm bells in Western circles.

which attracts us to one another? Nothing, since we've achieved peak uniformity! In traditional societies, men and women (yes, there were two genders back then) performed different roles, had different capacities and looked up to each other precisely for being different and for being able to perform tasks geared toward their different physiological and psychological natures. Men admired women for their intuitive nature, discretion and shrewdness in recognizing someone's personality and motives from the tiniest external details, and women admired men for their risk-taking adventurousness and pragmatism. They completed and looked up to each other for doing things differently. Why would I need someone who is my exact mirror reflection? Where is the interest and the adventure? What intrigue is there anymore, in a world where you can now order your fully programmable sex robot and even 'marry' it?? If in fifty years, Italy, France, Spain, England, Canada or Sweden will basically be resembling each other, what use will there be in visiting them?

Pursuing absolute Equality is finally showing its futility; since such ideology could never happen organically, it is being enforced by laws, surveillance cameras and intrusive social media. Equality is finally here and we're all now equally afraid to offend from fear of losing our livelihoods and social status, so we remain silent in terror.

The Protestant "Universal Church" is just another word for "Catholic", since "Catholic" means "Universal". The difference is that Protestantism is itself splintered into tens of thousands of sects (counting them all would fill a book), each with its handful number of followers, unwittingly executing the diabolical plan of dividing Christians to the point of total ineffectiveness. When everyone is their own priest, why would there be any need to listen to anyone other than one's own deluded narcissistic self? If we're all shepherds, then where are the sheep? And if only scripture should guide us, how can that be, when not two persons can have the exact same thought perspective and identical interpretation of any given text?

The Left has every right to mock the Church for failing to address paedophilia scandals. The Left has no inhibitions about its own moral decay and practices of legalized infanticide, witchcraft, drugs and paedophilia, but it is the Church which has the duty to uphold its own morals. The Left doesn't have morals to uphold, to begin with. Leftist 'morality' is as fickle as its own adherents' mood/gender shifts. The moral duty belongs to the Church, to resist and punish the above-mentioned degeneracy as in the good old days of the Inquisition. Failure to do so, signals a Church that has itself fallen prey to moral relativism, and in tough times like these, the people must keep the faith and weather the storm, with their holy books kept handy and close friends and relatives even closer. Some people are looking forward to the Collapse (of civilization) so that they can build anew. But most of them actually are attracted to the post-apocalyptic lawlessness they see in the movie and don't see much beyond it. They live in a fantasy movie, not knowing how much pain awaits those who take it upon themselves to actually rebuild from scratch. Avoid those people. You do not want them by your side when S.H.T.F.*

The modern push for no-excuse infanticide (abortion on demand) and child sexualization is simultaneously accompanied by another chilling trend: Seeking to normalize euthanasia, increase the retirement age and make

*Google it.

125

it harder for the elderly to seek healthcare. This points to one thing: The fiendish narcissism of a generation currently in charge, who wants to use kids for their own pleasures and simultaneously loot the pensions and retirement funds of the elderly.

Modernity takes every cultural element and empties it of its meaning. Through its Egalitarian political arms (democracy, multiculturalism, pluralism and a host of other 'isms') and its globalistic financial systems (socialism and capitalism) it seeks to transform the world into a bazaar where everything is a unit of production, of consumption or of utility. For example, tattoos used to have a sociocultural meaning. Slaves were branded/inked to be recognized as such, and so were criminals in certain cultures. In warlike cultures, a tribesman's tattoos would mean the number of battles he survived or warriors he has killed or the spirit animal/creature which represents him. Back then, a spirit animal or totem was no joke. Warrior chiefs, Shamans, druids, seers or medicine men had tattoos signaling their rank. Today, one gets a tattoo because everybody else is having one. In a world of convenience, our main occupation (when we're not on social media or not slaving away at our cubicle jobs), is aping each other. Tattoo artists will be happy to help modern men and women in their pretense and gladly sell them the tattoo they are willing to pay for. A tattoo becomes not a cultural statement anymore, but a topic of conversation, an item to remove from one's 'to do' checklist. A commodity with no meaning attached whatsoever and exceptions to that rule are very rare.

Tabula Rasa: Modernist worldview in its aversion for anything predating it adopts and implements the tabula rasa mentality; everything that came before the Modernist, either does not exist, or the Modernist will take credit for it if they found a use for it. Technology, institutions of learning, civilized behavior, moral standing, knowing right from wrong and many other manifestations of high culture, are useful to the modern, and he knows he did not invent them. The Modernist's arrogance resides in their subconscious, or sometimes, very conscious outlook of possessing moral rectitude *by default*. Seeking to erase the past, with its good and bad, betrays a sense of resentment, a chronic jealousy and an inferiority complex. If the Modern is in all ways superior to their past, why not then, keep it in order to laugh at it? But Modernism is not only resentful, it is also cheerless.

Qualitative Democracy: If democracy is to remain, a certain amount of voting power should be allocated to the person with the necessary cognitive capacities. A lower IQ score means the vote gets cut by a certain percentage.

Having a stake in deciding the future of a people should also be reserved to those who have the minimum required gray matter to perform the job. A basic example of such system is as follows:

IQ below 80 = no vote
IQ from 80 to 89 = 0.25 vote
IQ from 90 to 99 = 0.5 vote
IQ of 100 = 1 vote
IQ of 101 to 110 = 2 votes
IQ of 111 to 120 = 4 votes
IQ of 121 to 130 = 8 votes
IQ of 131 to 140 = 16 votes

and so on..

Newsflash: The science is never settled.

Self-loathing is prevalent in the modern atheistic West, because of Modernism's anti-traditional nature. The modern knows he inherited a society that is antithetical to his own nature in all points, so he wants to tear it down and create a society where absolute equality reigns and moral standards are customized to one's own preferences.

Christophobia is real. One of its earliest manifestations was the very subtle switching from the 'BC/AD' calendar to the 'BCE/CE' (common era). We went a long way from barely noticeable attempts to erase the christian worldview -like the one above- to literally torching whole Catholic cathedrals every other week.

A society insisting on having both Equality (all things being as valid as one another) and Democracy (majority rule over minority), is bound to self-destruct due to the paradoxal nature of its pursuit.

Still demonstrating its own absurdity, Modern society calls monogamy 'oppressive' and polygamy 'liberating' while at the same time, demanding Equality. The Equality that the moderns are calling for, is already under their noses. The so-called Patriarchy they're attacking, could have conserved the polygamous nature of its pagan times, but chose long-term commitment over sexual abundance, and found out that monogamy made for a much more stable social model. Let us not be fooled: Modernism, in its 'neo-pagan' strain, is not trying to reconnect with any ancestral practices, or traditions of old, but simply answering -and submitting to- its own bodily urges, regressing into animalism and calling it 'Progress'.

Rousseau's naive humanism permeates leftist thought; *'L'homme est foncièrement bon et c'est la société qui le corromp'* (Man is fundamentally good and is only corrupted by society) is a motto that animates Leftist hostility for borders, armed forces and national defense. Understanding Rousseau is understanding the modern Leftist. Both lived too long under someone else's protection, away from responsibility and from danger, resulting in disconnection from reality. Also how could one take Rousseau seriously when he abandoned his family and children for a life of irresponsibility and perpetual adolescence?

It is a Leftist trend to dig up anyone's past and then disgrace them because of a behaviour or a detail the Left finds 'offensive'. Authors, artists, geniuses and great people get the axe as the Left unearthes something 'racist', 'sexist' or 'xenophobic' they might have said. Tolkien, Shakespeare, Lovecraft and many others become shamed, not on any sound creative basis, but simply because they do not echo enough egalitarian values through their body of work, for the current post-Modernist tastes. Leftist creators on the other hand, are over-glorified creating an atmosphere where it is impossible to judge the quality of any work without marring it with political ideology. The Left however, fails to apply the same measuring stick to its own people; Che Guevara's anti-black sentiment is well documented, and so are the Ku Klux Klan's Democratic origins, to name but a few. More recently, Justin Trudeau in 'blackface' failed to get him 'cancelled' by hordes of rabid Leftists who would otherwise be howling for blood if the insensitive culprit happened to be right-wing.

The liberal mind is trained to innocently re-label realism or objective facts as 'hate'.

The more diverse a society becomes, the less religious it chooses to be. Getting rid of spiritual matters that could prove costly for business, PR and the newly formed social fabric, becomes a priority.

Democracy offers no accountability, unlike monarchy; instead of one clearly visible ruler, you'll have several thousand democratically elected/'appointed' bureaucrats who'll get rich off our hide.

Eastern & Western Catholicism: After Vatican II*, Catholicism added much water to its mixture in

*Vatican II: *The Second Ecumenical Council of the Vatican, commonly known as the Second Vatican Council or Vatican II, addressed relations between the Catholic Church and the modern world (1962-1965). (Source: Wikipedia.)*

the name of reform and became quasi indistinguishable from its own offshoot, Protestantism. The result was 'Catholics' with pro-LGBT and pro-abortion views going mainstream, as well as 'masses' incorporating 'youth-attracting gimmicks' like powerpoint presentations/screen projections, and pop band instrumentation. This of course, lead to the emptying of western churches and their subsequent conversion into either skating arenas or mosques.

When a void is created, it never stays void for long. Today we can distinguish 2 strains of Catholicism: A Liberalized, western one and a still traditional Eastern one. Traditional Catholicism still exists mainly in the Middle East. Is it a coincidence that in the 'Arab springs' that swept the region, Catholic monasteries were the first to be targeted and destroyed in Syria and Iraq? This traditional Eastern Catholicism** makes the western one feel queasy and uncomfortable. Maybe it's better that nobody knows it even existed...

The atheist worldview on the origins of the universe, in a nutshell: first, there was *nothing*. And then, *nothing exploded for no reason*. Then, life evolved somehow from dead matter, also for no reason. You must believe this, for this is *Science*, otherwise, you're a bigot!

Human Rights are a sham: In the dying days of 'Humanism', one still sees a funny display of shock among those who still believe in the 'human rights' myth. How come this or that country can do what they please to this

**Is it also a coincidence that the prefecture of Nagasaki, which was bombed by the US in WWII, happened to be the most densely Catholic area in Japan? The Nuclear charge was detonated right over the Urakami cathedral, during mass, killing mostly civilians and hitting no military targets - Source: www.mintpressnews.com

or that people and face no punishment from the 'international community'? The dumb look on whoever says that, is always priceless. Quite simply, Might is Right. And that rule has never really gone out of fashion, only carefully concealed under layers of political correctness.

Western college 'education' has been the most potent contraceptive for western society.

Feminists consider the male genome a 'defective' one, yet at the same time, accuse the Patriarchy of oppressing/controlling them. Genetically defective people bullying a genetically sound demographic: Twisted logic only a deluded Feminist is capable of.

Reconciling equality with hierarchy*: In the pointless war of Nature v/s Nurture, instead of taking sides, one can only look at how both can easily coexist; the 'nature' part is a being's genetically encoded capacities and aptitudes, while the 'nurture' part are the lessons this same being learns from their environment. A person with a natural capacity for martial arts, can become a worldclass athlete if their capacities are noticed and then properly trained. The same goes for an artist with a natural eye for Art or an innate gift for music. The more they nurture their natural capacities, the much higher they can reach. There exist examples of raw untrained nature, which does not evolve past its original state because it remained unexploited. One also can find examples of nurture alone; training someone without a natural capacity for the subject of

*: This is probably the most triggering pill, but if taken with an open mind, it could make for an interesting debate.

training, and still obtaining results. Curiosity and capacity to retain information play a great role in that case. Many egalitarians point out to the existence of modern, strong female leaders like Thatcher, Meir, Clinton or Merkel to justify *natural* female leadership. The truth is that Female empire builders only exist in sci-fi and other fantasy genres. The same egalitarians then point out that female queens do exist and have always existed. Yes, but the empires they inherited were built invariably by men - a historical fact, decried as sexism by history deniers, which leads to the question: Is the Y chromosome the gene for natural, built-in leadership and not just a sex switch?. A theory worth pursuing.

Men build, women nurture. Men are lousy nurturers and women make lousy builders. In today's inverted world however, we are witnessing glaring examples of women being bad nurturers and men being worse builders. This is mainly due to the fact that men and women are growing increasingly distant from one another and in the instances where they are together, their relationship is purely materialistic, physical, economical -like two business parties conducting a transaction. Dinners, gifts, sex and even children, become bargaining chips. In the midst of all this, the man finds no more purpose to build anything because of the fleeting nature of modern relationships, and the woman shifts her nurturing capacities to the tending of her own career and financial 'independence'.

Females who accept male leadership are simply confirming a scientific reality- The male genome contains both X and Y chromosomal variations while the female side has two X copies and cannot provide the Y, which is, as many scientific studies confirm, not only a 'sex switch'. The Y chromosome has yet to divulge all its secrets, providing that scientists looking for those secrets are not ideologically-driven misandrists busy bashing masculinity as can be shown in any basic online search about the X and Y chromosomes. Could the Y chromosome correlate with men's natural ability to be leaders, ie, a 'Nature Leadership' while women can become leaders by 'nurture' only

(Nurture Leadership), which explains the Boudiccas, Cleopatras and the Joanne of Arcs in recorded history? Some women clearly demonstrate clearer vision -as well as a more apt leadership- than many men, but could this be their 'nurture' leadership, drawing inspiration form previously existing leadership models like parents or forebears? Empire/culture building has invariably been a male-only venture, while its nurture/continuity has largely been made possible thanks to Woman (through counseling, inspiration, motivation and motherhood). Christian theology understands that complex reality by placing Man and Woman on the same level of importance in its sacrament of Marriage while at the same time, demanding from the wife to follow her husband, not because she is subservient to him, but because to be with him, she must love him, and to love him, she must trust his leadership and he, her counsel; two different, yet complementary powers.

Materialistic people view this relationship as 'oppressive' to women, because these people are unable to appreciate the non-material, non-financial importance of being a wife and a mother and equate fatherhood with purchasing power. They see motherhood as a hindrance because all they understand from the world is monthly salaries and whatever material satisfaction they provide.

To these creatures of a materialistic paradigm, the sexes compete like enemies for the material resources available. Neither Man nor Woman can advance on their own, and therefore they are equally as important but are suited for different tasks, a fact further underlined by their different biology. It is thanks to trust, that each component of a couple draws the needed confidence and finds the necessary serenity to fulfill their respective roles to perfection, fusing into a state where equality and hierarchy become one indivisible unit.

Individualism is the bane of change. Unbridled, it strokes the individual's ego to its farthest extents, atomizing societies and preventing any sustained, long-term cooperative undertaking. The day Individualism was enshrined as god in 'enlightened' societies was the day all hope of combating tyrannies by popular mobilization, ended. Individualism is an example of how too much of a good thing could prove detrimental- individualism is a sacred pillar of individual identity, but when It supersedes a political group's shared goals, it proves destructive. European inability to roll back tyrannical EU legislation, the Syrian revolution's failure, or the Lebanese rebellion's inability to produce a leadership or formulate common goals for its 2019 popular uprising, are but a few examples.

Pictures from the Lebanese revolution of October 2019. One of the fruits of egalitarian ideology: Women who have no issue objectifying themselves in public, but are offended when someone else objectifies them.

NATIONALISM OR PATRIOTISM?

American philosopher John Dewey viewed the State with distrust and favored the idea of global, centralized power, as a means to get rid of a "multitude of tyrannies" ruling over people by reducing them to a minimum. Viewed from this theoretical point of view, the Globalist sales pitch does have an apparent charm; like every sugar-coated deception, it promises freedom, and of course, presupposes Equality as its golden rule; it says we are equal. And due to humanity being more easily attracted to tangibles than to the abstract nature of concepts, this 'equality' becomes a very physical equality of very measurable and quantifiable, *outcomes*: Men can compete with women in women competitons, students would all get A's, or (even better!) no grades at all, a Universal Basic Income (UBI) that is seriously being discussed by our global elites...

'Inequality' is even being 'addressed' in pronouns and terms like 'father' and 'mother', becoming 'parent 1' and 'parent 2' in France and Italy , to name a couple of examples. Even here, one can expect 'parent 2' to howl at the injustice of being put in second place (to which, I humbly suggest color-coding so that we get 'parent purple' and 'parent indigo' for maximum utopian results!).

But how does the above have anything to do with Patriotism or Nationalism? Before Modernity took over from the old system (which can be traced back to the late Renaissance and Enlightenment periods, marked by Individualism, Liberalism and the French Revolution), Nations enjoyed culturally defined layers of identity: A clear outer border and a specific language, spread over the territory into a number of dialects; but those were the outer manifestations of a nation. Added to them were race, ethnicity and beliefs. To those factors is added a layer of environment. Geographic location and climate play a major role into the shaping of cultures. The resulting people, sharing all the above traits -visible and invisible, tangible and intangible- in common, are naturally bound to understand each other through a common language/system of communication, and therefore, each other's rights and duties. As the nation grows in complexity, the need for a written form of language emerges. Rights and duties are the means to preserve a people's continuity. Continuity births tradition, and tradition reflects a people's experience, through arts, crafts, and any cultural output produced by those people.

It is a complex, organically evolving system, where a people derive cultural pride from excellence in doing certain things better, or differently, than another culture. Building technology, agriculture, defence or transportation become a nation's pride. The Phoenicians were arguably the first to build ships strong enough to withstand lengthy sea-travel. They were the first to develop an alphabet and its initial purpose, was to document their inventories and trade-client accounts. They also accidentally learned about the special property of a local seashell, the Murex, to produce a reddish purple that would later be used as a highly expensive and sought after textile dye.

Conscious and accidental endeavors like the above mentioned ones, emanate from a culture's collective needs and reflect its collective behavior and character. Marks of cultural distinction come in the shape of feedback received from 'the outside' - the result of cultural, political, social and economic interaction between two peoples, building *reputation*. This is the precise point where Patriotism and Nationalism emerge. Warlike cultures do not necessarily wait for such 'feedback' to organically emerge from mere social and economic interaction; they unanimously agree about the need to expand their territory and discover that their neighbor can be conquered and its resources possessed.

Some define Patriotism as a love for one's country/nation while also recognizing its weaknesses. Nationalism, however, is the viewing of one's country/nation as beyond reproach and even superior to all others, despite its weaknesses. One is defined as a marginally tolerated feeling in our Globalist zeitgeist and the other is portrayed as an utter evil. The truth is that Patriotism and Nationalism are one and the same, but are, respectively, merely the states of a people, in times of peace and in time of war.

We are patriotic in times of peace while in the context of open or covert hostility, we become Nationalistic. This is doubtlessly why Nationalism has a more militaristic aura, but declaring it an evil is a ploy to brainwash any patriot into never 'crossing the line' from Patriotism into Nationalism in the event of political hostility. Dear Patriot, the Gobalist says you are free to love your country and people! But when another political entity threatens you, do not take arms! Do not resist! Just pack your things and seek your fortune elsewhere lest our medias paint you as another Hitler... Be a citizen of the world! If you do, we will speak nicely of you in our newspapers...

Worshiping Technology

"Speed is the absence of unnecessary movement. Technology is the engineering of speed for any given function, for which we are the directors. We are entering an era where WE will be given the directions from the technology in good faith that IT knows how to better enhance our function, we are becoming ITS technology. This is what I see as the road to utilitarianism, I could be wrong but I believe it's inevitable, given the human thirst

for convenience" -Jimbob Peltaire.

Ask anyone what mental image they have when you mention Modernity, and they'll tell you 'technology'. The term Technology has become synonymous with Modernity to a point where the terms can be almost interchangeable. The fallacy lies in forgetting that advanced technology was never due to the present (Modernity), but to *continuity*. And continuity's main ingredient is knowledge and experimentation done in the *past*. Modernity however, hates the past and credits itself for every human advancement.

Rabid Modernism, as soon as it has the floor, quickly loses its mask of equality and bears its fangs; it is here, to erase everything which came before it and views tradition as anathema. If the past is erased, then Modernism can take credit for anything it wants, without any opposition. Paul Edward Gottfried gives a potent example of modernist 'neophilia' in a passage exposing a democratic capitalist author's attitude and her relish to erase tradition and cultural tenets:

"(Virginia) Postrel's enthusiasms are a perfect example of democratic capitalist boosterism, characterized by support of open borders, the mixing of peoples and races, and a continuing redefinition of nations and cultures. [...] she frets over the "stasist policy" of those who say "I like my neighborhood the way it is".[1]

The idea of Progress itself presupposes an origin, a continuity, a slow build up from state A to state B. Modernists want to reach their futuristic utopia by burning bridges, conserving nothing, their blinders focused on the way

---

1   "Multiculturalism and the Politics of Guilt" (Gottfried) - p.27-28- (2004 edition).

forward, to achieve Progress and technological advancement *for the sake of it*.

The modern world, through all of its cultural outlets, never misses a chance to loath the very origins and society which gave it birth. With all its technological achievements, it knows that its own modern knowledge is doomed to be forgotten, a fragile victim of the elements of nature; when our ancestors' knowledge has survived thousands of years on stone, parchment and clay, we struggle to do the same with our own data. Hard drives can barely survive a 6 feet drop, let along several lifetimes; and even if they do, they are most likely to be unreadable due to rust or humidity.

Our methods of safeguarding precious knowledge are pathetic. We have yet to discover a data-transmission and reproduction technology that is really durable and resistant to nature- meaning that it could last several centuries and still be accessible. Of course we still have paper, a cheap way to reproduce knowledge that will nevertheless need to be stored in a humidity-proof container. Crystals, sunlight, tree rings, stone, or even water, might be means of storage, data reproduction and reading we have yet to harness. In any case, the link to our past must be restored. We also must keep in mind that technology is a means, a tool, and the tool must always be controlled by its wielder, not the opposite.

JUDEOCHRISTIANITY

(DECHRISTIANIZATION BY PROXY)

The world's three monotheistic religions, Christianity, Islam and Judaism, are vying for the heart, mind and soul of humanity and it is typical in political maneuvers involving several rivals to witness alliances. But in the case of JudeoChristianity, it is a bit more complicated than that; upon reading/hearing the term, the casual viewer would assume a Jewish/Christian alliance against Islam, but what is really happening is much less obvious and therefore, much more interesting: Jewish people are falsely mistaken, mainly by christians, to be sharing the Old Testament with their 'Christian brethren'. The truth is that Jews have long eschewed the Pentateuch in favor of their own, post-Christian rabbinical law: The Talmud.

In the Talmud, Jews practically switch religions, by abandoning their initial -inconvenient- Abrahamic teachings -where Christ is prophesized- and proceed to follow a much more materialistic and ideological worldview. The only thing they have preserved from their old Torah is the racial supremacist rhetoric. They still are YHWH's 'Chosen', but in the Talmud, Christ, his mother, Christians and all non-Jews, are thoroughly reviled. Christ in the Talmud is a petty sorcerer (Shabbath 104b), a heretic (Sanhedrin 43a), a summoned tormented spirit (Gittin 57a) or also, a bastard (Yebamoth 49b) while Mary is a prostitute (Sanhedrin 106a, b). Harming Christians (directly or indirectly) is not a sin, since they are considered heathens and apostates (Abodhah Zarah 26b)[1], and using the 'goyim' (non-jews) as planks for the advancement of God's 'Chosen' became the newly consecrated Jewish law. Talmudic references abound, where Christianity and Jesus are openly insulted, despite the best attempts of later Jewish scholars at defending their Talmud as 'not referring to Jesus' in its repeated insults. Eventually, Jews would finally stop justifying the Talmud, as more anti-Christian treatises by Rabbi

---

1   All Talmudic references verified in the Soncino Press English / Hebrew edition of the above-mentioned tractates (physical copies).

Maimonides, Rabbi Ben Asher's Yoreh De'ah, uncensored copies of the Talmud, the Toledot Yeshu become widely available.

However, as today's literacy decreases, it becomes far less likely for anyone to purchase expensive uncensored copies of the Talmud, which helps keep the prevailing idea that Jews share the Old Testament with their younger 'brothers' in the faith, perpetuating a lie that is most convenient to the Jewish political entity and the advancement of its people.

JudeoChristianity being a relatively recent term first encountered in the early 1800s and referring to 'a style of church that would keep with some Jewish traditions in order to convert Jews', it would morph into the standard religion of the United States and the Western world. This would permit the continuous Jewish stranglehold over top political positions in the United States, England and the European Union. It has also kept the Christian community oblivious to Jewish efforts aiming to erode and destroy the Christian faith. If there is anything to learn from those efforts, it is the eternal truth that groups only pursue their own interests, and Christian (mainly American Protestant) groups going out of their way to defend Judaism and uphold a religion whose oral and written laws are clear about the 'Goyim', are simply suicidal.

JudeoChristianity is a myth, but let us admire (and learn from!) Jewish craftiness in never appearing at the forefront of any major political endeavor and its perseverence in pursuing its own group interests:

Jewish Italian Emmanuel Carasso was instrumental in the founding of the Young Turks, and enabling 3 Turkish pawns (Anwar, Talaat and Jamal Pasha) groomed at the Thessaloniki Masonic Lodge (financed by the Jewish B'nai B'rith) to overthrow Sultan Mehmet II and conduct one of the bloodiest genocides on the non-Turk minorities, namely the Armenian Christians, and ushering the fall of the

Ottoman empire[2].

Jewish British prime minister Benjamin Disraeli even hints at jewish social engineering and racial supremacy in his novel 'Coningsby'. One particular passage being:"...the world is governed by very different personages from what is imagined by those who are not behind the scenes.").

Jewish origins and founding members of the Bolshevik movement are all but known today, after a century has passed on the weirding of Russia and its mutation into a godless and fearsome beast; Lev Bronstein (Trotsky) or Lazar Kaganovitch (instrumental in the Holodomor man-made famine which killed 5-7 million Ukrainians) are a few names worth researching.

Jews controlling the Weimar Republic were expelled from Germany and many of them formed the Frankfurt School from which Modernist, and post-Modernist fruits blossomed and wreaked havoc on Western Society. Jewish advancement of Jewish thought, from Darwin to Rousseau, to Marx, Freud and Marcuse, among others, resulted in the complete shaping of the western mind by Jewish hands. Jewish control of the world's collective mind is complete: An impressive feat that can not be ignored nor should it be belittled. Despite their number, Jews hold an astonishing 20% of all Nobel prizes. Through the direct and indirect efforts of Jewish genius, be it in thought, philosophy or economics, every success has resulted in the subsequent erosion of the Christian faith due to the church incorporating various amounts of the above-mentioned schools of thought, namely Marxism, Positivism, Liberalism, Socialism, Communism and the Frankfurt School's Modernism/post-Modernism movements. PragerU's founder, Dennis Prager recently confirmed during a video interview, that his own people are behind every modern 'ism' and 'ideology' as part of their

2   See: "Why won't Israel acknowledge the Armenian Genocide?" and "Why Were Jewish Zionists Behind The Armenian Holocaust? " (J. Manuelian) www.themilleniumreport.com

quest for the world's 'betterment'.

This is of course, not to mention the Catholic Church's complete financial subservience to the Rothschilds who became the Vatican's bankers in 1832[3]. The Church's decline has been already in motion since the Renaissance when the Vatican itself introduced 'reforms' showing leniency to usury, right before adopting those practices itself, and with Christian bankers (the Medici) help to boot. The irony is that nobody forced the Church's hand to be where it is today. It has itself to blame. When Peter himself, first Pope of the Church, thrice committed denial, was he infallible? Then why does today's Catholic church claim papal infallibility[4]? What use are all the cardinals, the bishops, the priests and the nuns, if anything the Pope says is infallible*?

Today, the Church is riddled with Liberalism**, diluted by Leftism, rotten by Humanism and neutered by cultural Marxism. The same cannot be said about Islam and Judaism, because Jews would not use their own weapon against themselves (except maybe in a controlled way), and they never actively directed it at Islam to begin with.

Today in 21st century Europe, Open-borders policies have resulted into waves of immigration flooding the European Union since 1968: Much of it is Islamic. And as previously mentioned, every sane political group works for its own interests, and the chief interest of Jews is a world with no political group pausing as a challenge to Jewish racial and ideological supremacy. This is ironic, given that they blamed Nazi germany for doing just that, or more recently, criticizing Trump for wanting to build a border wall, while Israel already has its protective walls. This means a world without Christianity and without Islam. The last two World Wars, did the Jewish cause enormous favor as tens of millions of European Christians slaughtered each other, paving the way to future decisions to 'repopulate' the

3   See: "God's Bankers: A History of Money and Power at the Vatican" (Posner) p12.
4   See: The First Ecumenical Council of the Vatican of 1869–1870 ('Pastor Aeternus').
*Infallibility should not be confused with Supremacy!
**Anomalies like 'Father' James Martin, 'catholic' women priests in the US and of course, pachamama rituals in the St Peter Basilica.

vacant old continent with new people. The Middle eastern turmoil also benefits them as Arabs, Muslims most of them, go at each other's throats. As Europe today is experiencing the result of the spiritual void it created with fifty years of full-blown Liberalism, contraception and open border policies implemented since 1968, something else has been filling the spiritual void: Islam. In France, Jewish ex-minister Jean-Pierre Chevènement, a gallicization of the original 'Schwenmann', took the administrative duties for the Fondation Pour L'Islam De France[5]. Why would a Jewish man lead an Islamic institution? And why would a 'non-profit' organization named IsraAid be monitoring the entry of Arab immigrants and refugees from Greece into Europe[6], while it could be easier for these so-called altruists to help Palestinians starving and homeless at their own doorstep?

When senator Ted Cruz was booed off a 'In Defence of Christians' conference, the media was quick to categorize the Christians who booed the senator offstage as 'pro-Syrian/pro-Hezbollah' shills. The issue is always more complex than how the media portrays it, but for the media, it's more important to dumb information down than to inform. What did Senator Cruz say, that earned him the booing from Levantine Church leaders? He quite simply adhered to the famous western 'JudeoChristian' paradigm, a Protestant, Western trend that simply has no traction in the Levant.

The proposal of considering the Jew as the Christian's older brother, is not a Middle eastern concept and doesn't work in this more realistic part of the world, the Middle East. The reasons are chiefly empirical and they happen to be plenty, if one should decide to look for them:

Whenever Al-Nusra or IS need to advance across open terrain, or are beaten by the combined forces of

---

5   See: "France : Chevènement va céder la place à un musulman à la tête de la FIF" (Reuters) - 2018.
6   See: "IsraAID sends team to help refugees in Europe" (www.israel21c. org) - 2015 & "IsraAid fighting to help refugees in Europe" (www.ynetnews.com) - 2015.

Putin, Assad and Hezbollah, Israel scrambles its jets to provide air cover to its protégés[7]. Whenever Al-Nusra cutthroats need urgent medical treatment, here comes Israel from across the Golan borders, with their ambulances to treat the wounded Islamists[8]. A casual look at the demographics of Israel shows only 2% of its population is Christian, with Muslims making 10 times that size, with 20% of the israeli population. How can senator Cruz and the neo-cons* pitch Israel as a 'Christian Ally' when Christians are not welcome in israel and repeatedly see their property destroyed for no reason[9]?

Talmudic excerpts are yet another plain truth about Jewish intentions towards the christian 'goy'. With the abundance of evidence of Jewish hostility towards the Christian, Christians should only blame their own ignorance, blindness or naivety for still believing that Jews are their 'elder brothers in the faith'. The Old testament (OT) is not, as many Christians falsely believe, a shared book between Christianity and Judaism. Jews have dropped the OT for the Talmud, now the official holy writ for the people of Israel. And since it has been written since the 1st century AD, and its main body was completed before the rise of Islam, one can safely confirm that what the Rabbis mean by 'goy', is essentially the Christian.

There is however, much more potential of Christian-Muslim political alliance and entente, than Christian-Jewish alliance as demonstrated in recent papal visits to the Gulf, Lebanese political power-sharing (Christians make barely 40% of the lebanese population-not counting diaspora- but control half the parliament), or on the military side, Christians enrolling in Hezbollah to fight off Al-Nusra on the Syrian-Lebanese border[10]. The Quran

---

7   See: "Israel raid on Raqqa led to ban on laptops on airplanes" (www.thenational.ae) - 2017 & "Israel bombs Damascus as Syrian Arab Army advances in Idlib" (www.thewallwillfall.org) - 2020.
8   See: "Israel acknowledges it is helping Syrian rebel fighters" (www.timesofisrael.com) - 2015 ,
9   See: "makhrour restaurant & home demolished" (Youtube.com).
10   See: "Christians joining forces with Muslim group, Hezbollah, to fight against jihadists" (www.pulse.ng) - 2015.
*neo-con: A shortened iteration of the term 'neoconservative'.

itself acknowledges the virginity of Mary while Protestants debate it. Surat Maryam in the Quran is one of the many times Islam honors the mother of Jesus, while Protestant Christians relentlessly accuse Catholics of Mariolatry - 'worshiping' an 'ordinary woman'.

Every group -ethnic, religious, racial- works to advance its own interests, and any group working against its own interests (like Liberalized Western Protestants) is serving someone else's interests be it knowingly (which is bad) or unknowingly (which is much worse) and therefore should only blame its own greed, stupidity or combination of both for its own downfall. While JudeoChristianity is mostly unpopular in Lebanon, a number of gullible Christian politicians demonstrate complete historical illiteracy and copious amounts of dhimmitude by naively adhering to it.

Political Talmudism is using Euro-Christian pathological altruism* and Islamic expansionism as useful proxies for its own immediate and long-term interests: Obliterating Christianity while staying in the background. But the JudeoChristian useful idiots would cry antisemitism at this 'evil' accusation. Christians in Israel being 2% of the general population[11], one would think that with such good 'brotherly' JudeoChristian relations, the number would be much bigger... But to cut it short, one can only be awed at the cunning, genius, perseverence and long-term strategy the Jewish collective keeps displaying. They're doing great for their own group. Everyone else should emulate their example and look for the interests of their own respective group.

---

11   See: "Israel Population 2020" (http://worldpopulationreview.com).
pathological altruism: *The urge to help other people to the detriment of one's own political interests.*

Kabbalism

Nietzsche, himself the son of a cleric, attacked the Church for being cheerless and devoid of the heroism which characterized older European paganism with its rich mythology. Many Freemasons and wiccans share that opinion.

They are however, most probably referring to Protestantism, the leading religion of Enlightenment-era Europe. Protestantism is a 'minimalistic' Christianity that eschewed the metaphysical trappings of Catholicism, resulting in a more 'humanistic', more 'modern', more 'rational' Christianity.

To a rationalistic Modern, Catholicism, with its seven sacraments is pure hocus pocus; the Transsubstantiation of the Host, the Immaculate conception, the Resurrection (in the flesh), the miracles and the Old Testament's supernatural events with their prophecies and revelations all refer to a metaphysical realm the Modern is allergic to. Ironically, that same Modern is attracted to witchcraft and has no problem practicing divination while aligning their shakras to exotic ritualistic background music. One's being always yearns for the metaphysical plane and recognizes its existence *à priori*, despite voluntary daily modernistic efforts to suppress it by discarding it as superstition. The practice of magick gives the individual the illusion of being in control as they seek to achieve supernatural results by way of spells and daemonic help[1]. This is yet another sign of a re-paganizing world, where people worship the elements instead of their actual source.

Attempts to 'reconcile' God with witchcraft are chiefly carried out by the esoteric discipline known as Kabbalah. Kabbalah is a Talmudist endeavor to create a sub-

---

1   See: "Millennials Are Turning to Witchcraft and Sorcery" (www.garydemar.com) - 2017 .

stitute religion to Judaism (after Jews abandoned Judaism along with the Old testament) and a system of spiritual and material aimed to rival and supplant Christianity, after Old Testament prophecies were fulfilled in the New Testament. This left Jews with the choice of either to convert to Christianity or invent a new religion...

And so they invented Kabbalah.

Kabbalah posits the existence of God in the form of 10 'emanations' (or Sephira) and divides itself into two distinct schools of mysticism: The Right Hand Path and the Left Hand Path. The Right Hand Path seeks to master Sephirotic 'good' magic (related to the ten sephira or emanations of God). The goal is to 'rejoin' God and reconcile with him, restoring the original state which existed when God created the universe, before the Fall of Man and of Lucifer, whose own star 'Daath' which was persent in the initial Sephirotic tree, went dark, as he was cast out of God's presence. The Left Hand Path employs Qlippothic (related to the Qliphoth, the dark doubles of the original ten emanations) 'dark' magic with the help of demonic entities to emphasize and restate Man's Fall and open up the path towards Man's own Divinity, diametrically opposed to God. This magic uses the 'double'of the original Sephirotic tree (or tree of Life), known as the Qliphotic tree or Tree of Death (or also, the tree of Knowledge)[2].

Kabbalah is a very popular religion in elitist Western circles, and is practised as a substitute to desacralized Christianity and boring atheism. Its main text is the sacred book of the Zohar. It is a direct adversary to Catholicism and Orthodoxy, which promote the controlling of base appetites and the delaying of self-gratification through family committment, fasting, prayer and strict moral commandments as ways to fight the entropy* controlling our existence.

---

2   See: "Qabale, Qliphoth et Magie Goétique" (Thomas Karlsson) - 2017.

Entropy: *the state of degradation that the world always slips towards, via inertia/passiveness/laziness.*

But what has Kabbalah achieved? It is a passtime for bored wealthy elites who want a fun break from their materialistic boring existence, but who also want to escape any serious commitment.

Christianity is the single worldwide institution with the largest number of universities, schools, literary/scientific publications, hospitals, orphanages, humanitarian networks and Nobel Prize recipients. It has shaped and molded the current worldview, culturally and morally, which explains why it's being under attack by Globalist Modernity and its mouthpieces. For Globalism to rule unopposed, any strong moral order and metaphysical, spiritual doctrine pauses a serious socio-cultural challenge and must be considerably weakened, or better, removed altogether.

LEARNING FROM THE JEWS

The jews are a group of people with important lessons we, as competing groups, could learn from regardless of feelings or political affiliations.

Jewish peculiarity lies in their self-designation as 'God's chosen people',automatically meaning that the rest of humanity were in fact, Not God's chosen. This prototype of racial supremacy was one of the reasons, aside from non-assimilation and usury, why Jews were persecuted throughout their history.

What everyone should be learning from the Jewish people, is their strong sense of identity, precisely their non-assimilation, which would work well within defined borders, and not among other host cultures welcoming them. When inside your own borders, preserving your own culture, race and ethnicity is paramount, whereas if you're in Rome, you do as the Romans do. Jews didn't do that however which earned them yet more persecution.

Persecution of the Jews predates Christianity and is mainly because of their self-professed racial supremacy as written in the Old Testament. This racial supremacy took on a much more aggressive tone in the later written rabbinical laws compiled in the Talmud, a body of Jewish legislative work which was written between the second and eigth century AD. The Talmud is not easily obtainable, as say a copy of the Quran or of the Bible, but non-Jewish scholars finally had written proof of what was previously an orally transmitted set of teachings. According to the Talmud, the Christian was far from being the 'younger brother in the faith', a misconception held by many Christians.

The Holy Virgin and Christ were given less than favorable treatment in the Talmud. Non-Jewish 'gentiles' or 'Goys' were according to Talmudic teachings mere disposable rabble, fit for every mistreatment the Jew directs at them. How could Christians and Pagans in ninth century Europe read the Talmud and not react to the people behind it as a clear existential and racially supremacist threat?

The Jewish question is then, one of double standards, where the racial supremacy of the Jew is unquestionable (and promoted by Judeo-Christians) but everyone else's national pride is a great danger to World Peace -whatever that thing is. Groups act in pure self-interest and Jews are no exception. They are a group with a strong racial identity, a stronger non-assimilation policy and an even stronger unity. Can we still talk of antisemitism when Rabbi (Rav) David Touitou explicitly declares Islam and Christianity to be the kingdom of Edom that must fall before the coming of the Mashiah (Messiah)[3]?

Every group, be it predominantly racial, religious or a mixture of both, should learn identity and unity from the Jew. Every community which aims to grow, progress and endure, has to conserve and protect its identity from competing foreign identities. Diverse groups tend to produce diverging political directions and end up fragmenting. Diverse groups are usually a phase of terminal decline in any given society. Being wary of other groups is key to the survival of one's own group. Altruism and charity, are better dispensed inside one's own group first, and then parcimoniously and in calculated measures, to the needy outsider.

While it's true that Jews control most of the world's media and pull the political strings of much of the world, blaming our own woes on this specific group is a sign of weakness, and of giving up. It's an easy getaway. It is not true that one group, no matter how strong it is internationally, controls the destiny of nearly 8 billion people without collaborator help. Falling into that trap is giving in to laziness and self-destructive fatalism, and will eventually lead to the illusion becoming true. Yes this is an extremely well

---

3   "Maschiach ou es tu" by Rav Touitou (youtube).

organized group. Yes this is an extremely well-connect-
ed, well financed group that is after its own interests and
whose 'advice' to you (as a member of another group)
should never be heeded; advice from a group to a competing group is always a trap. Let's learn from it, but also
conserve our own group identity and values. The main
ingredients of their success are simple: Identity, Unity, Fel-
lowship. Other winning strategies perfected by this group
are also well known: Manipulation by proxy, media control, two-party influence and controlled opposition, are but
a few examples. Let's learn those as well, not to practice
them, but to better recognize and counter them.

JEWISHPRESS.COM

**Jewish Billionaire's Fight for Top Office Against Jewish
Socialist Getting Nasty**

*Meanwhile,
in 'Christian' America...
2020 - (Source: www.Jewish-
Press.com)- As an update, it's
necessary to mention that both
candidates dropped out of the
presidential race.*

ALLIES?

Political Protestantism is allied with Political Judaism, which leaves Islam and Catholic/Orthodox Christianity open for a similar alliance- one which the Vatican is apparently actively pursuing, and which is much more natural despite its apparent impossibility. How can Islam and Christianity -who have waged so many wars on one another- become allies? In politics, everything is possible. It makes much more sense than a Christian/Jewish or Muslim/Jewish alliance, since the Jew considers every non-Jew as their inferior.

The bridges of alliance can be found in the Quran itself: It contains many references favorable to Christianity, unlike the Rabbinical Talmud. Islam even recognizes Mary's immaculate conception unlike Protestantism*. A Muslim-Christian would ensure a stable Middle East and consequently a more stable world since it involves the world's two most numerous religions with a whopping 3.5-4 billion people including the Orthodox Christian population of Russia and Eastern Europe.

by condescending to Islam in europe, Liberalism is fomenting radical islamism. Muslims in Europe notice the preferential treatment they're benefiting from, on behalf of leftist (read: anti-Christian) EU governments and see a continent open for conquest. They also notice that the Leftist/liberal is cocooning them through its academia and media, shielding them at every turn and this enrages them because they understand the game: The Left and its liberal cronies is using Islam as a tool** in Europe and no religion likes to be thought of as a proxy, least of all Islam. Protestantism's vocally anti-Islamic political rhetoric has one -not so- hidden aim: fomenting Islamic hostility towards Levantine Christians (Catholic and Orthodox) while many clueless Eastern Christians still view Judaized America and post-Christian Europe as 'allies'. Such hostility benefits both Jews and their judaized vassals as the Levant

*Luther himself, believed in the Immaculate Conception (according to Lutheran scholar Arthur Piepkorn). Subsequent generations of reformers, however, overrode him.
**To engineer Europe as a dechristianized social experiment.

is mopped clean of its last remnants of true Christianity and its traditions, using radicalized Islamist proxies which did not exist prior to the formation of the Hebrew state in the Middle East and the subsequent Western meddling in the region. The Arab world at the beginning of the twentieth century was modernizing and shedding all of its past barbarity with the death of the Ottoman Empire. Islamic communities and leaderships must consider the necessity of actively working towards a stabilizing Catholic-Orthodox-Sunni-Shia alliance to counterbalance the Rabbinical-Protestant-Wahabi-Leftist (yes, Leftism is a religion) hold on a world currently entering the death spiral.

PAGANIZED

The world today is witnessing an active and relent-less push to normalize things that were common currency in pagan times:

Polygamy & polyamory.

Infanticide (abortion as 'healthcare' or as a 'right').

Euthanasia.

Polytheism.

Veneration of the Self.

Obsession with sex (sex as an end in itself).

Pedophilia & homosexuality.

Witchcraft.

To re-enable a return to paganism, the current worldview is being erased by proxies: Jewish victimization (Antisemitism) and Islamophobia.

In the decaying West, Islamophobia keeps the de-generate European in line; here are a people you cannot even caricaturize, unless you want to be shot up in retali-ation for your views at a concert or during office hours, or ran over by a truck while walking your family in a public space*. So in the 'laique' systems of France, England or Germany, special exceptions are made for Islam to prac-tice its culture freely while Christian natives (mostly Catho-lics) are told to suppress their religious practices**, remove the cross from their necks and their classrooms, stop bring-ing ham sandwiches to school and surround their Oktober-fest markets with bollards. They also must use more neutral, more bland descriptions for their feast days, like 'Seasons Greetings' or 'Happy Holidays' because saying 'Merry Christmas' in a corporate setting today, will upset the

*The Bataclan shooting, The Charlie Hebdo shooting and the Nice truck incident, which all happened in France.
** EU communist regimes like France have gone full pagan with their 'vacances d'hiver, vacances de pringtemps' and other types of renamed school breaks in an effort to erase that offensive part of their identity which happens to be Catholic.

entire progressive staff and probably get the insensitive culprit fired or denied promotion for life.

In a nutshell, the spineless Eurocuck* is scared so dead by the rising and manly Islam, that she's actively censoring herself in order to avoid the Islamophobia stigma at all costs.

Then we have anti-semitism: Basically everything involving questioning Jewish influence in the media and world banking, or exposing blatantly inexact details about the Holocaust, falls into the anti-semitism category. By the time the attacks targeting synagogues, businesses, Jewish graves and even persons have been revealed to be false flags[1], the world would have moved on, but with yet another reminder of the eternal victimhood status of the Jewish people. The Jewish-controlled media makes sure those 'attacks' are sufficiently trumpeted and with enough sustain to keep the aura of Jewish victimhood floating around, even after later proof that most of them were false flags orchestrated by Jews themselves.

Such is the power of media and sustained propaganda that one would be excused should they feel a pang of jealousy for not wielding such magical power -the power to shape minds and influence the masses. In the midst of all this, attacks on Christianity[2] go totally unnoticed and fail to register the sustain that the above two buzzwords generate in terms of foaming frenzy among the general public. Syrian monasteries pillaged by ISIS? Nuns raped by Boko Haram? 'easter worshipers'* blown up in Sri Lanka? Priests beheaded during mass in Strasbourg, the Philippines or Iraq? Churches dynamited in China? Cathedrals in flames all over Europe? No matter how many attacks Christian people face daily, whether in the Far-East,

1   "Jewish suspects arrested over swastika graffiti on synagogues" (www.thetimesofisrael.com) - 2017, "Man's Apple watch proves he lied about anti-Semitic stabbing in West Bloomfield" (www.fox5ny.com) - 2020 , "Jussie Smollett Indicted by Special Prosecutor Over Allegedly Faked Racist, Anti-Gay Attack" (www.newsweek.com) - 2020 (Smollett is also Jewish from his father's side).
2   The Notre Dame cathedral fire, the Nantes Cathedral fire, The removal of statues of Catholic historical figures by Black Lives Matter rioters, the killing of Father Hamel during mass, are a few examples worth noting.

Eurocuck: The culturally cuckolded European.
Easter-Worshipers: Pseudo-christians Barack Obama and Hillary Clinton referred to Christians killed in a church bombing in Sri-Lanka as 'Easter Worshipers'. Their tweets received a wide backlash/condemnation. Christians do not 'worship' Easter, after all...

the Levant, Turkey, Egypt, South Africa, Nigeria, Europe or basically anywhere, the media simply moves on, and the public forgets in the next minute. Mass media controls the very sustain of the content it distills into the mind of its audience. Judaism and Islam constantly receive steady media attention covering anti-Jewish and Islamophobic bias, but not Christianity. This simply means that the 'secular' media reflects a general mood and that mood is plainly anti-Christian.

Islam is manly enough not to need any victimhood badge, but the uncalled 'honor' has been bestowed upon it by a media that is predominantly Jewish-controlled, joined by Leftist, atheist Western academia that shares a common dislike for Christianity- a fixed staple of every modernist footsoldier.

The moral relativism of the general public has reached a stage where it is increasingly incompatible with the traditional Christian moral code, and so we hear calls for the Church to 'modernize itself' and 'keep with the times', to 'evolve' with society. a call that is sadly echoed by many 'Christians' wanting to customize Christianity to fit their own modernist lifestyle. The real persecution happening, is not on a thriving religion like Islam, with a clear code regarding those who mock it, and who boasts the largest number of worshipers. It is certainly also not on the Jewish people, who have the undisputed power of information and coin and therefore control the material needs of an increasingly materialistic world; it is against a people whose hold on the world is cultural, *spiritual and moral*.

A successful return to paganism would require the breaking up and un-doing of that cultural, spiritual and moral essence which shaped the world and its thought for the last 2000 years.

In a full-on pagan world, Rabbinical Talmudists (Jews following the Talmud) and their allies are perfectly at home in a materialistic world ruled by Mammon, but will Muslims continue to be Talmudic proxies? Will Islam accept to live under the yoke of immoral paganism and Mammonism?

The world which sustained the Left is finally going away. Leftist success in 'deconstructing' the Christian worldview will be the end of it as well. A pagan or -more likely- an Islamic worldview is not expected to show any leniency or tolerance to Critical Theory proponents, SJWs and post-modern 'academics'.

Anti-christian atheists, feminists, positivists, humanists, and assorted Leftists are about to have their 'Careful what you wished for' moment very soon...

THE FRAGILE

A human being should be able to change a diaper, plan an invasion, butcher a hog, conn a ship, design a building, write a sonnet, balance accounts, build a wall, set a bone, comfort the dying, take orders, give orders, cooperate, act alone, solve equations, analyse a new problem, pitch manure, program a computer, cook a tasty meal, fight efficiently, die gallantly. Specialization is for insects.

—Robert Heinlein, Time Enough for Love

We must not mistake multitalentedness with multi-tasking. One is a natural state we are born with and have a duty to nurture and the latter is just a modernist two-dimensional substitute for the actual competence of the polymath. Modernity strikes again by telling us to stay in our lane, to microspecialize and be completely clueless in every area outside our training. A microspecialized society has successfully killed its innate curiosity and rendered itself highly vulnerable (modernists would rather say 'interdependent'!)to scarcity.

LAYERS OF IDENTITY

-Lebanon as a time-capsule-

When a citadel is under siege, The defenders of the citadel have several walls to fall back on; if the citadel successfully weathers the invader's storm, it would go back to gradually reinforce the walls it lost and regain its previous state. It is the same with people; the "outer wall" of any nation is its demarcated political borders. They are invisible unless marked by a walled structure, yet they are defensible by that nation's armed forces. The next barrier, if the outer wall is breached, is the individual cities, then the neighborhoods, then the individual homes.

Individuals also have that same type of "barriers" which define them. The outermost ones are the most generic (individual preferences of food, entertainment, clothing or hobbies), then come the tenets of real identity: Race, ethnicity, tribe and religion.

When a country is politically nullified as is the case with Lebanon, people can only fall back behind religious, tribal lines. The enlightened intelligentsia derisively calls this 'sectarianism', lamenting a people too entrenched in their so-called religious, superstitious mindset. The 'intellectual' does not understand that this 'sectarianism' is a symptom of a major problem:

absence of nationalistic concensus; the different sectarian/confessional components fundamentally disagree about the idea of what Lebanon is. Such problem was not at the forefront, back when Christian Maronites were the absolute demographic majority, but such is not the case anymore. In the West, one needs to add "Racial lines" as well because what is happening there, is as much a religious timebomb as it is a racial and ethnic one.

Those "walls" we fall back on, are the layers of

identity which define us. Before we ideologically

suppress and mock them, we need to embrace them and understand their usefulness as the result of centuries of social interaction, fine-tuning and self-calibration for an optimal reaction towards external stimuli, situations and threats.

Fifty years ago, Europeans laughed at the Lebanese for still showing a developed sectarian and confessional awareness, unlike their 'enlightened' European counterparts, who were now happily worshipping themselves.

They're not laughing now, especially not after they, themselves, voted to compromise their own borders, while adopting the pill-and-abortion 'lifestyle'.

Without outer borders and with plummeting demographics, the French and the remaining Europeans are slowly awakening to 'identitarianism'- a religious, racial and tribal sentiment that is the inner bulwark embedded in every individual by thousands of years of organic reality, not la-la-land 'humanistic' ideology.

Identitarians are the last defense wall in the faltering fortress of Europe, separating it from total anarchy: Empire is dead, borders are gone and native religion is suppressed in favor of the invading one, in the name of 'laicity' and 'secularism'. Who will you call? Your immediate family, tribe and parish, of course, but since family and parishes are also gone, Europeans are out of options and need to re-learn what it means to be a family, a clan and a tribe again.

The Europeans, could have studied the Lebanese and levantine time capsule before implementing their social engineering plans; it could have spared them so much tragedy.

Leftism seeks to dismantle this multilayered culture of "belonging" which makes every culture distinct; if you don't belong anywhere, you have nothing to fight or die for, and therefore lose your purpose. Doesn't that remind you of a very popular song by John Lennon? *Imagine* you have nothing to fight or strive for, nothing to work for, a being with no purpose, a cow placidly grazing in the fields of peace, love and equality. That is ironically the perverted view many modernized post-Vatican II Christians were told to believe is Paradise- People floating on a nimbus, greeting each other all day, plunking their harps, and smiling like idiots for all eternity... No wonder that people prefer to go to hell instead, which is described as some non-stop rock'n roll festival, with alcohol-drenched orgies.

This is the excessive abstraction we are currently living: simplifying things down to their dumbest form, and repeating that simplification until it replaces the initial concept.

The political reshuffling, demographic replacement and confessional tensions have long been happening in a tiny Middle Eastern country, since the 19th century: Lebanon has been a theater of many of today's socio-political woes currently metastasizing in Western Europe, North America and South Africa.

The formation of Greater Lebanon under its current borders, in 1920 during the French Mandate, saw a country with a Confessional majority of Christians (and at that time, uncontested rulers of Lebanon), forming an uneasy alliance with Muslim populations who still saw themselves as part of Syria, as well as citizens of the Islamic Ummah.

Prior to the formation of Greater Lebanon and even before the Ottoman occupation of the Lebanon region, the population which lived in that region was multiconfessional for centuries. As documented by Historian Kamal Salibi in his 1990 book 'A House of Many Mansions', although coexistence was never without some scuffles between different confessions or religious groups, Lebanon witnessed a history where Muslim and Christian populations would coexist alongside each other, enjoying a new-found security after being persecuted by -surprisingly- their respective co-religionists in Syria and Byzantium[1].

In the greater context of life in the Lebanon region, every group kept for itself and life evolved organically between the different groups that would later coexist behind Lebanese borders. Throughout the generations, Lebanese communities interacted with various degrees of civility, but sometimes with violent animosity as well. That resulted in massacres which happened notably between Maronite Christians and Druze communities, until both communities learned to get along, seeing opportunity in unity (notably under the Ottoman yoke, using their respective European connections).

The interconfessional tensions would fester again between the 1960s and 1980 during the Palestinian crisis, with Muslim confessions siding with the Palestinians stationed in Lebanon and the dwindling Christian communities seeing a clear demographic threat with the Palestinians settling within Lebanon. A violent 15 year war would ensue and more than 200000 Lebanese are killed, with countless more displaced. Christians irretrievably lost their political control (and demographic majority) in Lebanon, but were not removed. Conseqently, all other confessional communities considerably lost of their military and political power too, except the Shia community, which has been kept marginalized for centuries and found itself for the first time, in a dominating position as of 1983.

The co-existence of Lebanon's various communities happened organically, without an active social engineering program, as is the case in Europe. Greek, Persian, Roman and Egyptian invasions, the Islamic expansion, the Crusades, the Ottoman empire or the Sykes-Picot agreement all played a considerable role in the resulting confessional and ethnic melting pot that is Lebanon. Thus Lebanon is an indirect result of the above mentioned macropolitical events. Despite the confessional animosities which scarred the pre-Greater Lebanon people (notably

---

1   "A House of Many Mansions" (K. Salibi), p133-140.

the Druze-Maronite conflicts), The architects of today's Lebanon were Druze, Sunni and Maronites, who put away their confessional differences to work for a common goal.

Many proponents of multiculturalism cite Lebanon as an example of coexistence, but the problem is that these multiculturalism zealots believe in a multicultral utopia completely different from the Lebanese one: Their multicultural dream is a result of active and intense social, racial and ethnic engineering through open border policies and socially encouraged miscegenation. Lebanese communities are different in the fact that their confessional borders, although invisible, are very real and their people do not mix in the 'state & media -enforced' manner desired by the multicultural zealot. We do of course, witness interconfessional marriages (or even interracial ones) among Lebanese, but those are generally far from being the norm.

Today, identity-aware Europeans speak of a 'Great Replacement' and the rate of socio-cultural change these Europeans are witnessing, is astounding in its speed; today's European is the product of 50 years of pro-abortion and pro-contraception culture starting with the sexual revolution of 1968, and cannot keep pace with the very high fertility of the arriving migrant. Lebanon is only now catching up with the abortion/contraception trend and needs to snap out of it while it still can.

Another aspect where Lebanon is a time-capsule is the erasing of its collective memory, similarly to what is today happening in the West: Lebanon in the 1960's was in its golden age; as the US and Soviet Russia rushed into a space-conquering technological race, Lebanon was, amazingly enough, pursuing a similar goal: A bunch of Lebanese scientists from the Haigazian university proceeded to fly rockets between 1960 and 1966, which would go as high as 150 Km from Earth's surface. The Lebanese Space program was suddenly shut down in 1966 as tensions between Israel and neighboring countries reached a boiling point. All subsequent memory of the Lebanese space program was then systematically erased from Lebanese collective memory: Generations who lived in that time period discovered as if for the first time ever, the existence of the Lebanese Rocket Society in an eponymous movie released in 2012.

Three Years after the death of the Lebanese space program, the US put a man on the Moon, a huge achievement that would sadly not be repeated after 1972, ever again. Today, stories downplaying the moonlanding as a hoax are eerily similar to the suppressing of the Lebanese space program from Lebanese collective memory. This is not surprising, since NASA's main goals today are minority, racial, religious and gender quotas, instead of the actual exploration of space[2]. If that trend continues, the Moonlanding will soon take on the aspects of myth, a fantasy which never actually happened, and whoever still believes in it, would be branded a heretic -a view that was mentioned in the Sci-Fi movie 'Interstellar'. Today, Western Leftist political movements manned by activists who hate their own past are aggressively proceeding with the removal of historical artifacts, statues and monuments of Western history for the purpose of rewriting the West's history and origins[3], where its Christian past is erased[4].

Those who are sane, are too paralyzed by the madness they are witnessing on display. But time is not for paralysis; urgent measures are needed to secure a people's threatened history.

Meanwhile, Lebanon stands at its 'make it or break it' crossroads. Its constituent communities have fought each other, betrayed each other, conspired against each other, and allied with each other. All are weary from years of fratricidal backstabbing and of being used by foreign powers to advance foreign interests. After western foreign

---

2   See the book:"Whitey on the Moon" (P. Kersey)
3   See: "Deadly rally accelerates removal of Confederate statues" (www.ocregister.com) - 2017.
4   See: "Christopher Columbus Statue in Central Park Is Vandalized" (www.nytimes.com) - 2017. *update: guess what happened to it in 2020*

policies have left a trail of misery from Latin america, to Rhodesia-Zimbabwe (and now South africa) to the Middle east and the Far-east, the West itself is in grips with the results of its socially-engineered multiculturalism. It will manage to offset its impending collapse for a few years more, thanks to its robust economic and technological structure. Lebanon on the other hand, is back to square one. It has, so to speak, a 'headstart' and must grab the opportunity to rebuild while learning from its on mistakes and from the West's. Get rid of religions? We saw the result in Russia, East europe and today's Western countries. Forget our past and traditions by tearing down things that 'offend us'? It's not working so well for the West either. This is an opportunity that is felt by the Lebanese probably for the first time. The time to be a nation and work for our own interests -as the only *organically* multicultural nation in the region- is now or never.

PHOENICIANISM

After pioneering Pan-Arabism, Levantine Christians initially wore the Arabism mantle with pride, believing (and rightly so) that the term, in its original iteration encompassed all Arab populations, Christian and Muslim alike. Arab people are pre-Islamic, meaning that Muslims and non muslims could be referred to as Arab for sharing ethnic, geographic and linguistic cultural backgrounds. The Pan-Arabism movement itself was spearheaded by Christian orthodox Syrian and Lebanese citizens; Michel Aflaq (Syrian), Jurji Zeidan and Antoun Saade (Lebanese) were the main articulators of the Pan-arabism/Arab Nationalism idea, but soon the notion of Arabism, with the Rise of Nasser in Egypt and the founding of the Baath party in Syria, ended up referring exclusively to the Islamic constituents of the Arab population.

Christian demographics in the Arab Region (Spanning the Arabian peninsula and North Africa) did not help slow down that trend either, as they represented an ever dwindling (and in some parts, non-existing) minority. Christian Arabs found themselves excluded from the idea they themselves struggled to formulate.

The Christians of Lebanon needed a new identitarian bulwark to reaffirm their presence in the Levant, after Arabism ended up being 'appropriated' by the Arab world's Islamic constituents.

This bulwark is Phoenicianism. It does not seek to 'overlook 850 years of Arabisation' as affirms Historian Kamal Salibi, nor does it seek to negate them. It merely restates the lineage and heritage of modern day Lebanese to something that is much older and more inclusive than today's notion of (purely Islamic) Arabism. Since Arabism politically excluded Christians from its equation, they needed an alternative identitarian tenet to reaffirm their pedigree in that Land we call the Levant. Phoenicians are our common ancestors, whether Muslims or Christians, so Phoenicianism, far from negating later identitarian tendencies and layers, far from dividing and excluding, seeks to regroup the Lebanese under a common origin which predates Islam, Christianity and probably even the Arabs. Attempting to draw parallels and common points between Phoenicianism and European imperialism is not only a feeble attempt to discredit Phoenicianism but a blatant attempt at smearing an important part of Lebanese history that is commonly shared with the rest of the Arab world (Phoenician history).

Modernist ideologies do what they are designed to do: Mock, deride and seek to erase a people's earliest origins and ancestry, with every means at their disposal. Division is death. Unity is the way. If Arabism cannot unite the Lebanese, then perhaps Phoenicianism has a better chance, provided that we ignore modernist attempts at attacking, and discrediting our common history and origins. Of course, to some of its proponents possessed by sectarian aspirations , Phoenicianism is a pompous attempt at asserting supremacy (without any historical proof) through lineage, of one Lebanese group over another Lebanese group. This is an example of how an idea with great potential to unite a people, can be used to further divide it.

"These Phoenicians who came with Cadmus...brought with them to Greece, among many other kinds of learning, the alphabet, which had been unknown before this, I think, to the Greeks."
—Herodotus 5.58

THE LEBANESE NATIONALIST PARTY [LNP]

The earliest source where the name 'Lebanon' is mentioned is arguably the Bible (Deuteronomy 3:25). It refers to two mountainous ridges, where the northernmost part is almost permanently covered with snow (from where the 'Luban', or 'Lubnan' pronunciations are derived, and they mean 'milk'). The southernmost ridge is known as Hermon.

The Bible referred to the region as the Land of Canaan. It is only in 1920 that Lebanon, as a state with its current borders, was founded. The year 2020 marks the centenary of the formation of the Greater Lebanon. After its independence from the French Mandate in 1943, Lebanon enjoyed a couple of decades of prosperity. This 'golden era' did not last long however, as the formation of the State of Israel in 1948 drove numbers of Palestinian refugees into Lebanon. The Christian Lebanese viewed the Palestinian refugees staying indefinitely, as an attempt to socially engineer the Lebanese population by tipping the confessional scales in favor of the Muslim demographic... Fast forward to 2020: The Palestinian refugee issue still remains, with rumors of forgiving the Lebanese national debt in return for the naturalization of Lebanon's Palestinian population.

Lebanon is now roughly divided into three main demographics (Sunni, Shiaa and Christian) with each demographic representing about a third of the general population. The Druze demographic is a minority that is added to the muslim demographics and is often incorrectly considered to be muslim. Today, Lebanon is home to a multitude of political parties, including one particular party called the Syrian Social Nationalist Party (SSNP) which advocates the dissolution of Lebanon back inside the Syrian entity bordering it from the North and the East.

A full century after the formation of the political

entity known as Lebanon, parties with outdated political concepts should either update themselves or be condemned to irrelevance. The SSNP, despite its bylaws which accommodate for confessional pluralism, is antagonistic towards the very concept of the state of Lebanon. 100 years after the Greater Lebanon, it is time to ask ourselves: Do we want the dissolution of this country called Lebanon, back into Syrian territory or can we believe in the idea of living in a country we call our own? If the answer is the latter choice, the SSNP needs to make way to the LNP, the Lebanese Nationalist Party, where Christians, Muslims and Druze are welcome to envision and implement a system of governance and a new constitution which best represents the interests of the Lebanese people.

Tentative logo for a party yet to exist:

A cedar-shaped trident, with the bottom symbolizing a compass of a people with several millenia of heritage behind them. The bottom and largest branch is the nation. The middle branch is the family. The top branch is the individual. the tip of the trident is God, towards which all the below constituents aspire to. The opened branches mimick open books in their negative space to symbolize the endless pursuit of knowledge.

DEMONIZED

History has not been objective towards Ancient Phoenicia, Canaan and Carthage, but then again, history is written by the victor and is therefore always biased. To the overwhelming majority of the public, Punic/Canaanite culture is -essentially- one of bloodthirst and child sacrifice. Yet what is the historical/archeological evidence pointing towards such a grisly heritage? Historians like Thuclides and Polybus, who were contemporary to the Carthaginian culture, never mentioned the subject of phoenician child sacrifice *(Carthage: Fact & Myth- Docter- p.55)*.

Interestingly, The Old Testament mentions one of the tribes of Israel, the sons of Judah and among them King Ahaz, who actually did practice child sacrifice *(2 Kings 16:3; 2 Chronicles 28:3)*. The valley of Ge-Hinnom (Gehenna) in Jerusalem, is associated with child sacrifices by the Kings of Judah, who have departed from Yahveh's teachings (Ahaz and Manasseh).

Rabbinical sources were obviously hostile towards the Canaanites as mentioned in the Old Testament (since monotheistic Judaism was at the time, competing with Canaanite polytheism), as were the Romans, who battled the Phoenicians over the control of the Mediterranean. It becomes understandable from the viewpoint of history being written by the victors, that the defeated Phoenicians would be depicted under a negative light.

We get our views of Canaanites essentially from the Israelite and Roman sources. Literary sources (Rabbinical, Roman and later European ones) would portray Carthage as a bloodthirsty people who sacrificed their children to Cronus/Saturn. Roman historians such as Cleitarchus, Diodorus Siculus and Plutarch all took part in the ongoing/post-punic wars historical propaganda that would ensure the name of Carthage is sullied for posterity.

171

No archeological finds would confirm such a practice, nor even trophies from the defeated Carthage, kept by the Romans. Tophets (sacred burial grounds) would be used by historians to uphold their theory of child sacrifice but funerary urns with the remains of a child are hardly evidence that this child was killed or offered as a sacrifice. No inscriptions on any of the urns mention that those children were sacrificed. Where are the giant bronze statues of Moloch mentioned in rabbinical and Roman sources, where children were thrown alive into the smouldering maw of the bronze god? Historian M. E. Aubet concludes the following, after examining archeological evidence at Carthage:

" ...everything points to them dying of natural causes, at birth or a few weeks later. Although human sacrifice may have been practised, the high proportion of newborn babies in the tophets shows that these enclosures served as burial places for children who died at birth or had not reached the age of two. "

Another logical explanation would be the utter carnage perpetrated by the Romans themselves who, after a long and excruciating series of wars, the Punic Wars, finally achieved victory over an existential arch-enemy. It makes sense to the Romans to let no stone left standing in Carthage, and no one left alive- including children, that mortal enemy which was -under Hannibal- dead close to actually defeating Rome itself.

Force of repetition has ensured that we take a repeated theory as historical truth, despite no archeological evidence to confirm it. How sustainable can a culture be, if it were to routinely sacrifice its firstborn children to its own gods? How would such PR work in favor of the Phoenicians, who were the ancient world's leading salesmen? Despite the logical unlikeliness of such a practice, we need to remember that childbirth was not as easy as in modern times. Many children were born dead, or did not survive early childhood, which is a more sensible explanation for the sacred burial grounds of Carthage. A bronze statue of Moloch, like those described in the anti-

Canaanite writings of rabbis and Romans alike (a description further 'romanticized' by Gustave Flaubert in his novel 'Salammbo') would make an impressive war trophy for the Romans to bring back from their victorious campaign against Carthage, but no such artifact has ever been found. One would imagine the size of such a monstrous furnace with its articulated hands and gaping mouth to be between 4 and 7 meters high, would it be built. Surely such a large sacrificial device would be an easy find in an archeological excavation. And yet, in the Old Testament, it is the sons of Israel who, in their impatience at Moses' absence, melted their jewelry into a bull-shaped deity.

In nearly every pagan cuture, human sacrifice has been documented, and in many cases, archeologically confirmed, however rare its occurrence would be. But in the case of the Phoenicians, that is yet to be confirmed by archeological findings. There is strong evidence to suggest that The Romans and the Israelites wanted to cast an evil aura on their Phoenician adversary by depicting it as a child-killing beast, and the world has been forming an opinion based on biased written accounts more than on scientific, archeological evidence.

Culture Preservation

"If you can cut the people off from their history, then they can be easily persuaded."– Karl Marx (1818-1883)

Out of all the causes one could choose to work for, Heritage preservation has got to be the most difficult pursuit. It will always feel like a losing battle and never ending reserves of optimism are a must. Also having Bruce Wayne or Tony Stark kind of money would always come in handy, in which case, by all means, protect your country's heritage by financing your heritage projects yourself.

Almost everywhere, the Ministry of Culture is the most cash-strapped, not to mention riddled with dull bureaucrats with no vision. Additionally, cultural preservation is simply not *humanitarian* enough to trigger the emotions needed to make a donation or help in any way on a collective scale. There are no suffering women and children, no sick elders, no homeless refugees and no people who need emergency help, in the field of protecting heritage.

In 2013, more than half of the Byblos Museum's artifacts were stolen. The NGO *Protect Lebanese Heritage* contacted INTERPOL in vain and sent high-definition pictures of the stolen artifacts to help INTERPOL identify them. The Culture minister downplayed the crime by saying that most stolen artifacts had no cultural value. Ministerial incompetence would also shine in the earlier -and completely illegal- demolition of Phoenician vestiges in the Beirut Minat El Hosn area (Parcel 1398) in 2012, to make way for a private building.

Heritage preservation does not of course solely cover architectural and archaeological memory; artisanal trade, cuisine, fashion, music and arts, as well as the geographic environment are all integral elements of what makes a country's identity. Restoring and maintaining the above in good repair for the sake of tourism, is a laudable mission, but it is still not enough; all the above have to be not only restored, but *revived and kept alive*. And if it is dead, it is possible to resurrect it by re-practicing the various trades, techniques and methods we have inherited from our forebears and which are fortunately still available in documented form. Such trades, coupled with the current technological advancements available to us, could hold many good surprises in terms of design, thought, architecture, engineering, art, music and similar cultural emanations where past and present take part.

Our current modern outlook created a schism with the past. It severed the bridges to our origins, and that is why we look at our past the way one looks at a grave. We have been raised in the Enlightenment paradigm and taught by its media talking heads to mock and view the past in a kind of amused pity: Our poor superstitious ancestors didn't know better, with their outdated lifestyles, antiquated social structure and simpler life without iPads, social media and air-conditioning. What did they know about Augmented Reality? Ethnic fusion restaurants? About our current opulent and convenient cosmopolitanism? Heritage preservation is not about preserving buildings and places. These places and edifices are dead if the people who made them do not return. A people's collective consciousness needs to reawaken and restore the break caused by Modernity. Without this necessary step, a people can easily be relocated elsewhere, by the simple promise of a good job and material convenience. Countries would disappear overnight without the necessity to remove them through war; their people have surrendered already by uprooting themselves on their own. People shaped in the modernist worldview have trouble defining what heritage actually is. The average person believes that passed a certain amount of time, a place or a building is automatically eligible to be considered 'historic'.

Common people who think this way, are forgiven, but hearing ministers of culture and conservation 'specialists' reason that way, is cause for alarm. If all it takes is to wait, then every generic building would be considered heritage if it remains standing after a century or more. Thankfully, modernist horrors never last beyond fifty years without maintenance, while Roman sea-walls and roads, or medieval castles still stand today, unfazed by time.

So what criteria need to be reunited in a building or place for it to become heritage? A heritage relates to the people who created it, first. It is this people's cultural expression materializing itself in architecture or any other tangible (or intangible, as say music or philosophy) output. An edifice built by any given people, reflects **their way of life, language, behavior, customs, esthetic values and even their geographic location and climate**. This enables us to tell the difference between an Inca and an Egyptian Pyramid or between a Japanese and a Greek temple. It is through such an expression that the building gains its specific aspect/character and reflects the identity of the people who built it.

Utility is just one of the many ingredients which go into a historic work. Utility alone (as promoted by Modernism) produces soulless creations that fail to create any metaphysical bond with the people interacting with them. Modernism has rigorously taught us to despise any ornament or touch of beauty, through its dogmatic *'less is more' mantra* which is religiously followed in art schools everywhere, threatening the aspiring artist with a failing grade if not obeyed. Beauty is to be avoided. Utility is to be pursued under the guise of 'Purity'. As a result, every art student zealously auto-censors themself from fear of failing their course, by stripping down their work to its strict, boring, cold and stale minimum, proudly calling it 'minimalism'. Mediocre students are doubtless, happy to be provided with the ideal excuse to mask incompetence and laziness! Futurists promised us Atlantis and we got Asimov's bleak, metallic and dying Trantor. Worse, we did not even reach Trantor's technological paradigm because we were too busy being virtue-signalling egalitarians.

With Modernism, the tree of tradition has been severed from its trunk, leaving people disoriented and unsure of what it takes to perpetuate heritage. The very term now rings hollow to them, growing increasingly foreign to their understanding. The more foreign something becomes, the more we distrust it. Our defence instincts are peaked in the presence of the unknown. But to the ones who know, the severed trunk can still sprout life.

A people, should they so decide, can reconnect with their past and remember forgotten knowledge before it's too late. A people connected to their past, can produce cultural output in the present with all the criteria reunited to qualify it as Heritage. It does not need to dumbly wait centuries to gain that title! It already *is* eternal because it contains the soul of its people.

APLH[1] interview by a Scuola Politecnica di Milano graduate
-Originally Posted on March 24, 2019 on the APLH blog-

1. When, how and why did you start your organization?
The APLH originally started as a facebook group in march 2010, known as 'Stop Destroying Your Heritage'. It was created by Pascale Ingea as a reaction to the rapidly changing post-war urban landscape in Beirut and the systematic loss of traditional lebanese buildings as a result of post-war reconstruction. The group still exists and is still run by APLH. in october 2010, APLH became a fully registered NGO under permit number 1764. It is based in Zouk Mosbeh, Lebanon.

2. Briefly describe your organization task
To re-awaken cultural responsibility through published works (online, film and print), events and projects (lectures, workshops, archeological tours, etc...).

3. Are you supported by the community?
And what are the challenges you are facing?
Support is very limited, which is understandable in a country where people are too busy surviving. It is hard to stop a little and think about abstract notions like culture, collective memory and heritage when you have to make ends meet. Our greatest challenge is to make people understand that heritage doesn't mean a bunch of old buildings we need to be protecting. It's actually more than that.

4. Why do you think it is necessary as an activist to fight for this cause (saving and preserving old houses)? Some strong arguments?
We don't save old houses. Our cause is to revive a spirit we have lost around the beginning of the XXth century. We broke away with our past at roughly the 1930s, the start of Modernism as a cultural movement. Since then, anything we've built and used, has been of foreign origin and essence, and therefore not linked to us in any way. Before that period, whatever cultural ideas we borrowed from abroad, would still be laced with our own creative cultural insight and vernacular and that was especially evident in our levantine architecture where local design fused seamlessly with Venetian design into an original outcome, which is the famous triple-arched traditional lebanese house that still charms so many tourists. With Modernism religiously applied, architects were told that the past is dead, that only utilitarianism (pure function) matters, and this transpired into buildings completely disconnected from their people. If you want to understand the current malaise of the modern world, look no further than its cubicle jobs, anonymous/generic apartments and total disconnection of architecture from natural environment. This digression was necessary because we want to clarify that it's the builder of the house, not the house itself, who needs saving.

---

1   **APLH:** The Association for the Protection of the Lebanese Heritage.

5. Can you provide the approximate number of old properties in Beirut (Timeline for example from 1995 to present)?

Counting houses is missing the point. They can be a thousand or a few dozens. If the people have still not re-linked with their past, they are driftwood into an ocean of uncertainty.

6. Are there any documents or papers that prove what you are fighting for? (illegal papers, misconducting of properties)

We have so far conducted a large number of legal pursuits and complaints with the legal council (known as shura council) regarding illegalities and improper proceedings in obtaining demolition permits. All of it is documented.

7. As an expert, do you think the landlords have taken any juridical measures regarding this issue?

In the 90s, the APSAD[2] produced a grading list to be used for assessing traditional houses. Grades A, B and C were worth preserving and restoring, while D and E were not. We have heard of many cases of landlords deliberately degrading their houses to facilitate the obtention of a demolition permit. That practice has now been outlined in a decree that has yet to be implemented (it is now still a draft), so *technically*, it is not considered illegal.

8. Do you think Real estate companies and developers have a big influence on this issue? How?

They do, and their influence is predictably profit-oriented: It is more profitable to raze a single house and build a 60-apartment building in its place, maximizing space profitability.

9. Why do real estate companies and developers target these old houses? (could be related to the previous question)

Please see previous question. Also, it is not that they are targeting the old house for the sake of it, but simply because they want the plot on which the house is built, in order to have a skyscraper that would contain multiple living spaces where just one house used to stand. Urbanists would use that as an excuse to tackle the problem of overpopulation, but they don't seem to want to go through the effort of actually designing a skyscraper that looks 'lebanese' or incorporates the needs of the people who live here. Modern architecture is generic. Modern buildings could just as well be in Paris, Hong Kong, Moskow or New York, you cannot tell, so much they are interchangeable. We are not 'anti-tall buildings' and we are aware of overpopulation as a pressing problem, but we wish architects and urbanists could design spaces to look, feel and behave 'local', to reflect the identity of their creators. This is their challenge. A building could very well be built now and be a heritage building, because it carries the essence of the people who designed and built it. A building does not have to be 200 years old or more in order for it to be considered 'heritage'. This is what we want the reader to understand. Many falsely believe that in 500 years, the

---

2   **APSAD**: Association pour la Protection des Sites et Anciennes Demeures au Liban

buildings we live in, will (automatically) be considered heritage. It is not so, if those buildings only had utilitarian function.

10. This is a cultural matter: Have any of the ministers of culture taken any actions regarding saving the properties from demolition?

The actions taken are usually never done all the way to the end because the developer is usually linked to the political sphere, the same sphere who appoints the culture minister and who can force his hand at will or just tell him to look the other way. There is no political will to save lebanese heritage at the moment, and the awareness is still at the material level, i.e, the 'protectors' of our heritage think like most people, that protecting heritage is about preserving a bunch of houses/stones from demolition and/or degradation.

11. As some quoted: Cutting off "some" of these houses could bring benefit to the city? Do you agree? If yes, in what ways?

There is not much left to 'cut off'. Besides, it is sad to hear such cynicism on display- because what do they mean when they refer to 'the city'? Is it the mass of concrete buildings? Or is it the people whom they are building housing for? Shall we remind them that no lebanese citizen can afford the current housing being built in Beirut? So whom are the cynics benefiting? Could they tell us in what way will 'the city' benefit by cramming more generically designed 'housing' that outprices almost every economic stratum in lebanon? Architects learn the importance of preserving the environment while building, but never seem to apply their theories upon entering the market. Anyone looking at Beirut from afar would agree: Here is an urban tumor, and removing further traditional houses will not cure nor ease that tumor.

12. Does the Municipality of Beirut play any role on this behalf?

Yes, an irresponsible, ignorant and counterproductive one. the last green area left in Beirut (around the Beirut hippodrome) is the target of relentless efforts by the municipality to 'urbanize and rentabilize' that space.

13. Few years ago, the interior ministry has agreed to give the culture ministry power of first veto over any applications to destroy old buildings before the file is handed to the Beirut Municipality. Such regulation exists in practice? If yes how? State an example.

We have not heard of such a regulation [it does not exist]. The only regulation in existence is a law for the protection of archeological sites which dates from the French Mandate (1933). There is a draft to protect lebanese heritage, which has yet to be voted into law. Ex-culture minister Ghattas Khoury presented it but it has not been promulgated into law yet.

14. What areas in Beirut are being subject to demolition? The highest rate and why in your opinion?

All of Beirut is being actively disfigured. The trend has slowed a little as of late, due to the slump in the real estate market and of course the worldwide economic recession that has not yet abated since 2008.

15. As a local, living/ From Beirut, what can be done to bring these houses back to life?

Enact and enforce the law to protect built heritage, and most importantly, relink the people to their origins, and for this to happen, all modernist dogmas must be fought off from schools and universities. Currently, such speech is heresy, but decades of ugliness in art, architecture and thought, are proof enough that we went in the wrong direction and that it is necessary to reconnect with our past (i.e: identity) so that we better navigate the future. Modernism and identity cannot coexist. when modernism thrives, identity is suppressed (and people are aimless and frustrated without knowing why). Modernity failed to deliver on its promises.

16. How many properties did you save so far?

Only a few. And some of these properties ended up illegally destroyed later, which is why we came to the realization that it's really not about the houses but rather the mentality of people (cynical and profit-oriented) which needs to change. We have nothing against profit, but it shouldn't come at the expense of collective identity and culture.

17. In what ways could we save them? (Preservation, restoration, etc...) and do you think turning them into cultural spots (museums, art galleries, etc...) example Sursock Palaces could be a way to preserve them?

Repurposing these houses is definitely a valid solution but securing funds to do so, is the impossible mission (because it involves the purchase of the actual building first). It's made even more impossible with the absence of the heritage protection law. Once this law exists, the government (as well as NGOs) could under that law, raise funds for such projects.

18. Is this topic "Saving Beirut Heritage" been discussed in universities of fine arts?

Yes, the APLH for instance, has conducted several academic projects in that theme at the Lebanese University. We also conducted a workshop with students of the Lycee Verdun, Beirut.

19. Are students in schools and universities aware of the impact of changing Beirut's image?

They are, but the challenge is to make them interested.
A good suggestion would be to coordinate with schools and universities and include heritage-themed projects into the curricula. This is already being done at the Lebanese University fine arts faculty in the Chouf/Deir el Qamar area. What we lack is more members.

20. Have you collaborated with other local organizations or activists? State them. If yes, what project/s did you work on? And what was the outcome?

We did collaborate with the following entities: Nahnoo (a Beirut-based civil action NGO), Beirut Madinati (a civil action group)
Save beirut heritage (a Beirut-based NGO), The Lebanese Eco Movement (a Beirut-based grouping of environmental NGOs) and the Association for the

Protection of Jabal Moussa (a Mount Lebanon-based NGO).

21. Have you ever collaborated with international organizations?
If yes, in what ways?
The APLH has approached the EU organization Federculture for a large historical project that is still in the making.

22. As an organization, have you relied on some ideas made by other organizations (outside the country) fighting for the same reasons and tried to implement them in Lebanon? If yes, what organizations and countries? What were the ideas you used?
We do follow the news of regional and world heritage but every country and region has its distinct problems, but we surely are always self-updating in case any foreign-implemented idea could be of use to us in lebanon... We mainly rely on ourselves and devise our own projects internally.

23. What are your future plans/ actions/ aims regarding this subject?
Secure sponsors and/or donors who believe in our mission because we have a stream of ideas waiting to be implemented all over lebanon. Some of these ideas have their feasibility study already completed.

24. Please Feel free to add any additional comments, experiences and facts that would be beneficial for this thesis.
Many want to help but cannot get past the social media 'activism'phase. To help save heritage, real commitment, real members and real effort are needed. Social media 'awareness' is another modern-day non-solution that makes one feel good without actually doing any effort. We thank our volunteers and real-time members and wish we had more of them.

TRADITION V/S TREND

Every once in a while, a group of people agrees on a same set of values, beliefs, life goals, defensive concerns, lifestyle, etc... A civilization is thus born. To take but one example, the ancient Roman Civilization lasted 700 years (Western Roman empire), an impressive lifespan, from its birth, to the start of its decline (which took an entire millenium until the total demise of the Western and Eastern parts of the Roman Empire with the fall of Constantinople).

The early Romans of 300BC differ from the Romans of the 3rd century AD, but not so drastically as to be unrecognizable. In its infancy, Ancient Rome took much from its preceding Hellenic ancestors, but quickly developed its own identity. This identity, visually evident in Roman garb, military equipment and architecture, evolved and grew as the Romans forged their empire through the centuries. This is tradition in motion. It is only tangible via its material manifestations (architecture, arts, behavioral/cultural habits, rituals, clothing, etc) but otherwise, it is an abstract concept, difficult to build a mental image of, by many, if not most people.

As illustrated below, the same people's clothing and equipment evolved, but is still recognizable as 'Roman'.

1. 260 BC 2. 55 BC 3. 15 AD 4. 100 AD 5. 200 AD 6. 290 AD 7. 400 AD

Source: Dirondello on Pinterest

are all-inclusive, for obvious commercial reasons. Tradition, contrary to what we're told in these modern enlightened times, is not the dust-buried remnants of a dead past: It moves, it grows, slowly and steadily, with its people, according to their needs. It's an ongoing empirical experiment, trying things, adopting them when they work, discarding them when they don't. The growth is there but imperceptible within a single human lifespan. This is perhaps why humans invented trends; to have something that changes several times within one's lifetime, and give them the feeling that they are in control. Trends are centered around the individual, while traditions emanate from a functioning community with a defined shared identity. No wonder why in an age and paradigm of excessive individualism, traditions are mocked and disregarded as 'out of fashion' and 'outdated'.

Traditions were never meant to be a 'fashion' anyway, even if they may sometimes be regarded as such. One individual has no control over a tradition and if they did, as maybe an emperor could, chances are they still wouldn't live to see the full results of the changes they made in the forging and shaping of their reformed society. As society grows more atomized, the individual lives as an island of feelings and emotion, operating their fashion trend on their own social media page, basking in delusions of changing the world while actually mistaking a banal trend for something far more enduring, timeless and outside their grasp. Trends and fashions are attempts by humanity to influence others into adopting a certain way of clothing, cooking, behaving or making art. But because humans get bored, trends and fashions being the man-made devices that they are, must change with human emotion, feelings, moods and attitudes of the time. The shallowness of trend is evident in its cyclical nature. It always returns to square one under the name 'retro' or 'vintage', which are actually no more than camouflaged acknowledging of the relevance of an older lifestyle.

No matter how many fashion tendencies we'll see in the space of a few months, they'll always come back to ape whatever classical or timeless cultural trait they originally sprung from.

Left:
Parisian Gentleman Hugo Jacomet in a classic handmade suit. Right: Progress.

Trends do not require a shared set of values, beliefs, blood bond or lifestyle to admit a newcomer. They should be taken for the recreational human distractions they have always been, without confusing them with actual traditions, which live longer and will always constitute the benchmark from which trends spring and die out. Oscar Wilde called fashion an intolerable ugliness, but fashion/trends are actually a bit more than that.

Because we will never be able within our human lifespan, to experience the birth and maturation of a tradition, we've created a substitute, which we can control, depending on how prolific creators we can be. Imitation being a form of flattery, trends are an imitation of something intangible we humans can feel and see, thanks to artifacts, historical documents and records we inherited from our ancestors. Tradition is something we can only deduce and acknowledge, a tranquil force that shapes us over several centuries, even millennia.

We currently live in Leftist times. Leftism, an ideology that promotes equality, but not before God, is an anti-traditional force imbuing the zeitgeist of the past and current century, but whose seeds bloomed in the times of the Enlightenment era and French Revolution. Since then, trends took center stage and traditions were vilified. Instead of having people creating trends and fashion as a healthy creative expression of the human mind, trends became increasingly marketed as a replacement of actual tradition.

As societies 'modernize', individuality slowly mutates into individualism, giving us today's atomized societies where tradition and cultural roots are abhorred, and every single individual wants to be a trend setter with his/her horde of social media worshipers. We're mini gods and rockstars now, and we set the pace in our mini social media group.
Or at least we like to think so.

Signs of decline

Just like traditions are a reflection of the Eternal, trends are a reflection of the Eternal's creation: fluttering expressions of creativeness borne out of an ephemeral individual; movements taking place within the much larger timeframe of a tradition.

Trends are an imitation of traditions. They're either a conscious or subconscious flattery of those traditions, and ideally, should never be at odds. When a trend's purpose is to mock and degrade, it's a sign of something wrong that needs to be addressed promptly, because next time such frustration or negativity manifests itself, it will no doubt do so through less artistic and more violent means.

By building monuments and sponsoring skill, art and genius, nobles, aristocrats and kings worked towards eternity. It was their way of aspiring towards God, to emulate the eternal as faithfully as possible. The Pyramids, the Colosseum, the Great Wall, Baalbek, Stonehenge, The Roman aqueducts, the Sistinas Chapel, the Lifelike sculptures of Graeco-roman antiquity, and then again, of the renaissance are all manifestations of a quest heading towards God.

Aristocracy is never measured by one's financial wealth but by their vision, by looking at a stone and seeing an intricately shaped sculpture, looking at a ceiling and picturing it covered with a host of angels and saints battling demons, by fashioning perfection out of the raw material at hand. This is analogous to God in Genesis, who fashioned Man from soil.

Tourists of all creeds flock in their millions to admire and be awed by these works of eternity, be they Versailles, Vatican city, or the Pyramids of Egypt. It is a testament to an aristocratic vision.

It is ironic that Socialist and egalitarian regimes profit from these monuments and the art which keeps their coffers bulging, long after the kings, emperors, and aristocrats responsible for them, became dust, or were put to death. Some intellectual would promptly smirk and point out that the artists who did all the work were poor! A falsehood. The artists patroned never lacked anything and were treated even better than the useless courtesans that infested every king's hall, but still, there's the need to point out yet again, that aristocracy is not measured by financial wealth, but by vision, genius and most importantly, the ability to recognize that genius. These 'financially poor' artists, were 'aristocrats of the arts'. But it took someone to recognize their talents: Another aristocrat, blessed with soul, vision and wealth.

Kings and nobles of old knew how to recognize and elevate a genius. This is how this genius was able to work for years on a church's ceiling, or a series of sculptures or a castle, or a pharaoh's tomb, without starving and dying unrecognized. The resulting art shone like the sun. It was straight-forward in its beauty and greatness. There were no tricks in it. No lengthly meandering 'conceptual philosophies', no ArtSpeak to 'help' us appreciate it, because it touched our innermost being and broke the barriers of culture and time itself to inspire generations.

Not everyone, of course, can hope to achieve 'eternal' Art. Not everyone in the class can become the rocket scientist, so naturally, such elitism is bound to elicit resentment. People who make mediocre art outnumber those who make Eternal Art. In the age of democracy, popularity is what counts, which is why we now have the antipodal art, the art of the popular: The 'art' found at the Pompidou and the Guggenheim. The 'art' of the masses is the farthest from the eternal. It is unrecognizable from trash and yet ironically, it is celebrated. Celebrated by those who are jealous of the few who could channel the Infinite into our earthly world and shine a ray of eternity into our souls.

Culture, Liberty, Borders, and Charlie Hebdo

As the first civilisations were founded and states formed, each constituent group took it upon itself to fulfil a specific task: Politicians, priests, knights, teachers, masons, artists, doctors, lawyers and thinkers formed groups under the rule of kings, high priests or a mix of both.

Armies were formed and depending on the ambitions of the rulers who lead them, either set out to conquer nearby areas or resolved to defend their own land and borders. As armies grew more organized and efficient in their role, stability of the areas they protected, extended for decades, centuries, until the people living in said areas took them for granted. They forgot about their existence and even forgot the very notion of the vital need for security, which was a matter of life or death, when a civilization was in its budding stages.

As evolving technology and vast military experience allows an army to deter an invader, complacency begins to set into the non-military people of a nation. The excess security that the nation enjoys, has finally disconnected its people from ancient natural reality, where a lowered guard meant a brutal and violent demise. Death, doom and destruction become all a distant memory for those not bearing arms. The mere sight of a gun would throw them into a fit, now. Weapons gain a perverted meaning. They are now not only a symbol of evil but are *themselves, evil*, which means that their absence, is *good*! Death is also equated with evil (and so serial child rapists and similarpsychos are kept alive).

The complacent nation nowbelieves that death and killing only exist in movies and works of fiction. Then the government itself ends up believing its own delusions, that death and demise only happen to others, in movies, books and distant planets. The complacent government, under the pretext of cost-cutting, decides to downsize its own army (less weapons=less evil, remember?), open its borders,welcome everyone, in its naive benevolence. The disconnect is total, the guard is lowered and death is only a matter of time.

Modernity means we have disconnected ourselves from our past and from nature. Our scholars, artists and 'human science experts' preach of tolerance, open borders, holding each other's hands and being one big happy corporate family. They have forgotten that their security and lifestyle have been bought at the cost of countless lives, violently terminated with bullets, missiles, knives and swords.

Whether we like it or not, a culture becomes a culture at a great cost. People die, giving birth to their own culture. A nation and its borders are hard earned, and this is a reality people must never forget. Once they forget it and take it for granted, death awaits for thus is the law of nature: As one willingly ends one's own fight, and slips into inertia, nature steps in and weeds them out. Just like with sharks; movement must be continuous. Thinking must be continuous. The moment we stop, the moment we slack off, we die.

On the morning of the 7th of January 2015, a dozen Frenchmen* died, thinking they were still free, living in their own country, doing what their country permitted them to do at the cost of a great many lives.
It appears that time is past, now. A once great nation's guard has been lowered and the enemy struck where it hurts most: at the very pillars of liberty and freedom of expression, the very pillars of europe. Fourteen years earlier, the World Trade Center went down in flames as the enemy struck an unsuspecting, overconfident and

*Justin Trudeau would have preferred we say 'Frenchpersons'.

complacent America. The Charlie Hebdo massacre is even more sinister than 9/11: The 9/11 attack was an attack on US economy and its symbols. Economies can be replaced, reforged anew. The Charlie Hebdo attack was on a culture. From now on, in Europe, you will not dare speak your mind, because you might pay for it with your life.

A culture, a way of thought, a lifestyle, has just been kneecapped and is about to be beheaded. Britain and the US, already in bed with ISIS and Al-Qaeda, have understood that: Their media blares about the dangers of Islamophobia, almost vindicating the perpetrators and blaming it on Charlie Hebdo's staff, which is ironic, given that the Hebdo is a left-wing publication: One of *theirs*. Liberal cowardice is shown on that day, as liberal media and governments backstab a liberal journal for being liberal, killing Charlie Hebdo's staff a second time by implicitly blaming them[1].

Liberal delirium has also been shown to us that day, as the deaths of the Charlie Hebdo's staff are the direct result of pro-immigration liberal policies.

The West has allowed foreign cultures not tolerant of its own way of thinking, inside its borders. If the West is to pursue more open-border and pro-immigration policies, it will have to suppress its own lifestyle, accept the death of its own culture, deny its own past and the sacrifices of its founding fathers, or bear more murderous attacks on its own cultural foundations.

1   "Charlie Hebdo Paris shooting may deepen 'normalized Islamophobia' (www.cbc.ca) - 2015.

THE ISSUE WITH EXTREMISM

In recent elections all over the world, the public has been scared by the media's talking heads and their 'polls' about the popularity of certain leaders whom, the media judged, were too 'extremist'. Of course, extremism has always meant -for the last 80 or so years- right-wing 'extremism'. The voting public, cowed by 'scientific polls', and TV blowhards, begins regurgitating personalized versions of the things they were fed earlier online, on the radio, on TV and in newspapers, not to mention stand up 'comedians' and assorted 'artists'.

The word 'extremism' has not only shifted semantically to designate everything that does not align with the Leftist/Globalist Establishment, but has nowadays become a purely negative adjective, with heavily antagonistic connotations.

However, if we take an everyday example, as for instance, a case of mild flu, the solution for such a situation is usually an equally mild, but effective medicine, which is found in every household. As the flu worsens, more measures are taken such as additional quantities of medicine, hot soup, infusions, and some rest. To each action, a matching reaction is always needed, so when somebody's illness is beyond any immediate measures which are within the reach of almost any person, the patient needs to receive a more focused help, and goes to the hospital. Without this drastic measure, the patient has a good chance of succumbing to their illness.

Now should we call this drastic measure, an 'extremist' one, in the same negative connotation existing in politics, when hard times call for harder leaders? When tumors call for a good oncologist? Aren't the electors who keep voting for 'moderates' and weaklings in hard times, guilty of treating a severely sick body with only aspirin and soup, instead of taking it to the hospital? Aren't these voters guilty of cowardice because they preferred the scoring of Political Correctness points in a time where their collective destiny and future are in great -existential- danger?

The masses today are proving their ignorance, irresponsibility and irrationality by choosing as usual, the least worst candidate. They've been trained into the knee-jerk behavior of rejecting drastic,'extremist' measures, which they unconsciously consider as evil, worrisome and dangerous. Dangerous for their comfort zone, that is.

A wise man once warned us of the banality of Evil, and nothing better than choosing the 'good enough' illustrates that banality. The 'good enough', is the aspirin we take, when we are coughing blood. It will achieve nothing but extend our agony for a little while more, before our eventual and painful death. And what's worse is that we know it, but social peer pressure has proven a greater force than the instinct to survive. And so we choose the 'good enough', get extra social points, before biting the dust.

It is time, then, to un-demonize and celebrate Extremism, not the Al-Qaeda or FEMEN blend of extremism, but the drastic, pragmatic behavior of brisk leaders that are needed to get a sickly political body nursed back to full health. It is time to strip Extremism off its NatSoc, bogey man cultural baggage and recognize it for the necessary measure to cut down excess fat off an overweight body, or the removal of a deadly tumor to save a patient from certain death, or the cauterization of a deadly wound with fire to prevent gangrene.

It is time to make Extremism great again.

SEXUALIZING THE INNOCENT

In recent years, the public has been hearing some shy echoes in the mainstream media about grooming gangs in the UK, Italy, and the USA among other countries in the West.

The Maintream media (MSM) coverage was shy because most of these grooming gangs happen to be of immigrant origins, which doesn't sit well with the pro-immigration narrative of the MSM.

Most notable among those grooming scandals is the Rotherham sex trafficking gang, still smothered by the MSM which tried its best to minimize its amplitude. Plenty of sources about the Rotherham scandal exist online and the number of grooming gangs is on a steady rise, confirming the trend of paganization taking hold of the world. The normalizing of the sexualization and violence against children is, in our modern world, a growing phenomenon. We also see a growing number of TV-series not shying away from scenes featuring the death of a child or their violent treatment.

Such trend will, in the long run, anesthetize the public to possible real-life scenarios featuring violence or mistreatment of children. Among other trends is incest, glorified by popular TV series like Games of Thrones, Arrested Development or even the iconic cartoon series Futurama.

However, it is when such a sexually deviant agenda is carried on in plain sight that the public is most unaware of it. One of the largest (if not the largest) proponents of sexualizing the young is none other than Disney. Since Kids make up the bulk of Disney's audience, it is expected that youngsters look up to and try to imitate whatever their Disney teen idols do on screen. Well known Disney actors like Miley Cyrus, Lindsay Lohan, Demi Lovato, Vanessa Hudgens or Selena Gomez, went on to strip down in varying degrees of sauciness in their post-Disney careers.

This means that the millions of kids watching their idols during their Disney years, and kept following them later, would predictably adopt their idols' sexually charged lifestyle as something completely normal. Meanwhile, parents are too busy, being at work all day and too exhausted once they're home, to monitor what their kids are turning into. Disney is not the only culprit in this business; Nikelodeon has seen many of its tween and teen stars turn into sex-bombs later in their adolescent and adult years.

Is this a deliberately planned trend to wreck childhood by making a young generation attached to celebrities who would later adopt depraved lifestyles? I personally say yes. But why? My take is to turn children into commodities from their earliest age, because after women were seduced by salaries and joined men into the economic woodchipper, it's now children's turn to become money-making cogs for the Machine. What is the purpose of Drag Queen Story Hour[1]? All Boys Can Be Princesses Too[2]? Drag kids[3]? Cuties?[4] Seemingly innocent animated series like 'Zafari' shuffle animal attributes to further destabilize our kids (elephants with zebra stripes and koalas with cheetah spots, to name a couple of examples). Onwards to a Trans-species utopia?.

Our youth is in danger. In an appetite-controlled world, where money is the measuring stick, it makes sense to pervert the innocent young; sexualized kids feed the hormone and drug industry, the abortion industry and the organ traffic industry (among others!) under the guise of 'empowering' the youth. Through material enticement then through transforming them into consumables, one last taboo is conveniently removed through the desacralization of children and childhood.

---

1   https://www.dragqueenstoryhour.org/
2   https://www.littlethings.com/boys-dress-like-princesses
3   https://desmondisamazing.com/
4   https://www.netflix.com/lb-en/title/81111198

SEXUAL IDENTITY

Sexual Identity is the most basic and the very first 'unit' of definition we are born with. And it's a very simply identifiable criterion right from the start. We are either Male or Female *intersectional genderfluid heads popping in some nearby university dorm*. Once one gets this simple matter sorted out, begins one's journey of exploration.

Enriching one's soul, mind and body with different skills, arts and forms of knowledge adds to the original seed of identity. A girl could thus become a pianist, an athlete, a professor, a scientist, a cashier, an entrepreneur, a mom, a mom with a career,...

Same is the man; initially a boy, he picks up various interests along the road: football, reading, playing an instrument, rafting, solving math problems, or poetry. Whether man or woman, we encounter several environmental, social, cultural and economic factors that contribute to the shaping of a person's identity. One is not just 'a man' or 'a woman' anymore, defined by their sex. We become whatever our interests are: a loving father, a construction worker, a deployed soldier, a doctor, a writer, a martial artist or a teacher.

The original sexual identity phase that defines us since birth gives us anchorage in the real world.

You're a man. You're a woman. This is the starting point for everybody. And now it's up to you to become men and women *of purpose*.

However simple that definition is, it has now encountered (and in the more learned circles nonetheless!) a hurdle. This hurdle is called 'gender-fluidity theory'. This theory distorts language and when it tells you 'you can be anything you want!!!', it doesn't mean you can be an astronaut, a stunt actor, a producer or an architect.

Unfortunately you cannot be anything anymore because what this theory wants you to be is solely hinged upon your sexuality and appetites. So 'Male' and 'Female' are binary, outdated and archaic conceptions that are so *passé!* Today you can be a rainbow, tomorrow, a unicorn, and the day after, an elf, or a cat! Who's that backward oppressive patriarchal pretentious has-been who said there are only two sexes and not 16 billion?

And so, as Western 'academia' gushes over gender fluidity, and governments enforcing that ideology, young people cannot anymore focus on becoming teachers, thinkers, architects, doctors, artisans and builders of tomorrow, because they can't actually figure out what toilet they should be using first. The gender-fluidity theory has kept youngsters perpetually stuck at the starting point, told by the media to 'celebrate' the 'spectrum' of their sexuality, while they miss out on the most important thing in their life, which is having a purpose.

This is a clear sign of dying societies, where weak-minded adults who were never stable nor particularly useful at anything, decide to experiment with their own kids, with vampiric encouragement from the media and the governments (specifically western ones). History should, and will record their moral depravity and evil, with the hopes that their children somehow get the help to recover from the poison of gender-fluidity theory before it's too late. There are more important things in life than gender-hopping.

PURPOSE

'Follow the Profession Of Your Passion'. - Ruth Obeng Mensah

The above quote elegantly summarizes the 'Do what you love' advice, which, in a time of strict materialism, is continuously being ignored.

No matter how many thousands of times we've heard this clichéd and frankly tired slogan, let us take a second from our everyday frenzy and think about it for a moment. There are people with highly placed jobs but with a miserable life. Why? Most likely and on some subconscious level, they haven't realized their purpose. Purpose is when one can do something and be fulfilled, regardless of the amount of money being made. Eventually, the more we do what we are purposed to do, the more money will come as well. Contentment is key.

It is important that 'work' doesn't become a 'job' and thus lose its meaning, making us miserable, pessimistic and out of options. Our children today are caught in a maelstrom of quick decisions to make while still in school. Too many studies divert their focus on discovering what their purpose is. And then suddenly they're 18 and it's time to go to college, choose a degree. The decisions are made on the fly, because everybody is enrolling. And so many students enrol without even pausing to think " am I made for a lifetime of this?" or " will I even love what I'm getting into?" And with a fatalistic shrug, they lie to themselves: "Hell, I'll learn to love it, but now I can't afford to lose time! The semester is starting"...

Students get the illusion that they're 'choosing' a career while most of them are playing it safe and picking majors which are already saturated with graduates. Yet, they keep making the mistake because somewhere on Google, they saw an article that says their major is one of the ten likeliest **not** to become automated in the next ten years. Purpose is lost in the process and hordes of miserable and very likely jobless graduates roll off the academic assembly line. Those who ever find a job in a two square-meter cubicle will learn to live with that sense of misery clinging to them every day in traffic, commuting to work: Is this my purpose? They will learn to live with that tiny voice until they stop hearing it.

They'd address the question later. Right now there's paperwork to fill and a very important soul-killing meeting to catch, where we will exchange lousy ideas and nothing gets done.

We call this the age of speed for a simple reason:- Modernity favors quickness. It caters to the 'here and now' exclusively. It cuddles the individual to satisfy whatever they crave 'at the moment'. Modernity is therefore, the age of impulse and emotion. The age of short-term preferences. People in this age must face such a barrage of immediate pleasure that the long-term forest lies completely hidden from them. But It's not hard to find one's purpose, though in this age of noise, fast moving trends and volumes of useless clutter marketed as information, it is hard to keep track for just enough time to focus a little on what is important and what is of less importance and plan ahead accordignly. Take some time off your smartphone. Take some time off your friends, even. You'll see them later, I assure you. Turn off your earbuds and take out a pencil and a paper. Write down the things you like, the things that really move you. You should have a nice little list of five to ten things you really can't live without. These are your career prospects and your long-term plans. The things you love are the stuff you are willing to do for free. Choose with a cool head and nothing your friends or parents will say is going to make a difference. These are your choices and you are going to succeed in them.

EXPENDABLE YOUTH

-Edited by Brett Stevens for www.amerika.org-

Before modernity, people began the adult portion of their lives at age fourteen, which meant that they realized that they had to become responsible for their futures at an early age. As a result, life, though short due to illness and lack of medical technology, was intense. Flash forward to our age; at age eighteen, the average human has completed a dozen years of obedience and conformity in school, and is now ready for their first four years of further domestication through higher education.

I say "first", because soon afterwards, they are told their diploma is worthless so they must pursue graduate education or a certification program. Everyone has a masters degree which makes that post graduate pursuit equally worthless, and so, the helpless youngster is told to respond with even more "education" and get a doctorate. Then of course come a couple of years of "training" and then suddenly one realizes that they are thirty-five and still living at their parents, yet are too "overqualified" to be hired anywhere despite all those fancy degrees they have earned.

This is a true story. Many are living it daily, which explains not all but a good part of the current malaise of contemporary youth. The young have been robbed of their best years of life and vitality. Between fourteen and thirty-two, they are told that there is no way other than wasting years of their life mindlessly gobbling data as the world rushes past them. Time waits for no one, not even PhD graduates, and so this pathological emphasis on "education" robs them of time to ponder on their true calling and what they truly want to be doing with their life.

The jobs -once called professions, trades or crafts- on offer are pre-programmed by the system which has been placing blinders -with parental cooperation, no less!- on these youths since their earliest school years limiting their field of vision in a systematic will to break the youth by making it conform to the unfolding consumerist utopia. Today, few see any future outside of a wage-paying job, which understandably creates a sense of helplessness among the youth.

Many do not make it out of this narrow corridor and spend their entire life too "busy" to realize they have given the best years of their life for... A cubicle job, a condominium, a divorce with kids, and a whole lot of paperwork. The average career consists of a replaceable desk job loaded with stress that follows you home and intrudes on the weekends, to be served like a prison term until you drop dead or quit -and are quickly replaced.

This *replaceability* is also what gnaws at today's youth who is ironically told in every ad, in every Hollywood feel-good movie and in every pop song, how "special" they are. A long time ago, people worked a few hours a day, had time for leisure and still managed to have a fulfilling life and a dignified retirement. One paycheck sustained a thriving and often numerous household. Today, paychecks are easily in the four-figure category, but cannot afford much of anything, especially not a respectable and unique place in a pleasant town surrounded by intelligent, caring people.

Historians mentioning history's greatest figures, point out that these had already achieved immense things by the time they turned thirty. Today thirty-year old people are "living" fake lives on Facebook, or playing their game console in the basement of the house in which they grew up. We are surfing on the achievements of the pre-World War I generations who contributed the blueprints and ideas of all the scientific and technological prowess which makes our life so convenient today.

Once the last people who grasped that technological thought are no more, we will return to the stone age in no time. However, some hope persists, and more youths are realizing the uselessness of today's "education" and are opting out of college, choosing a riskier but more challenging and fulfilling path by breaking out of the Matrix. We will owe to these people alone any progress that humanity might make in the future because they dared to go into dark and uncharted places looking for new ways when the "established" ones rotted and failed.

These are the true creatives. Some people are suited for a cubicle job, but who decided that such a fate had to be shared by the entirety of humanity? When everyone has a Masters or a PhD, then no one has one. When everyone gets an 'A,' that grade becomes meaningless. Today's most frequently given grade is an 'A,' reports The New York Times. Are people becoming smarter or are standards being lowered for the sake of all-inclusiveness? Everything points towards the latter. Universities wanting to keep their scam from being discovered are willing to give good grades to keep the students (read: clients) coming and the money flowing.

We suffer in our souls from these wasted years. Each year of our lives is irreplaceable, especially the sweet spring of youth, but we treat them as a means to an end of bringing in money so that we can pay off society to keep its dysfunction at bay. Each year comes only once.

Wasting these years collecting degrees without a moment of pause as to how useful these degrees are is the tragedy of our times. As a result, time feels as if it is spinning faster, adding to the human frenzy, resulting in more hasty decisions and more irrational choices to the vast detriment of both individual and social life.

FAMILY AND MARRIAGE

"Every man who truly loves a woman, and every woman who truly loves a man, hopes and dreams that their companionship will last forever. But marriage is a covenant sealed by authority. If that authority is of the state alone, it will endure only while the state has jurisdiction, and that jurisdiction ends with death. But add to the authority of the state the power of the endowment given by Him who overcame death, and that companionship will endure beyond life if the parties to the marriage live worthy of the promise. . . . ". . . love and marriage under the revealed plan of the Lord are not like the rose that withers with the passing of summer. Rather, they are eternal, as surely as the God of heaven is eternal." - President Gordon B. Hinckley, "The Marriage That Endures," General Conference, April, 1974

Today, most people are confused about the purpose and finality of marriage as an institution. Some believe that people marry 'for love',some 'for happiness', and some 'to share life as a couple'. A couple can do all that without the necessity to actually marry. People can love each other, live together, be happy together and grow old together without the need for marriage. This will trigger many modernists and even some who consider themselves 'conservatives'. Marriage has one purpose and only one purpose: the founding of a family that is biologically connected, forming the smallest functional molecule of a society, to be added to the greater social body. Love, happiness, devotion and creativity are not the purposes of marriage, but are actually what cements it and keeps it going. Love, happiness, devotion and creativity should not be mistaken for the 'ends' toward which we marry, but the 'means' by which we keep our marriage and family alive, functional, fulfilling, meaningful and ongoing.

Some couples marry and find out they cannot have kids. This is an unfortunate condition and can be remediated through adoption, because the will to have a family exists, but family is prevented by a biological condition. Political correctness aside, no combination other than heterosexual, can form a biological family. The drive behind homosexual 'marriage' is particularly interesting since, according to a survey published on www.liveabout.com *"The*

Williams Institute at the UCLA School of Law, a sexual orientation law and public policy think tank, estimates that 9 million (about 3.8%) of Americans identify as gay, lesbian, bisexual or transgender (2011). The institute also found that bisexuals make up 1.8% of the population, while 1.7% are gay or lesbian. Transgender adults make up 0.3% of the population." This is a much smaller figure than the Kinsey studies suggested. And according to a 2013 article by The Guardian, *"the Office for National Statistics estimated the number of UK people who identified as gay or lesbian, to be about 1.5% of the general population"*.

Out of the estimated 3.5% of US population who are homosexual, not all of them want to actually marry (www.usatoday.com) and a sizeable portion, 48%, reported to be either unsure or averse to getting married. There are around 594000 same-sex couples in the US according to www.lifelongadoptions.com and less than 20% of them actually decide to have kids. This leaves us with an infinitesimal percentage of people who belong to the LGBT community, who actually want to get married and want to become parents. Why does the media and big corporations -through their bought legislators- go through all the hassle of legalizing something that will eventually be adopted by at most, less than 1% of the general population? They're not doing it for the LGBT community obviously -who is, despite its propensity for shopping, remains meaningless as far as commercial volume is concerned. They have 2 goals:

1-Using the LGBT community as a springboard to reach their real commercial target: Virtue-signaling liberals who support the LGBT lobby because it makes them appear as morally superior and open-minded; this is a sizeable population made up of generally affluent, media-savvy and 'educated' (read: college-indoctrinated) shopping-oriented people; those liberals are going to buy its line of products even if they don't actually need them. So if a company is 'pro-LGBT', it is not necessarily because it genuinely cares about LGBT people; it's just that gay demographics are a good revenue-generating proxy.

2-Undermining the actual institution of marriage as a stable societal molecule by removing its exclusivity as a hetero-only club, and consequently its meaning, rendering it available to whomever feels like getting married. An institution which was traditionally only open to a heterosexual couple who wants to start a family, is now open to anyone. This translates into more business for big pharma and its hormone industry, for pseudo-sciences like psychoanalysis and its assorted charlatans, expertly devised legal loopholes, divorce industry, and all major global businesses which could benefit from an atomized society with 'standards' that change as frequently as the trends and fashions of the minute.

The bottomline is: the definition of marriage is simple. The purpose of marriage is simple. It's the mutual agreement of a heterosexual couple to form a family and therefore have a descendance, and a stake in the future of humanity. This couple therefore accepts to go through the hardships of raising kids and transmitting its knowledge and experience to those kids in the hope of producing better human beings than their parents, and so on. The glue that keeps a marriage together is love, mutual respect, reason, faith and creativity. It's no simple thing to stay with the same spouse for the duration of one's life. Creativity is paramount to help avoid redundancy, repetitiveness and a boring lifestyle that would eventually undermine the couple's life. To go into marriage is to be realistic and reasonable. It takes mental fortitude to keep a marriage not just together, but enjoyable and thriving. With the array of temptations available at our fingertips, it's more and more difficult to keep a marriage afloat. More and more expensive too. All the more reason to question why would a promiscuous community like the LGBT want to get married in the first place, knowing that most LGBT people regularly change partners. To go into marriage is to be mentally stable, focused and morally sound. The LGBT lobby is known to promote paedophilia, 1 in 5 Men who have sex with Men in the USA has HIV -and that statistic is on the rise, according to www.poz.com. LGBT people have 40 times more AIDS incidence than heterosexuals. In 2016 in the US, around 40000 people were diagnosed with HIV, and 67% (26500) were gay and bisexual men (www. hiv.gov).Gay and bisexual men account for the majority of cases of syphilis -nearly 75 percent (www.stdcheck.com)- and according to a 2012 article in www.lavendermaga-zine.com, *"Within the last 5 years, the incidence of anal cancer within the gay male community and MSM (men who have sex with men)has risen by as much as an astounding 1800%"*.

The above information is a clear indicator that the drive behind the LGBT marriage scam is purely for commercial and corporate ends. Pulling the strings are multinational corporations (and big pharma) who would benefit from the commercial boom and social laxity that would result from a vulgarization of the institution of marriage; more puberty-blocking pills, more demand for abortion and more transgender surgery will boost big pharma's already fat margins. Grand parents will be a thing of the past, as people are delaying marriage and parenthood until well into their forties. They'll be lucky if they even manage to become parents. Progressivism is death, but I digress. Clearly with its established lifestyle, the LGBT 'community' has no interest in marriage or family rearing. The whole issue is a corporate crackdown on the family to increase profit off an atomized society while providing a way for virtue-signalling liberals to have something to fill their tedium with, while sipping their tall latte at the local Starbucks.

THE ENDGAME OF FEMINISM

Let us look at the achievements of the latest wave of feminism in western societies:

-Easily available divorce is 70% of the times initiated by women (www.psychologytoday.com)

-Late-term abortion without any valid medical reasons.

-Fighting 'oppressive patriarchy' at home while supporting immigration from male-dominated, hardline patriarcal societies.

-Supporting transgenderism, which allowed biological men to defeat women in every sport.

-Corporate wage-slavery instead of founding a family.

-The sexes are now competitors not partners. All men are rapists.

-Traditional family is viewed as and oppressive. Abortion is glorified and called a 'human right', or also a 'choice', which is another way to avoid responsibility.

-Feminism spites itself by siding with anyone against traditional morality represented by Christianity.

-Any pursuit of perfection and physical discipline shunned (by feminism). Feminism glorifies the grotesque and the submission to one's immediate urges, like binging and leading an unhealthy lifestyle. Feminism seeks to distort and erode language and consensus over what is "beauty" or "perfection".

Leftism centered the world around the individual and feminism took the hubris further and centered it around women and, specifically, their genitals; such a sex-obsessed 'philosophy' (as shown in all feminist 'art' and demos) is bound to mislead women from what makes them women- namely their feminity and their care-giver nature. By antagonizing roughly half of humanity (males) and building its ideology on victimhood culture and sex-obsession, Feminism has degraded many women and made them into hate-filled beastly creatures. The 'successes' of feminism have not emancipated women and have not created a better world.

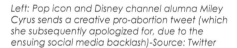

Left: Pop icon and Disney channel alumna Miley Cyrus sends a creative pro-abortion tweet (which she subsequently apologized for, due to the ensuing social media backlash)-Source: Twitter

Right: A pro-abortion 'art' performance where the blood-drenched feminist 'artist' rips a baby doll, no doubt to show the world how 'empowered' and 'brave' she is. Source: Twitter.

CONTRACEPTION

"Demography is destiny", the saying goes. This is what the enlightened Western world is beginning to find out, after decades of using contraception on itself and at the same time, admitting waves of migrants with high fertility rates. What does contraception mean in our modern multicultural world? It means that whoever limits their fertility is at a demographic disadvantage and is bound to be replaced by those who do not play by the contraception rule. Israelis in the 1960s discovered that Arabs living with them in their newly founded state had a much higher fertility and will soon be taking over the Jewish settlers, demographically and therefore, democratically. This motivated Israelis to rev up their fertility rate to match that of the Arabs.

In the meantime (still in the 60's), Europeans and westerners were lauding the benefits of contraception from an *environmental* standpoint and were in the midst of a sexual revolution, which, four decades later, resulted in booming divorce rates, loneliness, mistrust among the sexes, declining familial cohesion, single-parent households, and general social misery.

In that dark hour of western culture, open borders policies allowed the arrival of immigrant communities that did not believe in contraception nor were convinced by it. It is hard to believe that the marketing for contraception, the sexual revolution and open borders policies in the West happened all at random, without any smart orchestration. The "contraception for the benefit of the environment" was a façade; not everyone buys into this 'grand' idea to save the planet and reduce CO2 emissions through population control, except Liberal white Europeans and North Americans.

They believe humans shouldn't have children. Who are the anti-natalists - and how far are they willing to push their ideas?

THE TIMES OF INDIA

Kids are cute but they're not really eco-friendly

One less baby helps the planet more than giving up meat, car

10 Jul 2017 · 19 more

Having children is the most destructive thing a person can do to the environment, according to a new study. Researchers from Lund University in Sweden found having one fewer child per family can save "an average of 58.6 tonnes of CO_2-equivalent emissions per year".

Eating meat, driving a car and travelling by aeroplane made up the list of the most polluting things people can do to the planet.

But having children was top, according to the new study, published in the journal Environmental Research Letters.

"A US family who chooses to have one fewer child would provide the same level of emissions reductions as 684 teenagers who choose to adopt comprehensive recycling for the rest of their lives," it said.

Lead author Seth Wynes told The

Local: "We found there are four actions that could result in substantial decreases in an individual's carbon footprint: eating a plant-based diet, avoiding air travel, living car free and having smaller families.

"For example, living car-free saves about 2.4 tonnes of CO_2 equivalent per year, while eating a plant-based diet saves 0.8 tonnes of CO_2 equivalent a year."

The paper, which studied analysed 39-peer reviewed journals studying the environmental policies of several major economies,

found most governments focused on incremental changes which have "much smaller poten- tial

Top left: Why doesn't this enlightened youtuber lead by example and hold his breath for just a few hours? - Top right: A BBC article on the 'benefits' of having less babies.
Middle picture: Why does the Times of India illustrate their anti-natalist article with a white family? Could it be subliminally directed towards other demographics?

Contraception is an excuse for a civilization in its end stage, to indulge in unlimited sexual activity without its finality (having a progeny). Caring for the environment is a lame excuse, and eventually, in a vote-based system coupled with open-border policy, destructive and suicidal. The most popular political system currently being Democracy, people who have been limiting their own population are bound to be out-voted by those who have been actively maintaining or even increasing their fertility and population replacement rates.

Contraception is then, the best way for a population to commit collective suicide. It's too narcissistic and lazy to have a stake in its own future, and rather prefers to 'live in the now', 'enjoy the moment' and other similar cosmopolitan slogans glorifying a hedonistic self-centered lifestyle.

This is of course, not to say that one should have more children than they can realistically have the time and finances to handle. Overpopulation is a massive problem and cause of much of today's human misery. Yet, where is contraception mostly applied? Western countries. Countries who already efficiently manage their population volume. In a yet another semantic twist by the Left, contraception is given a new name:
Protection. Protection from what? Condoms were synonymous with protection in the times when AIDS was a serious threat. But 'protection' has quietly grown to define all forms of contraceptives now.

It is time to realise that the topic of contraception is not as it is being marketed, a way to regulate overpopulation in order to save the planet. Rather, it's an ideological weapon used by certain groups against other groups, in the social war for domination that humanity has been waging upon itself since the dawn of time.

WHY ARE GAY PEOPLE SO VOCAL ABOUT THEIR SEXUAL 'ORIENTATION'

When two straight people mate, a result happens: new life is conceived. This quite simply tells us that the act of mating is a means to an end, which ultimately results in Life.

This simple, and yet at the same time, mind-blowing process does not exist for the gay person. Two gay persons will 'mate' and mate again, and again and again, and nothing will happen as a result (except some horrible STD*). So the gay person has to consciously do something to add 'meaning' to their sexual activity. If the means or methods are dysfunctional, or used wrongly, i.e, opposite to their nature-intended meaning, there can be no finality, no raison d'être to them, no purpose.

Thus, obviously, the gay person will glorify the means itself, since there is no end, no outcome to their sexual activity. They will trumpet their lifestyle over the roofs, on the streets, on the radio, on camera, everywhere they possibly can. Even on ATMs. They will glorify the act of homosexual mating as an end in itself, in a desperate bid to change the course of nature, to deny reality, to create an alternate world. The gay person today will happily go on TV and seek to shock the audience with twerking, depraved dances or gross behavior, while there's no point for a straight person to indulge in the same behaviour.

Straight people know that sex is enjoyable. There's no need to say the obvious. But they also know, at least the smarter ones, that sex is a means to an end. It has a finality, and is not itself **the** finality.

Not for the gay person, though.

A gay person knows that glorifying their sexuality is a

*STD: Sexually Transmitted Disease

sign of insecurity, a way of bending reality, to compensate for something they're unable to do: Naturally producing life, through sexual union. I'm sure many gay people are realistic enough to recognize that. Author Jack Donovan is an Alpha example of that. You wont find Mr Donovan taking part in a gay pride. There exists instances where gay people have mustered enough will to revert back to a straight sexual lifestyle[1], shattering the 'born that way' myth[2].

Legalizing gay marriage is not a sign of openness, or progress, or whatever the Liberal lobby chooses as a fancy name for it. Nor will that make it *right* -in the same way that legalizing infanticide won't make that *right* either. Legalization of depravity through legal lobbying is the best way to normalize degeneracy by making it 'legal' and therefore, accepted among those automatons of modern society. It's a sign that an entire society has deviated from from reality, and in its embrace of the Self, has decided to live in their own bubble. Instead of being in one world, interacting with one reality, each of us is now will have their custom-made reality, and since each customized world -whether functional or not- is, according to Liberal ideology, equal to the next, nothing makes any difference anymore. even in one same language, we now have unlimited personal interpretations for it. It's the proverbial Tower of Babel, where everything is equal to everything else, beating its own purpose.

---

1   "Former LGBTQers Testify: If You No Longer Want to Be Gay or Transgender, You Don't Have to Be" - January 2020 - (Youtube).
2   "Denials that ex-homosexuals exist" - www.conservapedia.com

DIVIDERS

U.S. Democratic presidential candidate and mayor Pete Buttigieg was campaigning on a pro-abortion platform, calling it 'pro-choice', as a much more sellable pitch. In his address to potential voters, he throws an enticing bait to his female audience:

women should have the 'right' to end a pregnancy at any term, no matter how advanced, no questions asked.

There is an interesting observation to make from Buttigieg's proposal: the absolute absence of the unborn child's father. The presidential hopeful completely nullifies the role of the male parent, reducing it to the bodily emission necessary for fecundating the female egg. For Buttigieg, a so-called *Catholic*, there is absolutely no relevance to the traditional family unit composed of husband and wife, and in the event of conception, the mother is the decider while the father ceases to exist. This kind of thought is yet one more modernistic manifestation of the anti-family hostility which modernism and leftism bears the monogamous family structure. We understand where Buttigieg is coming once we know about his homosexuality, which means his lifestyle excludes the other sex completely, while he ironically campaigns for 'all-inclusiveness'.

Remember how Leftism overturns every concept into its own opposite? That is the goal. Deconstruction is the name of the game. But deconstruction of what? Of the Christian worldview, of course. But I just said he is a Catholic, didn't I, so how come? Is there a better strategy than subversion from within? The enemy inside is always the most lethal because defense awareness is at its minimum.

Where the Church consecrated equality of man

and woman through the bond of monogamous marriage, neo-churchism seeks to divide man from woman, glorify homosexual 'marriage' where the opposed sex is completely banned, and pit father against mother in the decision-making concerning the life and care of their future born. A church of *convenience and impulse* replaces a church of committment and maturity.

In some instances like in the modernist debate of nature v/s nurture or form v/s content, we further see that same dividing trend, typical of Modernism. One is forced to take sides where there really is no need.

A BRAVE NEW HOMOSEXUAL WORLD

Edited by Brett Stevens for www.amerika.org

Today the total earth population is hovering around eight billion, most of whom are not very bright and show minimal concern for the future of nature, humanity or common sense. We know that the fuse is lit, and at some point, this bomb will go off and destroy us. At the back of our minds, we hope for some deliverance from this inevitable disaster.

Imagine that a new and extremely popular leader emerges today who is so persuasive and charismatic that he convinces the voters that we must cut the world population in half. This leader has Colgate teeth, a benevolent face, the most soothing voice and the most handsome face you could ever imagine, combined with poise, swag and a posture which embodies every archetype you hold in awe. And yet, he is talking about eliminating four billion people. What might we call this person? Stalin 2.0, or Hitler, the sequel? Maybe Satan.

Take your pick.

But he is merely advocating homosexuality.

If enough of humanity accepts homosexuality, and it becomes massively trendy, we can successfully negate the human breeding colossus. Men cannot breed with men, nor women with other women, so each person converted means two people taken out of circulation. And it might just succeed. With enough manipulative advertising, you can brand any poison into the latest fad, getting people to wait in line for it. Homosexuality is the most celebrated fad in today's decadent world, thanks to smart branding: love, rainbows, freedom to choose, all-inclusiveness, forward-thinking, progress... The perfect formula for a new gay planet.

The opposite sex has no place in a homosexual world. Humanity is thus effectively divided in two perfect halves, each wanting to be independent of the other, disgusted by the other, repulsed by the other, but don't forget, it's all under the aegis of freedom to choose whom you want to *love*! A trifle to pay for all the progress that lies in wait.

It takes Adam and Eve to create humanity. Adam and Steve will have to borrow someone else's kid to fake a family. They can also use "science" to turn them into freaks that can get pregnant, give birth and lactate, and if they can't afford it, the state will happily oblige[3]. But nonetheless, they want to exist away from the opposite sex. Not quite the all-inclusiveness that's advertised, but think of the ecological impact: fewer people means less pollution and more grass to munch upon, more job opportunities and higher wages too!

It's really a win-win situation. Families and reproduction lead to overpopulation. Homosexuality means open-mindedness and lower population. Even more, it allows each person to exist without the burden of family which could restrict their pursuit of their own ideas and urges. One more nail in the coffin of the outdated heterosexual model!

---

3   "Warren And Biden Support Taxpayer-Funded Transgender Surgery" -2019-(verified by www.snopes.com).

In the case of a homosexual Earth scenario, some-one — most likely the state — needs to take things in charge to avoid a complete extinction of humanity. It can factory-farm foetuses to keep economies running, pro-viding them with the needed amount of cattle. This way, the homosexual utopia can finally become a reality, and the state can manage our lives from cradle to grade in its infinite benevolence.

A REPLY TO A PRO-LGBT BLOGGER

Lebanese Blogger Elie Fares (**"A Separate State of Mind"**) has published a pro-LGBT piece where he attempts to refute the arguments presented to him by what he calls 'Lebanese Homophobes'. He wrote down the 'opinions' of the so-called bigoted homophobes and then he proceed-ed to 'debunk' them with links, scientific 'facts and logic'.

Those links, scientific facts and logical counter-ar-guments were heavily skewed, as will be demonstrated. In short, it's ideologically manipulated propaganda that only *looks* scientific.

For the full article, go to:

https://stateofmind13.com/2017/05/17/dear-lebanese-homophobes/

Here is a one-by-one rundown of Elie Fares' **(EF)** counter-opinions where he attempts to 'educate' the bigoted homophobic Lebanese, and my personal take on Fares' answers:

'Bigoted' Opinion #1: Homosexuality is against nature

EF-[This is factually incorrect. If you're going to use the nature argument, you can't disregard the fact that all species on Earth exhibit homosexual behavior. From penguins to dolphins to a ton of species in between them, almost all species walking the Earth exhibit homosexuality. And yet, the only species that has homophobia is humans. Food for thought.**]**

1-NOT all species on earth exhibit homosexual behavior, as Fares claims. Out of 8.7 million of animal species on earth, only 1500 (0.017%) exhibit homosexual behavior (www.news-medical.net). And yet, Elie Fares -quite unscientifically- confirms that (I quote) *'almost all species walking the Earth exhibit homosexuality'*.

2- Another important fact carefully omitted by Fares is the purpose and finality of sex. He only talks about playful sex, points out that some animal species exhibit it, and then reduces the sexual union to play exclusively, before falsely blanketing it over the entire fauna. Sex, while enjoyable (at least to us humans), is also (and chiefly) for procreation. Every species alive, outside of protozoae, needs to sexually mate in order to reproduce. When dolphins, penguins and a handful of other species do exhibit homosexual behavior, it is strictly for play, until they find a mating partner to procreate with. Even animals understand that the survival of their species depends on their heterosexual mating, but Fares and his LGBT lobby apparently are the only humans who fail to understand that most basic biological thing.

Nowhere in Fares' article, or in any LGBT article, is mentioned biological reproduction because biology exposes the LGBT lobby as the exclusively recreational, reproductively barren club it actually is. It has zero contribution to the genetic advancement of humanity, zero stake in the future of the human race and therefore is irrelevant in terms of reproduction and the continuation of the human species. This does not sit well with the ideology of Equality peddled by the Left and its LGBT cronies. No wonder why the LGBT and the Left, presumably the Party of Science, have a raw hatred for biology and an affinity for the 'soft' (i.e., easily skewable) sciences like psychology, sociology and anthropology.

3-Fares, the LGBT and the wider Leftist umbrella behind them, are experts in language distortion but get lost in the process of their own semantic acrobatics. They postulate that if something exists in Nature, it is therefore 'natural=good', implying therefore that it's OK for humans to practice it. They point out that bonobos indulge in homosexuality and therefore it is fine that humans behave like bonobos. Baby spiders keep eating each other until only a few surviving spiders remain. This occurs in nature. It is therefore 'natural', and maybe, according to Mr Fares' logic, we should practice it as well. Beheadings are part of the folklore of the Islamic State. IS is part of humanity and therefore, of nature. Their practices are thus, 'natural' and therefore, would probably be OK'd by a rationalist like Fares. Bowel movements, cancer and AIDS are also 'part of nature'. Plenty of disgusting things are part of nature. This skewed logic governs modern, equality-obsessed thinking, but what gives it more leverage is that its proponents claim it does not hurt anybody, unlike IS beheadings, and is a private act by two consenting adults -also unlike beheadings. As long as they stick to that definition -except that they don't*- the rest of us are totally fine with it, but then this invalidates the need to promote homosexuality via Gay Prides, because the rest of humanity -statistically more than 95%- does not consent, nor adheres to the homosexual lifestyle and it will not be forced to observe it, adults and children alike.

Homosexuality is not 'against nature', it's however, an exercise that has no value beyond the recreational and cannot be equated with heterosexuality, since the latter can produce new life, naturally. Homosexuality however, is against Humanity in the sense that it cannot biologically and genetically advance it. Modern ideologists would point out that with 'Science', we can make a man have ovaries and a woman have an erection, to which I answer: this is merely an exercise in precision meat-cut-

*A TEDx speaker gave a talk in Germany, that referred to pedophilia as an 'unchangeable sexual orientation.' (verified by www.snopes.com) - this shows that children, when enough manipulated, will give their consent to pedophiles, and if consent is legalized, it will be the last obstacle to normalizing pedophilia.

ting, akin to the part-removal and replacement that we do for hardware, cars and other customizable equipment. The common man calls it 'science' but it's actually only scientific in its outer method -by cutting and pasting with precision instruments- not in essence. We have successfully grafted an ear on the back of a mouse. That doesn't make mice with human ears the norm for the mouse population.

'Bigoted' Opinion #2: Anal sex is the root of all STDs:

EF-[This is factually incorrect as well. I mean, if you're going to talk medicine, you should really back up your claim with hard medical data not what your local priest or sheikh told you once upon a time. It is statistically significant that HIV has a higher rate of transmission through anal sex compared to vaginal sex, yes, but that doesn't mean that anal sex created HIV or other STDs for that matter or that "doing it from behind" (as one comment said) is "scientifically proven" to be the root of all sexual diseases. You see, there are more STDs than HIV, and the key to combatting all of them – regardless of the genitals you're sleeping with – is to practice safe and clean sexual habits.

If you're straight, bisexual, gay, trans or intersex, regardless of whoever you sleep with if that person is not a long term partner whom you are aware is healthy, safe sex is a key towards prevention of all major STDs.]

Mr Fares is of course right when he says STDs do not all originate from anal sex, but something tells me this is a made-up 'opinion' because when someone makes such a preposterous claim, they should be quoted, but Fares somehow chose not to. STD causes are of course NOT all rooted in anal sex. One can get STDs from vaginal sex just as well, however, Fares skews the claim by implying it says anal sex is the origin of HIV. This whole 'opinion Number 2' is a rambling non-issue where Fares is trying to imply that opponents of homosexuality falsely claim that homosexuality means anal sex and that anal sex is the only source of STDs, in an attempt to make his opponents look like illiterates.

'Bigoted' Opinion #3: If homosexuality is okay, then why do they have a high prevalence of HIV?

EF-[While anal sex is proven to have a higher risk of transmissibility compared to vaginal sex, due to the type of cells in the anal mucosa and the viral load in penile secretions, that is not the full story. The reason why HIV has a higher prevalence among homosexual and bisexual men is because of the stigma that their community faced over the years, leading them not to have access to healthcare or needed awareness that is needed.

It's almost ironic that an argument whose answer is discrimination is used to defend one's bigoted views about that which you're discriminating against. Instead of fostering a world of non-judgemental healthcare, you are discriminating against someone based on the disease they contracted. This is not okay in any day and age. To quote a dear friend: Epidemiology ALWAYS has social reasons. Now that is a fact.]

1-According to the Centers for Disease Control, in a 2016 article reported by CNS News, *"gay men, who make 2% of the US population, account for 67% of all new HIV diagnoses"*. 28% (that's more than a quarter) of US transgender women have tested HIV
positive in a 2008 statistic.

Anal sex is potentially far more risky because the anus is designed to hold in feces, and therefore, no matter how 'clean' it might look to the naked eye, it's still full of bacteria that will infect the giving partner especially if no condom is used, but Mr Fares chooses to ignore once again scientific statistics because those numbers do not add up for his agenda.

2- Fares claims that HIV-positive gay people outnumber HIV-positive straight people mainly because of medical treatment discrimination. This is a preposterous claim where an advocate of science is baselessly accusing doctors with the unfounded claim that homophobic doctors are denying treatment to gay HIV-positive people, which explains the higher incidence of HIV within the gay community. This propaganda sounds like it was copy-past-ed directly from some APA psychologist essay because, as usual, the APA always blames society for the risky lifestyles of its protected LGBT minorities. Fares has yet to provide a single instance where a gay HIV-positive person has been denied treatment while another HIV-positive straight person has been admitted. Anyone who wishes to, can freely have medical tests and see whether they test positive to HIV or not. I personally have never read about any case where an HIV-positive person has been denied treatment due to homophobia and yet, the APA -and its mouthpieces- continues to peddle such unfounded propaganda in its 'scientific' newspapers. This shocking claim ignores the biological risks inherent in anal sex (14 times more likely to result in HIV than vaginal sex and the fact that gay, bisexual, and other Men who have sex with men acquire HIV at rates 44 times greater than heterosexuals, according to www.healthnewsdigest.com) and is built on no basis whatsoever other than false assumptions. He provides no research to back up his claims and no hard factual numbers to demonstrate that homophobia is the main cause of medical discrimination when HIV-positive gay people are involved.

'Bigoted' Opinion #4: Kids brought up by same-sex parents will grow up to be gay:

EF-[No, this is incorrect. All psychologic studies to this date have not shown this to be accurate. Being gay is not a matter of upbringing. It's a complex interaction between genetics, hormones, environmental factors, etc... Science has not even fully understood why homosexuality exists as the issue is that complex, but I'm glad you can reduce it to someone's upbringing. It sure saves every scientist a lot of effort and future accolades into the study of human sexuality.

And yet, despite all of this, the science is clear. Not only are children brought up by same-sex parents not at an increased "risk" of not being straight, but they're also not at a disadvantage when it comes to life (link: https://qz.com/438469/the-science-is-clear-children-raised-by-same-sex-parents-are-at-no-disadvantage/).]

Notice how Mr Fares' chief sources are psychologists and sociologists, NEVER biologists or professionals in the 'hard' sciences.

1-Psychology is sadly, and in the words of an eminent psychologist, not a science[4]. Contrary to hard sciences like physics, chemistry or astronomy, it is a conflicting tissue of theories that clash with each other, with jungian, freudian, skinnerian and outsider psychologists rattling sabers and destroying each other's methods, disagreeing about the fundamentals of psychology itself! A science with no consensus over its methods and subjects is NO science.

Psychologist Timothy Wilson says: 'psychology often does not meet the five basic requirements for a field to be considered scientifically rigorous: clearly defined terminology, quantifiability, highly controlled experimental conditions, reproducibility and, finally, predictability and testability.'

No wonder why the LGBT have this love story with psychology; it's a practice that has demonstrated its vulnerability to social and political pressure, as in the time when the APA was pressured (consistently from 1970 till 1973) to remove homosexuality from the list of mental illnesses -which it finally did- by sheer and continuous demonstrations from LGBT activists outside the building of the APA. No science was involved in that historical removal. Only bullying.

2-Mr Fares involves genetics in his explanation of what causes one to be gay. Coming from someone who says has a medical degree, this is a saddening claim, because it is based on no biological proof. On the contrary, there is a growing body of evidence of people who used to be gay, but overcame this sexual orientation back into a heterosexual lifestyle. The media however, is always silent on those, and any doctor who produces biological evidence disproving any genetic link to homosexuality, is being savagely attacked by a gay lobby growing increas-

4   "Why Psychology is not a Science", by Alex Berezow -2012 (Source: www.latimes.com).

ignly more rabid, influential and experienced in the arts of bullying.

Dr Robert Knight compiled the following research PDF, that shows how the removal of homosexuality from the list of mental illnesses in 1974, was a purely political stunt and had no basis in science whatsoever: **https://con-cernedwomen.org/images/content/bornorbred.pdf**

Mr Fares' claim that genetics has something to do with being homosexual, is pure LGBT, non-scientific propaganda. He is using his own medical degree as a scarecrow to add credibility to his propaganda. Homosexuality has so far no genetic origin and is therefore, a product of psychological and environmental factors, as many homosexual people managed enough will power to revert back to a heterosexual lifestyle:

"Some Gays Can Go Straight, Study Says"

http://abcnews.go.com/Health/Sex/story?id=117465

"'Ex-Gay' Men Fight Back Against View That Homosexuality Can't Be Changed"

http://www.nytimes.com/2012/11/01/us/ex-gay-men-fight-view-that-homosexuality-cant-be-changed.html

"Gay Conversion: I Slept With Over 200 Men, Now I\'m a Happily Married Heterosexual Dad"

http://www.ibtimes.co.uk/gay-conversion-i-slept-over-200-men-now-im-happily-married-heterosexual-dad-1443188

This shows that homosexuality is not physiological/biological/genetic but rather psychological, and as a medical degree holder, Mr Fares more than anyone else, knows that one cannot change their genes through sheer willpower.

The below links are testimonies of children of same-sex couples, who are speaking from experience, against same-sex marriage, and FOR traditional heterosexual marriage. Somehow, Mr Fares chose to use a pro-LGBT marriage study, but ignored real life situations like the below testimonials:

"Children raised by same-sex parents speak up for traditional families"

http://www.smh.com.au/comment/children-raised-by-samesex-parents-speak-up-for-traditional-families-20150417-1mn8ue.html

"Adults with gay parents say same-sex marriage isn't good for kids"

http://www.washingtontimes.com/news/2015/mar/27/adult-children-of-gays-say-gay-marriage-isnt-good-/

"Adults Raised by Gay Couples Speak Out Against Gay 'Marriage' in Federal Court"

http://www.cnsnews.com/news/article/lauretta-brown/adults-raised-gay-couples-speak-out-against-gay-marriage-federal-court

"Children of Homosexuals Fare Worse on Most Outcomes" Peter Sprigg sets the tone in his research, which can be downloaded via this link:

'new study on homosexual parents tops all previous research': **https://downloads.frc.org/EF/EF13I75.pdf**

Mr Fares is saying gay parents will not result in gay children because sexuality is a choice, contradicting his initial premise that homosexuality is rooted in genetics. While the sexual organs are a biological fixture, sexuality and sexual preference can be greatly influenced by social and environmental factors, as Mr Fares previously mentioned in his article (the part where he tried to smuggle in some genetics), and since parents will always teach their kids their own values, is Mr Fares expecting his readers to believe that homosexual parents would not be an environmental and immediate social influence upon the sexual preferences of their kids? A slow read of the above research will hold a trove of information of the social risks that kids of a gay union are likely to go through, but Fares will blame society -a typical APA ploy- instead of blaming the actual people for their own personal choices.

So far, all of Mr Fares' arguments were rooted in pseudoscientific psychoanalitical 'evidence' disproven by biology, genetics and hard reality.

Thankfully, the mind is powerful enough to over-come social engineering propaganda championed by the powerful LGBT lobby (and its shills); the media is more and more unable to obscure the testimonies of kids of same-sex parents advocating for traditional marriage, and of ex-gay people reverting back to a heterosexual life-style. Renowned Psychologist Dr Spitzer was forced by the media, the LGBT lobby and the APA to apologize for the results of his research where he advanced the hypothesis that one can revert from a homosexual, back to a het-erosexual lifestyle. No counter evidence was produced to discredit Spitzer, but a relentless ten-year long bullying campaign forced him to retract his research in order to enjoy his retirement, free from media encroaching.

'Bigoted' Opinion #5: Same-sex couples have higher divorce rates:

EF-[Literally incorrect. The biggest study on the matter surveyed 150,000 married same-sex couples and found their divorce rate to be at 1%/year, whereas it is 2% for opposite-sex couples.

Yet again, if you're literally telling someone they can't love another person because of that person's gender, I would assume it's unfathomable for you to believe that two people who love together can stay together.]

This is of course, assuming that a homosexual union can actually be defined as a marriage, which it isn't, at least not in communities who are still immune to political correctness, like Lebanon, the Far-East or Eastern Europe. Fares is again banking on the recreational nature of the union -just sex- rather than its true finality -progeny and descendance. According to www.lifelongadoptions.com, out of 594000 same-sex couples in the US, only 115000 have kids (either from one of the spouses or adopted).The large majority of same sex couples choose NOT to raise kids. This is not the case with heterosexual couples who, in their majority, choose to have kids, and therefore, have much more responsibilities raising them with all the stress on the marriage that this entails. This has been conveniently ignored by Fares and his LGBT friends.

Mr Fares plays his favorite language-distorting gambit again when he says "you're literally telling someone they can't love another person because of that person's gender", painting heterosexual society with a stalinist or khmer rouge brush, where a majority is literally forbidding a minority to 'be in love'; No, Mr Fares, we're telling those who refuse to understand, that marriage has a purpose, and it's to build a family, and a family is something only a heterosexual couple is capable of doing. LGBT couples can still love each other, and live

together and do whatever they feel like doing under one roof, without the need to ape a heterosexual union by wanting to get *married*.

Last and not least, in his skewed statistics, Fares shows that divorce rates among heterosexual couples are double that of the homosexual ones, forgetting that homosexuals are less than 5% of the general population and only a small portion of them chooses to marry.

'Bigoted' Opinion #6: If you like homosexuality, why don't you approve of beastiality or pedophilia?

EF-[It's actually quite simple. The whole point behind Lebanon's Pride Week is to advance the mantra of "live and let live," which is to say it's none of anyone's business who people love and why they love them.

How the hell is sex between two consenting adults, regardless of their gender, the same as when someone forces oneself on a helpless animal who doesn't possess the agency nor the mental capacity to give consent to whtat they're being forced into?

Or even worse, how is a sexual relation between two consenting adults the same as when one adult forces themselves on a child who doesn't possess the agency or legality to give sexual consent?

The only resemblance between beastiality, pedophilia, and homosexuality is, you know, the fact that both involve sex, which – gasp – also applies to heterosexuality.]

Then it is settled! Since it's 'none of anyone's business who people love and why they love them', there is no need to organize a 1-week long Gay Pride to promote something that is none of anyone's business. Mr Fares and friends need to address this obvious contradiction.

Mr. Fares also needs to update his own information regarding paedophilia, which is well documented to be supported by the LGBT lobby. This is a slippery slope where already beastiality is being in the process of normalization, and has already been legalized under some forms in 'progressive', pro-LGBT countries like Canada[5], for example.

'Bigoted' Opinion #7: It's a Western ploy to ruin our societies:

EF-[You'd be surprised to know that Arab society was much more open to homosexuality and other manifestations of human sexuality than it is today. Abu Nawwas, the famous Arab poet whose works on love and wine and even sex are taught in schools and universities today, was an open bisexual. He was embraced by society, because his "behavior" was more

---

5   "Most bestiality is legal, declares Canada's Supreme Court" -Source: www.independent.co.uk- 2016.

accepted back then.

In fact, homosexual behavior can be traced back to earlier civilizations that existed in these parts of the world and our neighboring countries and regions. There's literally nothing Western about it. If anything, our regions "exported" it to the West when we started emigrating from our own countries to the New World.

Regardless of what politicians want to tell you or what your own "we're better than the West" mantra, human behavior is very similar across the Earth. This is why we can find common ground between two individuals who are worlds apart. And yet, it sure is telling that anything that Arabs find to be at odds with what they know gets attributed to the "West." It's a major shortcoming of our own societies, if anything.]

Here, Mr. Fares is carefully skirting the obvious; while homosexuality exists in all societies, The LGBT lobby is firmly a western political power, and its policy is starting to show through today's crop of western kids, who are increasingly growing disoriented an confused about their sexuality, 'coming out' as transgender, and requesting reassignment surgery -out of their own accord, and without any adult manipulation, I swear!. Mr. Fares is implying that the LGBT movement in Lebanon does not have the same devious targets like the western one, and is only about being free to love whomever one wants.

Come now, sir, your movement is backed by a multinational establishment, by multinational corporations like Starbucks, Walmart, Apple, Target, Levi's, Microsoft, Amazon, Disney, Gap, Pepsi, Absolute, Smirnoff, Citigroup, Nike, Google, Facebook, Mercedes, Audi, etc and you expect to tell your readers you're completely independent from this immense behemoth whose political, mediatic, publishing, and cultural reach can model the thinking and perception of entire generations any time it chooses? Do you seriously think you're the one who is oppressed? You're painting the LGBT as victims, while in reality, you're the establishment, and anyone who dares speak up a dissenting opinion, is flattened by that establishment[6].

The gender theory supported by the LGBT aims to atomize people and render the traditional family obsolete. When every child questions their sexuality, and can be freely reassigned to another gender, the most basic identity unit - gender- is gone. And you, a medical degree holder, a scientist, are defending that. Yes, the LGBT lobby looks like a bunch of nice people who just want to 'live and let live' on the outside, and I disagree with the humiliation they're subjected to, while incarcerated, but at the same time, as people connected to the rest of the world, we've seen the lawsuits against private hetero-owned businesses (always Christians, as the LGBT bully dares not play their scam on Jewish or Islamic businesses). We've seen the bullying on the corporate levels and in the media, we've seen the media brainwashing, the children forced to watch gay prides, drag queens reading to kids in school libraries, how children are used as props on magazines heralding a transgender age (National Geographic, Cadeau, etc). We've seen the schools forcing children to learn about gay sex, reading gay 'literature' and watching gay cartoons. It's all gone crazy on social media, proposing more than 60 different gender options for their new users.

And we want none of that.

The LGBT lobby is the ruin not just of our Eastern societies, but of ALL societies. There are 2 genders, Mr Fares. Two. Male, and female. XX and XY. You're a scientist, remember? Snap out of your politically correct scientism and re-embrace true Science.

Isn't it ironic that religious authorities in Lebanon are siding with Science and biological realities while 'scientists' like Fares, are siding with hocus-pocus Bill Nye gibberish about a gender infinity spectrum? People like Fares are religious zealots, believe it or not, and their religion is

---

6   "Barclays Close Christian Charity Bank Account Offering LGBT Conversion Therapy" - (Source: www.forbes.com) 2020.

late-stage liberal ideology.

'Bigoted' Opinion #8: I don't know any gay people:

EF-[Yes, you do. 10% of the population falls among the LGBTQI+ spectrum at the most conservative of estimates. Your class of 20 people [in 9th grade] had at least 2 people among your classmates, and maybe even your friends, are LGBTQI+. That 300+ biology course you took in university has around 30 LGBTQI+ people, maybe even that person sitting next to you. Your family and extended family has a couple people or more who are too afraid to be who they are because of you.

Don't live in denial. Embrace others and be open to the people you love for them to find a beacon of safety in you.]

I know quite a few gay people, and work with quite a few. Some of my favorite writers and artists are gay people. Jack Donovan and Philippe Verdier, who are both gay, are extremely talented writers and thinkers, who keep their lifestyles to themselves. They don't go to Gay prides. They don't need that extra reassurance. They are achievers and they do not need a lobby to give them relevance. They do not need Elie Fares' support or his 'open-mindedness'. They TRULY live and let live, without relentlessly blogging about their sexual preferences. They don't crave the attention. They dont live off their homosexuality nor are defining themselves by it. Their sexual choices are their own business, and as a fan of their work, I accidentally discovered their sexual orientation because they don't advertise it. That's the kind of gay people I can fully support and respect.

Mr. Fares belongs to a lobby and the second a gay person reverts back to a heterosexual lifestyle, or proclaims some non-conformist political views, he will not hesitate to attack them. His LGBT friends say one thing and practice another. Not wanting someone to rub their sexual preference in people's face, is not homophobia. It's not bigotry. Fares contradicts himself when he says gay people's choice is nobody's business then he goes out of his

way to promote a lifestyle that is not even his, for a whole week. Mr Fares needs to start practicing what he preaches. Society is the majority and the minorities need to adapt to the rest, not bend the rest to
the minority's will.

Fares also needs to update his 'scientific' figures; the 10% statistic of the Kinsey study which dates from the 1940s, has now been proven false and the numbers are closer to 3% ...

'Bigoted' Opinion #9: Medicine says it's an illness:

EF-[This is not true at all. Psychiatry has declassified homosexuality as a disease for over 50 years now. The Lebanese Psychiatric Association declared it not an illness more than 4 years ago. The Lebanese Order of Physicians has restricted its physicians from practicing any anti-LGBT medical practices and, if a physician was found doing such illegal practices, their license could be revoked.

So if you find a "doctor" who's giving a "lecture" about why homosexuality is bad, know that that doctor is a fraud who is not practicing medicine. Hocus pocus would apply more in that case.]

First, let's agree that homosexuality is not an 'illness' but rather a 'psychological condition' one can overcome. Now that we have that detail behind us, it's good to remind Mr. Fares that homosexuality was removed from the list of mental illnesses, not because of any groundbreaking scientific evidence on that
subject, but simply due to massive and relentless demonstrations from the gay community, finally forcing Dr. Spitzer to make that declassification (under sheer pressure) in 1973-74 and later in 2001 when Dr Spitzer again enraged the LGBT community by advancing a research where he hilights the possibility of reverting back from homosexuality into a heterosexual lifestyle.

Based on no scientific evidence whatsoever, but

solely from great political pressure, a professor was forced twice to give a political community what it wanted, and it was enshrined into law. And now we've got lobbyists mindlessly parroting to the rest of the world that 'the Science is Clear'... Again, Mr Fares looks as if he's being scientific, but in fact he knows the homosexual condition was unlisted by sheer bullying alone, and involved zero scientific rebuttal:

"Psychiatrist famous for declassifying homosexuality as mental illness under heavy pressure from activists, dies at 83":

https://www.lifesitenews.com/news/psychiatrist-famous-for-declassifying-homosexuality-as-mental-illness-under

"Homosexuality: The Mental Illness That Went Away"

http://behaviorismandmentalhealth.com/2011/10/08/homosexuality-the-mental-illness-that-went-away/

Ironically, ADHD is still listed as a 'mental disorder' by the APA, but transgenderism and homosexuality are not... Food for thought!

'Bigoted' Opinion #10: When will we have straight pride week?

EF-[Straight people in Lebanon are not being persecuted, discriminated against, put in jails, and subjected to all kinds of human rights violations against their bodies just because they happened to have that particular sexual orientation.

No one's walking around the street telling people they like vagina or penis or whatever other body part you seem to have a problem with people liking. The point is them asking you not to point your finger at them and judge them and call for them to be shamed and persecuted because they like to sleep with people who have that body part.]

1-No one wants to have a straight Pride. It's a pointless exercise in attention-seeking. And we all know that attention-seeking is a personality disorder.

2-Actually the rest of the world wants to really live and let live, so the LGBT lobby needs to instruct its adherents that some discretion is advised, and that there's no need to openly advertise a sexual lifestyle everywhere one wishes, and I'm sure that all will be well. Invariably, all gay prides include explicit sexual symbolism, which denotes an obvious obsession with sex. Obsession with sex is often linked to mental disorders and predatory behaviors...

The unrealistic demands of the LGBT lobby do not make the rest of us -the overwhelming majority- homophobes. It just shows Fares and friends to be out of touch with reality. It also shows them as unable to focus on more important issues or aim towards meaningful, more fulfilling purposes in life, outside their obsession with sex, as all the lobby membership's 'literature', discussions, articles and 'art' clearly show.

The LGBT community and its supporters, simply use and abuse the term 'science' without supplying any scientific evidence (outside the occasional and heavily skewed psychology 'study') . Their whole talk is supported by the pseudo-science of psychology, an institution which is demonstrably highly vulnerable to political bullying. This political bullying has forced entire establishments to change their views, influencing billions of people across generations, under the false belief that 'The Science is Settled'.

The Left and its LGBT cronies has demonstrated on many instances its abuse of science and its distortion of scientific facts as well as its bullying of professors and researchers into submission, through career threat, social ostracism and demonetization.

The Left is the party of Scientism, not Science. The LGBT people are of course, humans, who should themselves NOT be bullied or humiliated because of their sexual choices, but seeing their unbridled power in the West, I think Lebanon is right to be wary of the LGBT as a lobby.

Also, and while gay people in Lebanon have the social right to be with whomever they wish to be, Lebanese law should never grant any LGBT 'marriage' permit. Nor should gay couples raise children, also based on the links provided above, which show real-life situations, and not Leftism-based pseudoscientific 'studies' sponsored by a pro-LGBT establishment.

Marriage is not a 'right', it's the sole privilege of the heterosexual union being the only natural way to advance humanity through biological reproduction. Without the heterosexual union, humanity has no future -and gay couples will never be able to borrow children and imitate a traditional family structure.

For more in-depth information on this extremely

important subject and to discover how the LGBT lobby manipulated, pressured the APA, and bullied its doctors, read or search for the book "Homosexuality & American Psychiatry - the Politics of Diagnosis" by Dr Ronald Bayer.

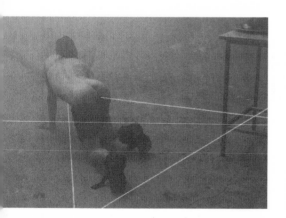

Yes, our 'art' consists of twerking with a laser inserted where the sun doesn't shine. You must take us seriously, or else...

"This Dance Troupe Performs with Lasers in Their Butts" - *Young Boy Dancing Group's co-founder on challenging gender and sexuality with a laser in your anal sphincter. (March 1, 2017) -*
Source: www.vice.com

There is absolutely 'no' agenda to wreck your kids and prey upon their curiosity... - Source: www.notimeforflashcards.com

Quebec, Canada: The CSQ (committee for sexual diversity and gender theory) is advising a series of LGBTQ books for preschool and primary levels: http://www.pouruneécolelibre.com/2014/07/le-syndicat-csn-suggere-des-livres.html

Below: taken from www.enfantsquebec.com, we have yet another example of the west's rabid child abuse via sexualization of kids and youngsters in an effort to destroy mankind's most precious gift: Children and their innocence (nice picture, Shutterstock. Thanks...).

Mon Enfant Est Gai *(My Kid Is Gay)*

Crédit: Shutterstock

Aujourd'hui, de plus en plus de gens acceptent que leur enfant soit homosexuel. Mais lorsque des préados font leur *coming out*, une foule de questions et d'inquiétudes traversent encore la tête de leurs parents... *Sophie Marcotte*

« Maman, je pense que je suis amoureux de Samuel », vous annonce votre fils de 11 ans. Surprise, inquiétude, malaise, panique, envie de banaliser le sujet peuvent pointer le bout de leur nez. Vous croyez que 11 ans, c'est tôt pour savoir si on est gai ou hétéro ? Vous n'avez pas tort. Selon l'enquête à la base du livre *De la honte à la fierté – 250 jeunes de la diversité sexuelle se révèlent* (VLB éditeur, 2014), les jeunes Québécois LGBT (lesbiennes, gais, bisexuels et transgenres) découvriraient leur orientation sexuelle à l'âge moyen de 13,3 ans, et feraient leur *coming out* un

An internet meme highlighting mainstream media hypocrisy in its obvious collusion with a pedophiliac agenda.

When you're so oppressed that companies
just can't seem to endorse you hard enough

*When you're so oppressed that companies just can't
seem to endorse you hard enough - Aaron Clarey*

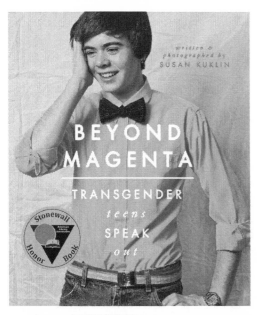

*Right page: Front cover and
excerpt (below) from the
book 'Beyond Magenta',
by by Susan Kuklin.*

*This is the account of a
'transgender' youth's sexual
'coming of age', which
started at age 6.*

only wear boy clothes.

I was sexually mature. What I mean by sexually mature is that I knew about sex. From six up, I used to kiss other guys in my neighborhood, make out with them, and perform oral sex on them. I liked it. I used to love oral. And I touched their you-know-whats. We were really young, but that's what we did.

I was making out with girls too. I used to love making out with girls 'cause everybody thought I was cool. Everybody was encouraging me. "Look, Frank's not gay—he's making out with a girl!" They wanted to know how the hell I learned to kiss like that. I didn't know how I learned. It was pretty weird.

Guys used to hit on me—perverts—pedophiles. I'd see guys giving me a look, and it kinda creeped me out. They would touch themselves, saying, "Come here, sweetie." Something told me not to go. I ran away. I ran to where there was a lot of people.

Top picture: A transgender 'being' hungrily sampling a drag kid at the Ru Paul transgender convention.

Bottom picture: A kid brought to a Pride parade, and taught to view animalized freaks as part of normal everyday life.

PSYCHOLOGY: A SCIENCE?

Psychology is a discipline that studies human behavior and the human conscious/subconscious mind. It uses scientific methodology -mainly statistics/surveying, case studying, and observation- to verify its findings.

Its main problem is, as many scientists and researchers have already pointed out: **Replicability**. When a scientific method fails to replicate the same results of an experiment using the same paramenters initially used, we have a problem. This problem gets bigger as replicability issues happen most frequently in Psychology and Sociology than in other fields. An article published in Areo Magazine states

"one group of around 200 psychologists have been involved in checking the results of previous experiments and these have failed to replicate in 14 out of 28 cases."*

This recalls the criticism leveled by positivist philosopher Henry Bergson, at Biology, a science claiming to study life, yet has to immobilize the subject (by killing/anesthetizing/dismembering it) to actually be able to study it. The study is also only able to show the subject 'at the moment' where it is immobilized and not really alive, which is bound to produce inaccurate observations that are only partially reflective of 'actual life'.

The above reflection by Bergson is also true for psychology, where the data collected only reflects the subject 'at the moment' and in the social/physiological/psychological circumstances during which the subject gave this data. This means that the data collected is bound to be very subjective and will be different when given in a different context, which could explain a significant part of the replicability problem of Psychology. The human being is probably too complex a subject for psychology and its available tools, because it seeks to replicate that which cannot be replicated: the human mind with all its scientifically immeasurable, meta-physical complexities.

**"Psychology Replication Crisis" www.areomagazine.com - 2019.*

Another serious obstacle to the credibility of Psychology lies in ideological data manipulation. Psychology is a tool of knowledge. Tools depend on their wielder's intentions, so that even a spoon can become a deadly weapon.

Psychology in modern times has turned from being a beneficial tool for the exploration of human behavior and consciousness, to a tool of ideological propaganda and political pressure. When reading about ADHD on the APA website, one finds a very succint description of that condition affecting kids (its main symptoms are inattention and hyperactivity) summed up as a mental disorder. So if your kid displays inattention or is hyperactive, they are, according to the APA, a mental case. Next step, is looking up 'Gender Dysphoria' on the APA website, and weirdly enough, no mention of mental disorder is to be found. This means that if you have a kid who wants to transition into the opposite sex, that's fine and there is nothing to worry about.

The double standards displayed by the APA are not the only instance of flagrant scientific dishonesty from authorities in the field of psychology and psychiatry. Research team reports that deviate from their initial research plan seldom disclose their deviations, seriously detrimenting the scientific accuracy of the report *(www.psychologicalscience.org)*. More than the replicability handicap, Psychology in the hands of ideologues, has influenced generations of people who believed the APA's reports out of blind trust. 'The Science is settled' has become the warcry of mainly the LGBT lobby in its ideological jihad to bend the worldview in its favor. The removal of homosexuality as a mental disorder by the APA in 1973, is seen by many as a scientific victory over myths and an unfair demonization of LGBT people. What really happened was a power politics tour-de-force, complete with threats, intimidation and coercion of the panel of psychologists, who were forced to make their move not based on any new scientific discovery, but through a political vote *(Bayer, Homosexuality & Psychiatry - The Politics of Diagnosis)*. Bullying, not science, normalized homosexuality and every self-respecting psychiatrist and scientist knows this. The power of the LGBT lobby today is such that speaking this truth is somewhat like denying the Holocaust- an assured political, professional and social suicide.

Psychology is not the only discipline to face political bullying. Anthropology, sociology and biology are other fields which keep suffering from vicious ideological attacks from leftist groups who want to socially engineer the perception and consciousness of our future generations, through a most perfidious strategy: science-coated bullying. These groups of ideological bullies want to enforce their religion of equality everywhere: we all have the same IQ, race does not exist, we all evolved from amoeba or apes, genders do not exist, etc... This is why these same groups who pressured the APA are infuriated by hard sciences like Biology/genetics and anthropological finds that disrupt their political/ideological narratives on race, evolution, IQ and sex. In its inability to prove the existence of genetic explanations for homosexuality, the LGBT lobby today is trending the term 'Epigenetics' (the study of external/environmental/non-genetic phenomena and how they affect phenotypic -external appearence- variation). Here we see the LGBT desperately trying to dress their circus with yet another scientific fig leaf. We are witnessing the taking over of scientific fields by ideologically-driven zealots but that is a topic that would fill a book or two all by itself.

Perhaps when psychology is wielded by responsible scientists who do not give in to socio-political pressure and its 'politics of feels', one could then expect a truer, more credible discipline which, despite its replicability issues, would remain a helpful tool to map the human psyche.

One last question remains: could it be because of the inability of psychology to predict the human mind, and merely describe its current behavior, that its ideological manipulators are working a long-term project of

modeling the human mind in a way to make it fully predictable by psychology and sociology? By infusing school
curricula with the right propaganda, taking the child-raising role off the family unit, and sowing the seeds of sexual
confusion, the brains and minds of the future could be
sufficiently modeled and *reformatted* for
optimal predictability...

TRANSGENDERISM AS A SOCIAL PHENOMENON

Gender reassignment surgeries are en vogue in the
decaying West. Proponents of gender theory assure us
that there is an infinity of genders. Pseudoscientist Bill Nye
'confirms' that gender is not binary but more like 'a spectrum', a 16-million technicolor rainbow of love and progress. Youngsters with psycho parents are encouraged to
'reassign' themselves into their preferred gender and the
trend is sadly picking up steam. But since we're being told
that genders are infinite, one cannot help but wonder why
the reassignment surgery options only specify female-to-
male and male-to-female? Why are we being prevented
from achieving that unique pansexual dolphinkin look we
have always dreamt we actually were, since even before
birth? Clearly scientific and medical advances have much
to do yet, in order to help unlock and usher the much
awaited new age of progressive nonbinary, gender-fluid,
full-spectrum utopia.

The ongoing case of James younger, whose mother, *Dr* Anne Georgulas wants to turn into a girl, is still making ripples. The fate of the boy is still undecided as US courts are showing clear bias for the mother as opposed to the father (and ex-husband) who wants to protect his boy from the madness of gender re-assignment. - *Photo source: Facebook.*

INTERSECTIONALITY

Victimhood culture is a profitable business, and profitable businesses expend their lingo for added credibility and PR reach. *"Intersectionality is a theoretical framework for understanding how aspects of one's social and political identities might combine to create unique modes of discrimination" -Wikipedia.*

There are many fancy ways to articulate one's degree of oppression and victimhood. For example, *"Intersectional feminism aims to separate itself from white feminism by acknowledging the fact that all women have different experiences and identities."- Wikipedia.*

Intersectionality is the latest victimhood culture mouthpiece. It continuously looks for creative ways to make colorful injustice cocktails with the social categories at hand - racial, sexual, cultural, economic, political and social categories blend into a vibrant orchestra of social justice terms the modern Left cranks out on a daily basis. The aim is of course, not social justice, but attention-seeking through a new kind of bullying: Entitlement through victimization. Intersectionality also seeks to explain a demographic's continuous underperformance in any given sector, and blame some 'oppressor' for it.

The 'oppressed', seeing the opportunity for sizeable material gain and attention, will gladly play along and would stop crying only when they are given a substantial financial compensation and the needed morphine shot of social media/mainstream attention. This is yet another example where social justice, instead of righting social wrongs, further exacerbates them by creating more social division and animosity on an irrational victim/oppressor basis. The supposed victim is encouraged to remain immature and 'problems' are solved with money thrown at them. The result is a society nurturing hatred while creating 'positions' for losers who become tenured 'intersectionality professors/specialists', charging fortunes for their blabber. Modernity and the social sciences itmanipulates have created a society that rewards the mediocre and punishes everyone else with a functioning brain and an actual purpose.

DEMOCRATIC SOCIALISM
OR UNIFICATION THROUGH IDEOLOGY

In a modernist world, there is no place for culture and tradition. Both are reduced to consumable gimmicks and mocked. Therefore, the only feasible way to unite a people is through ideology. All modern ideologies are materialistic and Man-centered by nature and are confined to the realm of the five senses. Their focus and scope is essentially geared towards the tangible and is therefore, purely economical.

Uniting a people today, is *culturally* impossible. Modernism means the systematic removal of culture, heritage and collective memory, and their replacement with Multiculturalism, materializing Israel Zangwill's "Melting Pot" concept- Every multiculturalist's wet dream.

The only way left to unite the public is through money: Economic Growth, Prosperity, Trade and Markets are the pillars of the measurable, quantifiable and materialistic ideology that moves the Modern world. Today's rising ideology is known as Democratic Socialism, but do not be fooled; it is still the same old, outdated and failed ideology spawned from Marx's 'The Communist Manifesto':

'Traditional' socialism, back in the early twentieth century, was summed up by the seizing and nationalizing of all resources by the State, for their eventual equal redistribution. Since its earliest applied version was too bloody under Lenin, Stalin and Mao, it had to rebrand itself as 'Socialism' in post WWII Europe. Today, in the globalist zeitgeist, the State no longer exists due to open borders and free markets; the world is owned by corporations, and 'conservative' governments are as guilty as 'progressive/leftist' ones of aggressively offshoring and privatizing the national resources of their own peoples. So now, 'the State owning all the resources' is replaced with 'Social Ownership of all the resources' -whatever that means- (www.difference.wiki)

Thus, Socialism needed to rebrand itself for a third time: *Democratic* Socialism!

The term implies that before Democratic Socialism, Socialism was... Un-democratic. Socialists finally admit that socialism is an authoritarian system. How else would one enforce equality? So this time, Democratic Socialism is 'democratic' and hilariously enough, adds anonymous corporations and companies (ie, huge capital) into its rebranding efforts:

"A balance between government and enterprises mean the power remains with people" (www.difference.wiki).

Since many corporations -and their capital- can be physically elsewhere, there goes the centralized concept of resource control advocated by communism/socialism 1.0 and 2.0.

Democratic Socialism *"Does not advocate complete nationalization of all properties" (www.differencebetween. com)* since of course, most of these properties have been offshored by previous socialist governments. No matter how many times Marxism rebrands itself (Communism, Socialism, Democratic Socialism, ...) it will be always recognizable as an ideology viewing people as production units and seeking to enforce economic equality via the weapon of the democratic vote knowing that the majority of people are mediocre and resentful, their tyrannical self-obsessed vote will rule the more intelligent, but helplessly out-voted minority.

Economic equality will always appeal to the mediocre because it makes them feel secure. Why would you make any effort if you'd rather cash your Universal Basic Income and do nothing? The lazy majority will hide behind grand slogans like 'Against Inequality' or economically clueless ones like 'Fight for 15'* to hide their laziness and demand more state/corporation-enforced social justice equalizing humanity, but from the bottom. Corporations, like the State, have now the power to punish the

---

*"Fight for 15": A US activism movement fighting for a $15/hour minimum wage (unwittingly paving the way for earlier job automation). Such movements ignore that nobody is meant to flip burgers all their life and that such menial jobs are only transitional.

individual; demonetized bloggers, blocked users, and banned accounts are proof that monopoly on punishment are increasingly becoming a corporate prerogative and not anymore confined to the State. This is the Equality of the Modernists and their latest economic stunt - ::DEMO-CRATIC SOCIALISM:: - We have shifted from obeying God's commandments, to obeying the Self, and now obeying the State and its megacorporate sponsors and patrons.

The main problem with enforcing equality upon humanity is that it removes all that which makes an individual distinctive. No individual is equal to another and equality does not exist in nature. Back when societies worshiped one or several gods, and the concept of deity was more 'mainstream', the people were equal in the eyes of their creator, not equal to each other.

Now, since the Creator has been removed from the equation and Man is God, people have declared themselves gods through the religion of Humanism and egalitarian neo-Christianity (Protestantism and Teilhard De Chardin's Jesuitic Trans-humanism) and therefore they are equal to each other, but only in their hubris- drenched mindset. Such a worldview is bound to create continuous disappointment as people's dreams clash with their everyday reality: we are not equal what makes us unique are our individual choices.

Uniting a people through materialistic ideologies like Democratic Socialism -and neutering religion by turning it from transcendental to egalitarian- will bind these people together as long as their financial requirements are met. Otherwise, nothing much will keep those people together. The result will be a consumer-oriented society where the individual will only worry about their own immediate needs and whom, at the sight of any threat, would feel no need to defend a society which looks more and more like an apathetic non-place such as an airport or a shopping mall.

Financial wealth V/S Cultural wealth

Both unbridled Capitalism* and standard issue Communism/Socialism focus on financial and economic wealth, ignoring (or in the case of Capitalism, transforming culture into a consumable gimmick) or actively fighting culture as a non-material form of wealth.

How did it come to This?

In older, saner times, society used to reward the productive, the organized, those most in touch with immutable reality. This created stability, prosperity and a surplus of material wealth. As More liberal times rolled in, Man -and by consequence, society- became more self-centered and therefore multiple versions of 'reality' popped up like yeast. The age of pragmatism was over, nature was tamed and humanity could sleep securely, so now comes the time to express one's feelings and desires. A time of decadence.

In older, saner times, Reality was One. Consensus was shared among people of the same culture. The world was spiritual and produced the rich mythology which populates our imagination, and yet it also produced scientific and technological progress.

But then the Break happened. Man denied God and proclaimed himself 'caliph instead of the caliph'. Instead of one reality and one moral system, we ended up with billions of realities and as many moral systems. In that cacophony of tiny gods, each self-made deity needed to desperately win the most attention, and the most followers. Gradually, the world split in two neat groups: The old-school realists, who produced, assumed responsibility and wanted standards, and those who simply *acted* like the first group. Little by little, the latter group -the actors- overtook the former in terms of numbers, and since we live in a democratic paradigm, where quantity primes over

*An extremely narrowed down definition of capitalism: Using private resources to shape a market- Not only providing it with the commodities it needs (capitalism 1.0) but going the extra mile in **creating** needs where no such needs previously existed. That makes capitalism a creative force and if operating outside of moral bounds, a devastatingly destructive one.

quality, the mediocre started to consistently win elections, effectively becoming in charge of society. Today's world is ruled by actors and fakers, rewarding those who act and punishing those who still produce and create. Thus people with standards feel increasingly alien living in it.

Those who dispensed standards, vision and culture, commanded society, but as their numbers faded in an increasingly democratic (egalitarian, as opposed to hierarchical) world, their social power shifted from their hands and into those of the masses. This is why this world is louder and more disoriented than ever before; **cultural power** (the power dispensed by the gifted few) faded and became **social power**, the power of the multitude.

As more gods are self-proclaimed on their own social platforms, their need to stay relevant is proportional to the increase in the total number of gods. This urgent need explains the increasingly aggressive and anti-moral means employed to assert one's self as the newest deity into an increasingly crowded god market. It is like each sailing ship is devising its own north star and venting its merits over other ships' north stars. In the absence of standards, material standards are the defacto replacement. Consequently, today's individual is measured by 'net worth', and not much else. One begins to understand why socialists and communists look suspiciously at rich people today; in our current no-standards time, it is impossible to amass wealth in a 'clean' way! Aristocrats of the mind and the soul have disappeared a long time ago and we're only left with low-life nouveaux riches who are being recognized for the con artists that they are.

It takes a Leftist to know another Leftist.

RATIONALISM LEADS TO ATHEISM

Rationalists tend to agree that the best explanation -excluding God- for the existence of the world is that some random explosion happened and particles just randomly fell into place, creating orderly organisms, ecosystems and life by the most random chance. Nothing caused it, so your culture, civilization, and the pride you take from it, your family tree and the talents you accumulated over centuries of evolution in any trade or practice, are all absolutely random, come from nothing and are therefore, pointless.

If you don't see where this ideology is going, here it is: when nothing matters, when excellence, perseverence, pedigree and the cultivation of character over centuries count for nothing, we might as well degrade ourselves into anything our base urges call for. We can lead depraved lifestyles, murder at will, betray, lie , cheat, not bathe and then self-destruct. Yes we can do that, because we're all here at random and there is no meaning to anything we do, so why strive to be better? When positive effort, negative effort and no effort are all equal, then why even remain alive? We will die, disintegrate, and our atoms will reassemble, totally at random into a new existence elsewhere.

When this 'rationalistic' thought is broken down, and existence explained away as sheer randomness without any raison d'etre, it becomes obvious that this explanation is completely irrational in its total negation of the laws of probability. How likely are we to have a random explosion in which things, instead of disintegrating into flaming bits, are created alive and evolving? We have been making explosions here on Earth ever since we invented gunpowder, and instead of creating tiny ecosystems and worlds, everything and everyone keeps dying and flying into gory pieces!

It probably makes more sense to see the bigger likeliness of an external will/intelligence, above ours, which caused the infinite universe and all its yet undiscovered intricacies, to exist. But for the Rationalist/Atheist, we are organic machines, devoid of will and of mind, leading a pointless mechanistic existence, deconstructed into banal chemical reactions.

Since the atheist mind is essentially geared towards what is perceived stricly by the five senses - i.e. the material world- it is only receptive to materialistic ideologies and concepts. The five senses being demonstrably and scientifically shared by the rest of the fauna, atheists willingly place themselves on the same level as animals, standing at the antipodes of the Nietzschean Superman/Transcendental archetype. No wonder why bestiality laws and pedophilia are always being pushed by Atheists and assorted moral relativists. This is also why Darwin's ape-to-human 'evolution' theory makes so much sense to the Atheist. The ape is the ancestor of the Atheist.

Religious fundamentalists share with atheists the same animalistic blind fanaticism (as opposed to religious fervor). The object of their fanaticism is, however, not a transcendental spiritual dimension but a very earthly, material and quantifiable ideology. Both religious Fundamentalists and Atheists share this same phariseism in dispensing and enforcing blind and soulless dogma.

Atheists are the most fervent believers. When you firmly believe that an infinite cluster of lifeless matter and energy organized itself completely by chance, forming galaxies, star systems and living organisms, you can be made to believe in anything -Including becoming a guitar virtuoso by simply and without any structured method or focused effort, plucking randomly at your instrument, or just buying it and leaving it unused.

The void inside every Atheist is a fertile soil for any kind of ideology which is why they readily adopt the easiest ones to follow, but follow them religiously. They even

culturally appropriated 'Science', making it the sole pro-
prietorship of atheists, and thanks to media complicity, the
consuming masses today equate atheism with science
despite most science Nobel Prize recipients being religious
people (sorry, atheists, but those are hard numbers). It is
time for the public to remind itself that Science and the
Scientific method are no atheist inventions nor are they
the property of atheists.

Rational & Meta-rational

The world is now split down to its very atoms: Women against Men, Rationalists against Religionists, Communists against Capitalists, Modernists against Classicists, Salafists against Futurists, Fascists against Anarchists, etc... But this is all a diversion to prevent us from noticing the real clash, which is mainly between partisans of the *striclty* material world and those who see beyond the realm of the five senses.

The rationalist mistakes the biological manifestation of non-quantifiable concepts -love, fear, anger, happiness- for the concepts themselvee. This means that those concepts, are reduced/deconstructed into their banal and purely mechanical, chemical, physiological external manifestations. Secretions, muscular activity and metabolic activity -the outer physiological manifestations- *are the actual* phenomenon, the rationalist reasons.

What the rationalist observes becomes strictly what *is*, and therefore ignores the unquantifiable factors that resulted into the observable phenomena.

And since 'Science' (read: Scientism!) cannot quantify those factors, they do not exist!

So convenient! So... Rational!

Rationalism becomes an extremist ideology when it claims that anything not measurable or quantifiable by reason, i.e. the five senses, *simply is not there*.

The rationalist paradigm has witnessed the highest number of laws to govern a supposedly 'rational' people. Why do rational people need so many laws?

'Laws become superfluous if the people were reasonable', says Will Durant in his 'The Story of Philosophy', so how come we require a law outlawing the sale of one's own

children (as such law exists in the state of Florida) in the age of 'reason' and 'common sense'? In 'darker' ages there would never have been a need to pass a law criminalizing advertising on tombstones or cannibalism, as common sense could have easily prevailed in such cases.

The Self-Defeating Nature of Atheism

Depicting God as a bearded, venerable man, or a man-animal, is an understandable anthropocentric behavior observed in countless civilizations across history. Believers do it as a sort of bridge between their world and the Eternal.

Atheists 'deconstruct' that concept, by bringing literally nothing to the table, like a cat that just throws things off a counter. By making light of their own religious sentiment through voluntary suppression, atheists reduce themselves to simply living, consuming, defecating, dying and decomposing. When your life is reduced to its mechanical behavior, why bother reproduce, raising children and having a family?

Between 37% (Pew Center) and 51% (*American Religious Identification Survey - ARIS*) of Atheists in the US never marry[1]. Countries with pronounced Atheism (Most western countries including the US, where Christianity is almost unrecognizable from its historical origins) have sub-replacement fertility rates (Eric Kaufmann)[2].

Atheists are more likely to commit suicide than religiously affiliated individuals and less likely to have meaningful and strong familial ties (psychiatryonline.org). Given the media's, and social sciences, strongly pro-atheist stance, and despite grudgingly admitting that religious communities have lower suicide rates than secular/atheist

---

1   "Atheism and Divorce"- Source: www.conservapedia.com
2   "Atheism and Fertility Rates" - Eric Kaufmann.
       Source: www.conservapedia.com

countries due to stronger moral and familial values, it is impossible to get any relevant comparative statistics from those sites and any statistical tables are purposefully made indecipherable in a desperately anti-scientific attempt to cloud the glaring truth.

There is a problem with (some) religiously-affiliated people which atheists are right to make fun of: the tendency to 'ask God' to give us stuff. Praying to receive something is a delusion many religious people fall into. Wanting God to intervene on our behalf if we just ask him nicely is giving up our own free will and agency. We cannot 'order' a miracle. And even in the event of a true mircale happening -as in recovering a still-alive baby from under the rubble of an earthquake, days after the search parties have given up all hope- the atheist would still not buy into it. Their excuse is the non-existence of a scientifically 'rational' method to quantify, explain or dissect that event into gluten-free bits that the atheist mind could then safely digest.

Last but not least, and with all things being equally meaningless for them, atheists are the most supportive of abortion with 87% in favor(Pew Research Center). With no archetypes, ideals or objective morals to help them get by through life, atheists are continuously turning inwards, seeking to satisfy personal and immediate urges, since they see no point in conserving or building beyond one's lifespan. Extreme individualism leads to social atomization and we finally understand the turmoil of the West or how the *enlightened* majority fell prey to small groups of immigrating conquerors and is helpless against them. It looks so similar to a bank heist: Five or six armed robbers managing to subdue an entire bank's staff and the people inside. The robbers have a clear aim and are working as a team, the rest, who are only thinking of their own individual wellbeing, surrender when told to do so. When you have a small minority of the population (say 5 or 10%) who is united, and has a clear set of targets and the remaining 90-95% are atomized, and/or directionless, they (the so-called majority) are no longer a majority; they become single individuals and the real majority would be those 10% who are united by a purpose: Conquest.

And so, one has achieved atheism! What then? From the outset, the atheist desacralizes everything that matters, tears down every archetype and dynamites every piece of inspiration which could give them hope and courage when they need it most. Atheists say they do not need all that clutter. Good luck to them!

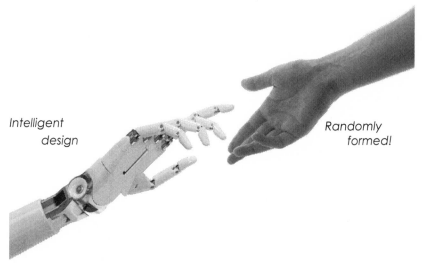

Intelligent design

Randomly formed!

Picture source: Pinterest

The Sad Reasoning of Neo Paganism

Paganism subjects gods to geographical locations, beating the purpose of actual godhood. Confining gods to geographical and temporal paradigms reduces pagan gods to being mere kings with superpowers. Assigning a geographical location to a god reveals the limitations and materialism of the pagan mind. What the Norse, the Red Indians, the Greeks, the Romans, the Saharans or the Mongolian steppe-dwellers see is a supernatural projection of their own environment, mixed with their own earthly culture. All are, in essence, experiencing the same thing: A primal creative and driving force governing the universe.

A similar example would be the visual representation of evil across differing cultures, in location and historical context: One can see a common denominator to the myriads depictions of monsters, dragons, vampires and chimeras populating the lore of cultures which are oceans and centuries apart. A common Essence.

Neo-pagans look at a religion which has demonstrably given Europe a common identity for the last 1000 years without erasing the underlying pagan one which preceded it, and see a 'semitic religion from the desert'. Neo pagan genius assigns 1000 years of Christian European identity with its Gothic churches and Baroque or Medieval art to the Middle-Eastern desert and the Semitic race. Meanwhile, the Neo-pagans are busy parading in their funny wiccan costume they bought on ebay. They outdo the most fanatical marxist in their denial of history.

The Neo-pagan gang is adamant: The 'semitic god of the desert' has no place in Europe! Take those gothic arches, spires and castles, those studies of perspective, and those astrophysics and genetics breakthroughs back into that semitic desert where you came from, Christianity! And no thanks to your monks for writing down all of our oral folklore and tradition so that we could LARP* to it...

For Neo Pagans, Gods are a product of localized culture and geographic location, exactly like a temporal king. But at the same time, their inner viking wants to conquer and plunder other lands. The neo-Pagan wants to break out of their own borders but their gods must remain confined in them.

Sheer comedy!

This is how you know that the people who want gods inside nice and tidy geographic borders, are defeated People, with weak gods and *weaker minds*.

PORTIONS OF GOD

Atheism is obsessed with denying God's existence, but not just any god. If an Atheist is confronted by a Muslim or a Jew professing their faith in Allah or Jehovah, the atheist adopts the conciliatory 'let's agree to disagree' stance and choose to let it slide. Atheism is actually in denial not of God, but of the Christian worldview which has been shaping the world for the last 2 millenia and sees in Leftism, Modernism and Globalism (with its anti-traditional stance, open markets, open borders policy and waves of incompatible cultures migrating into the west) an opportunity to erase and replace this worldview on which the atheist stacks all of humanity's woes.

The Atheist believes that an organized universe arose from nothing. Where is proof of God, they ask. I only believe whatever it is I can see. I believe in what science can measure... Infinity cannot be measured nor quantified by science, yet, science and religion agree over its existence. Thoughts and ideas are another non-measurable, non-quantifiable aspect of existence and yet they do exist. The closest science has got to measuring consciousness is by sensing the *effect* of said consciousness on our bodily constitution, but without the (living) body as a vessel of our consciousness, no scientific method can measure or quantify disembodied thought.

Disembodied imagination is just as elusive to the material tools of science and only becomes visible once we have 'willed' it onto canvas, film or any material support. If consciousness/will does not exist inside the living body, and that only the body's mechanistic properties are its own 'consciousness' (as most rationalists would have us believe), then all living humans should have more or less the same capacities for expressing their will, and from observation, we all know this to be false. What is athletism other than will exercising its power over matter, shaping it to its farthest extents? The same goes for the training of the mind: It never is a random process happening outside of the will and consciousness steering it. It most importantly, never exists in equal measures among people, as is demonstrated by the simple observation of a full classroom.

So why shouldn't the universe, which we are part of, be an emanation of God's own consciousness? In any case, the idea is much more attractive than a universe which formed itself from exploded bits, which randomly went off, without any intervention whatsoever, zillions of years ago...

Immeasurable and unquantifiable, infinity is 'there', nonetheless, and God, who is creation, infinity and eternity (all of them acknowledged by science), is just as incomprehensible to the finite mind. The explanation that something beyond our understanding is at the origin of the universe makes more sense than organized, evolving life emerging from a chaotic explosion of dead matter.

How does one prove the existence of a talent? Someone who's good at drawing, another who is good at poetry, or at baking fine cakes or at performing comedy... The gift of politics and artful lying, the gift of foresight and careful planning, etc... Where do these abilities come from and how can some people have them and others not?

If the point looks out of focus, let's just say that a certain gift cannot be scientifically proven or measured until someone exercises it; only then does the talent become visible, could be compared To others, measured graded and assessed. Only then can we say the gift 'exists'. But to exercise a talent, one has to *will* it. And this *will* can not, as Modernist 'philosophers' claim, be the result of random mechanistic and mechanical bodily reactions. As human creatures, gifted with varying degrees of talents, whom, or what gave us this or that capacity to be better than others in a certain field or activity? The rationalist would say 'Our two parents gave us those talents!', and then would add more factors like ' the environments we're born in'. Of course those are correct answers but are half the truth because they don't explain how our parents gained those capacities to transmit them to us, nor what caused our environment to exist in the first place.

So the rationalists keep adding more and more descriptions, mistaking them for explanations, while going ever further back in time, until they give up with 'Random chemical reactions (which came out of nowhere and exercised themselves for no reason!) formed in completely disorderly limbo, to give us people like Stephen Hawking or Plato or Da vinci. How can the doctrine of Rationalism reconcile itself with the fact that it offered such an irrational and scientifically unprovable explanation to explain the existence of brilliant and acute minds? How did the rationalist calculate the passage of random reactions and their sublimation into the orderly coherent consciousness of a Kant, Hawking or Michaelangelo? They didn't! They just believe it to be this way and command you to submit to their religion like a good progressive.

Proving the existence of God is not something that can be measured with computers and sensors.Irreverent rationalists, liberals and atheists more or less 'agree' on picturing God as some great spaghetti monster fairie floating in the sky and smiting sinners, exaggerating a symbolism that people devise to explain what their reason cannot grasp. They are simply mistaking the subject for its human representation, but their rationalistic philosophy is unable to explain anything outside the five senses.

What animates the universe we live in? Scientific simulations show planets, star systems and galaxies moving, expanding and pulsating in an astounding choreography of chaos and order, drawing graceful curves in space. At the same time, this same universe is insanely brutal; nothing pictures such immense galactic annihilation as that of a black hole or the death of a star, and yet, scientific instruments record all that, describe it minutely, suggesting theories as how all this came to be. By force of repetition, those suggestions become dogma. We are back at believing the scientists who gave us those theories. We validate the theories out of trust in the scientist's higher than average intellect, and research, but not out of irrefutable proof.

We can describe and make crude replicas of the universe but its origins, truths and reason to be are beyond us. At least beyond the atheist's anthropocentric views. Contemplating the death and disease in our world makes some of us hate its creator, and such emotional reaction denotes an immature, human-centered, emotional idea of the world. It also denotes the good/evil theistic moral code the atheists are themselves shaped by. To understand the world, we need to be able to control our emotions, and the atheist is the most emotional type of human, no matter how well they can hide their feelings.

Death and disease do not disprove God's existence but rather are evidence of a vast order where all things obey the laws of causality and where nature is a-moral. Order does not simply 'happen'. The marriage between chaos and order, evident in the cosmic movement recorded by our telescopes and space labs, is evidence of something far bigger than what our finite brains can fathom. Our minds, however, understand and admit its existence. Even atheistic minds. In their contempt for it, they admit its existence because you cannot hate (or be triggered by) a 'nothing'.

And so it exists, that prime mover. There is no use debating who or what created that prime mover itself, as this not only provides further proof it exists, but is already beyond our intellect's reach. Here we have to admit our own limits, but also we have to congratulate ourselves at how far we have come in understanding the world around us. The point here, is to recognize our finite and fallible nature and the need for a higher being than us, to use as our compass. This higher being/force/creative energy (call it what you will) caused this universe to exist and is infinitely greater than us. It is a suitable existential compass and a higher example to aspire to.

Now why do we give this prime mover human traits, like love, mercy, wisdom or kingship. Because it comforts us and gives us a way to identify with this higher power which we can only define in human-made terms, and in our human-made language. This is the atheist's biggest shortfall: mistaking religious sentiment for creation, and equating divinity with religion. The atheist believes we have made God, while actually it is more like we are trying to identify with and communicate with God using our own language and our own imagination. Religion is man-made, yes, but the object of our religion, the object of our worship already exists and caused this world to exist.

The earliest historical documentations and the re-mains of early humans show a violent and brutal lifestyle. Then further and more recent evidence shows an evident effort towards a more civilized, controlled and refined existence. Man invented language, tools, technologies and laws which improved human existence and this is ev-idence of a consciously individual as well as collective will to improve for the better. Religions were the vessel of the moral codes of their respective cultures. Culture is shaped by the environment. But that environment didn't make itself by accident, nor out of nothing.

Beauty is Objective

The Degradation of Art as Part of the Erosion of Language

In ancient times, artistic expression was inspired subconsciously by one's own culture. Today artistic expression is drawn consciously from one's politics. And since it is well known that 'politics are downstream from culture', our 'art' is a severe regression from what used to be considered Art, back then...

Art has been degraded from being a cultural manifestation of the group which produced it, into becoming a political one. And since the prevailing political paradigm today is democratic, art has, like politics, equated quality with popularity. The more people vote for something, the more it must be good. Politics has always been downstream of Culture but not so in our age. When culture is degraded, consumerized and forgotten, politics is all we have left, and today's art is by default, political.

Politics being an ever-shifting swamp of quicksand, its resulting 'art' is as shape-shifting as the politics that give it birth. It is an 'art' borne of trends, whims, and ephemereal situations, not out of tradition. It is a moody expression of the self, which can easily change into its complete opposite the next day, as the winds of politics change into another direction. There is nothing consistent about such 'art' and, therefore, one is easily bored by it. Such is the function of trends: to provide the masses with enough short-lived entertainment until the next trend is released for public consumption.

Today's art is an ephemereal gimmick, designed to be 'consumed' right away, because next week, another 'art' piece will be 'trending'. It is flashy, electric, loud and glitzy. It's made to hold your attention over all the other 'art' versions vying for your attention at that very moment. It has nothing in essence and you will forget it the next day. What matters is that you clicked, you liked (or were offended) and you shared it, therefore successfully consumed it and put a tick next to the 'successful art' tick box. It received a billion views, therefore it's 'good'!

Classical Art combined techniques of composition and rendering, message and genius to produce Art that defied time and stood eternal in its greatness. True art wants to transcend the realism of a mere photograph by showing the *soul* of the subject. Technique and composition alone do not create True Art. Art has a Soul. And to show the soul of the matter whether that matter is canvas, stone, wood or any artistic support, takes Genius. To define genius is to go into philosophical abstractions dismissable by the cynical rationalist. But to simplify it so that even a rationalist could understand it, genius is a state not available to everyone because it is a higher sphere of *Will*: It seamlessly combines both imagination and physical conquest of the matter in a way that seems unconscious, natural.

Many of us can imagine the most beautiful things but have not yet mastered enough the sphere of the will where matter is conquered so that we can do with it as we please, and make its soul visible for all to see. It will take a lot of time (and self-criticism) for the world to get used again to the idea of Beauty being Objective.This involves the eschewing of the concept of Humanism (Man as God, which makes all man-made expressions equally valid) and a revival of the spirit of hierarchy prevalent in the old system. That hierarchy drew its relevance and existence from God -an unchanging, perfect, unattainable absolute and 'Good' being whose nature is infinite and beyond our finite minds. Such infinity, though unattainable, provides Man with the impetus to continuously pursue it. In the process, Man refines himself and although always short from attaining infinity (God), Man is never tired of this pursuit and in the process, finds himself better off than where he initially was. Man also grows wiser; in his pursuit to reach God (Perfection), Man has successfully competed against himself.

And that is indeed **Good**.

That is probably what Friedrich Nietzsche wanted to convey, with his Overman archetype. Before reaching God -which we have 'killed' and replaced with ourselves in the Enlightenment- let us first overcome our own weaknesses.

In the Case of Humanism (the religion of Man as God), Man, a finite creature, is already 'attained' and therefore, there are no hills or mountains left to climb, no adventure from the outset! Worshipping the self is a boring religion. Humanism defeats itself. This is the reason why we always have to rationalize our boredom and our self-worshipping practices. We hide our mediocrity behind Artspeak: Minimalism, Less is More, Beauty is in the eye of the Beholder, Everything is art, Everyone is special, etc... Modernism itself, is the art of deception; it paints a diabolically ensnaring picture which flatters our ego. Its palette is rich in positive, benevolent-sounding spells: Humanism, Socialism, Pluralism, Feminism, Diversity, Equality, Globalism, Progress,... A seductive voice continuously whispering in Modern man's ear: Remember, you're already a god...

"The secret of genius is to carry the spirit of the child into old age, which means never losing your enthusiasm." - Aldous Huxley

Genius*:

IQ is the measurable, quantifiable part of human intellect. It determines one's speed at processing and understanding data, memorization, organizational abilities and raw mental power. It in no way translates into creativity. And creativity alone, hindered by a slow intellect, cannot go far.

So is genius a combination of Raw intellect and cre-

Genius: *It is necessary to point out the existence of an evil genius as well. This superlative state of creativity is not necessarily benevolent and is always a reflection of its owner's character.*

ativity? We're getting warmer. Is it the ability to see farther ahead than most and have the presence of mind to act upon that sharp intuitive spark 'in the moment'? That's definitely one of the many facets of genius. It can only be recognized by other people as some kind of magic. Genius is an ability to get a glimpse of the future (a parallel world even) and using one's being (body and mind) to snipe the opportunity and put it down on paper, canvas or whatever means of expression available. But how does that translate into the Arts?

Genius in Entrepreneurship and Business is the ability to capture the opportunity where no one else is aware of its existence. In Art, it's the ability to capture Eternity on a material support. To represent an image or a facet of the Eternal, on a piece of canvas or in a block of marble. Now how do we know it's Eternity? Because it speaks to the part of us which does not die. It stirs the souls of generations in a mysterious, universal way, transcending language, borders, culture, religion, ideology and time itself. It's simply the ability to produce an artistic work outside the boundaries of time, place or even language. Whether in its cultural appeal/relatability, mystery or combination of both, the artistic output only gets better with time, like fine wine. Its technical execution only adds to its greatness but it is only the gorgeous body to an even more beautiful soul.

To recapitualte, raw intellect and power of logic/deduction can be measured. But many high IQ minds do not see ahead, so other ingredients are still missing. **Creativity** can be assessed by a third party based on result. **Intuition** is a purely personal experience and its presence cannot be anticipated, not even by the first person. **Curiosity** is another trait which combines innate (but genetically untraceable!) and environmental factors that help sharpen that gift. an example is parents recognizing their offspring's natural thirst for discovery and encouraging them along that path.

So there we have it. Portions of unpredictable

creative drive exist in us in varying degrees and intensities. Portions of infinity. Hints of God. Should they be declared non-existant because of the inability of science or the 5 senses to accurately quantify, measure, anticipate or replicate them?

Art & Science are closer than we think:

In his magnum opus 'The Mathematical Basis of the Arts' Joseph Schillinger takes a cartesian approach to Art; where ideologically driven modernist ideologues claim absolute artistic freedom*, he, a scientist and an artist, applies a rigorous scientific methodology to create artistic output that is carefully planned and scientifically dissect-able. This approach, though clinical, gives Art a much needed objective leverage in terms of defining clear criteria for its scientific evaluation[1]. However, by displaying an almost obsessive dedication to reduce creativity into scientifically measurable bits, the author falls into the ratio-nalist trap, leaving the non-measurable parts mentioned earlier, outside of his equations. thankfully, Schillinger does not give in to Modernist ideology and even criticizes the impulsive, arbitrary, subjective brush that Modernists use to depict contemporary Art. Schillinger advocates the return to the scientific method already used by the classical art-ists, but which was infused with the curiosity to tap into the farthest metaphysical confines of both tangible creation and the intangible void- a detail the author voluntarily omits for practical reasons.

Nevertheless, Schillinger's work succeeds in presenting 'facts pertaining to the arts', resulting in a 'scientific theory of the arts' (MBA P.3) with its three main branches:

"-Semantics of esthetic expression.

-Theory of regularity and coordination.

-technology of art production."

---

1   See: 'The Mathematical Basis of the Arts' [MBA] - J. Schillinger- (P.3)
*The artistic soul/mind is 'free', yes. It is so, because the artistic mind wanders into spheres not accessible to the common folk and not even measurable by science or the 5 senses. In that sense only, can we say art is free, but not through the distorted and misleading defini-tion of modernity artspeak scammers.

Such a theory, while dismantling the modernist arbitrary definition of the arts, can be taken to a scary extreme: Creating robots that could produce art, but with a small caveat: An originator of the artistic idea is still needed to input its conceptual coordinates into the machine, reducing the machine yet again to being the artistic tool of expression, but unburdening man from the effort of applying artistic technique and skill. Such obstacle is being overcome with 'free' artificial intelligence writing aid software, where a central server receives written input from writers all over the globe and could later be able to 'create' books written in the style of any living writer.

In the event of losing such a technology, Man would have completely lost his manual ability to express art using traditional tools and his own hands. But let us put such a bleak scenario back into the drawer, as Schillinger's art theory demonstrates that the artistic 'spark' still eludes any man-made technology, but the *materialization* of this spark is now made much more understandable in scientific terms, thanks to Schillinger's effort. Nothing demonstrates the scientific/mathematical basis of visual arts like 3D design. Complex compositions start with basic geometric shapes, which are then sculpted, refined and detailed through a wide array of technical actions and tools available to the artist, who is also - and in the same manner of the classical masters- a mathematician/anatomist/scientist balancing the logic and magic bustling inside his/her mind, driving the creative pulse from its journey, from a disembodied idea into the realm of the five senses.

Inventiveness can be scientific or artistic (MBA P.7) but artistic genius consists in successfully translating the scientifically immeasurable and elusive creative spark onto the artistic medium, enabling the audience to sense its presence using the earthly, scientifically measurable five senses. Now how do we determine that 'success'? Simply by whether the art creation keeps retaining people's awe and interest long after their initial exposure to it. A 'Classic' is an example of a successful capture of the 'spark' into the finite realm of the senses.

Purpose in Art:

In his 'Varieties of esthetic Experience' chapter, Schillinger warns of the 'disintegration' of art into becoming 'art for art's sake'; unwittingly prophesizing the coming of post-modernism! The earliest forms of musical expression had a purpose; contemplative, religious, therapeutic, magical. As they evolved, they ironically devolved into rigid, formalistic 'dead-end of musical theory & practice' (MBA P.14).

Art, as any creative output, can be ranked. There is mediocre art, there is average art and there is high Art, with an infinity of nuances in between but to achieve Eternity, Art and Science must become one. Ranking is made according to physical and non physical criteria. The physical ones are those measured by the scientific method. The non-physical are the emotional, cultural, or behavioral effects which can more or less, be registered through observation or the examination of the biological impact displayed by the exposed subject -hormonal changes, muscular tension and other physiological manifestations. The physical manifestations recorded while measuring emotional reaction from the exposure to art, only show the 'outward result' of organic affectability. They should not be confused with the *reaction* itself. The disembodied reaction reflects a metaphysical plane involving the spirit animating the living organism. A dead organism is in no way affected by the same exposure to the work of art.

This tells us that the more an art form encapsulates the creative essence of its creator, the more it resonates with the soul of a living organism -there are recorded experiences conducted on the effect of music on living plants- and tuning with its anima.

Careful Planning or Spontaneous Creation?

We see artists once again, in typical Modernist fashion, divided between art as a carefully 'engineered' output or art as a spontaneous creative burst. First, as Schillinger rightfully states, all meaningful art throughout history has been carefully and meticulously planned (MBA P.30), which exposes the notion of 'spontaneous art' as a preposterous idea. The 'engineering' v/s spontaneous art is a non-issue from the outset because it's only with continuity in the mastery of technique and its application that the seasoned artist reaches that level of 'spontaneity' a less trained, less proficient artist has yet to attain.

Mind/body coordination gives the illusion of spontaneity to the casual viewer, but to the discerning audience, this spontaneity is recognized for the artistic virtuosity it actually is. What the casual viewer sees is an artistic ability whose 'spontaneous' qualities are actually *controlled and willed* by the artist, similar to the athlete who makes a record-braking effort look so effortless on TV. Months, years and much sweat and training of mind and body went into this flawless gold medal performance. It is the same with any enduring art.

Architect Donald Ruggles explores the way patterns in nature and architecture affect us in his work *'Beauty, Neuroscience & Architecture'* [BNA]. He goes beyond the emotional first stage of interacting with architecture and art in general. This first level is expanded upon, into a science studying 'the impact of architecture on our brains and well-being [...]: **Neuro-Architectology** (preface by B. Sallick, 2017).

We no longer need to 'assess' art with vague adjectives like 'nice', 'beautiful', or 'interesting'; we can scientifically explain the impact and beauty of the art at hand or its lack thereof.

The Ancient Brain[2]

'Humans, throughout the course of 2.4 million years of adaptive evolution, have developed an ability to recognize visual patterns [in nature] which can subconsciously activate survival (sympathetic) and pleasure (parasympathetic) responses, confirming that art and architecture are schemes of visual patterns and have a direct role to play in our health and well-being '(P.12-13)

So the more architecture and Art are dissociated from nature and its patterns, the more their human audience will grow disoriented, disconnected. Does it surprise anyone that modern generations are the most depressed and medicated, ever? So much for progress.

Pattern, repetition, rhythmic composition, geometric grids, progressions, scale and a myriad other mathematical tools make of Math 'our one and only strategy to understand the complexity of nature' (BNA P.22). The earthly key to our soul is through the one discipline most of us were scared of, in high school: good old pragmatic Math and Geometry.

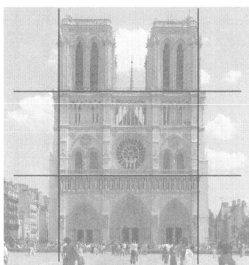

The Notre Dame De Paris cathedral follows th 9-square compositional grid discovered and adopted since the classical period. It is considered to be among the timelessly beautiful buildings in existence. - Original grid study is found in 'Beauty, Neuroscience & Architecture' - D. Ruggles

---

See: 'Beauty, Neuroscience & Architecture' - D. Ruggles (p.12)

Ancient principles of beauty encoded in our sub-conscious (BNA P.45) prove to be cross-cultural, reinforcing Jung's collective unconscious theory. 9-Square grids are used in Asian architecture as well as Arabian or European architecture. Concepts of good and evil are also similarly depicted as in the example of dragons, vampires and mythological creatures sharing cross-cultural similarities mentioned earlier.

With the advent of Modernism as an art movement and Modernity as an ideology, the very notion of art as an intricate practice that bridges the physical with the meta-physical, was upended. The Bauhaus movement, Ruggles states, was obsessed with utilitarianism, an ideology rooted in the industrial revolution of the 1800's. Time and cost were of essence, and a devastated continent needed to be rebuilt post WWI and in record time. Rationalizing the result as 'beautiful' came later...

The Musée des Confluences (Lyon, France)

The above-pictured *Musée des Confluences (Lyon, France)* designed by the architecture firm Coop Himmel-blau represents a clean break with every architectural or artistic tradition, embodying the tabula rasa ideology of modernism. There's not even room to speculate in modernistic relativism on whether the building is beautiful or not; the architect himself was quoted saying *'Ugliness is the next step in the pursuit of beauty'* (BNA P.10).

As late contemporary thinker Roger Scruton demonstrated in his video documentary *'Why Beauty Matters'*, no amount of ArtSpeak could ever succeed in polishing the proverbial modernist turd. Such 'artistic' output cannot survive without continuous media sustain and hype. Buildings with a strictly utilitarian purpose will sooner or later be abandoned, since they do not establish any soulful connection with the people inside them.

Modern Art as a money scam:

Author Brendan Heard briefly mentioned in his 2018 book *'The Decline and Fall of Western Art'* that modern art can and is being used as a way to launder money. The process is a medium/long-term one, meaning that it has a starting phase, a developing phase and a maturation. Here are the basic steps on how it is done:

A-Be a rich, well connected tycoon.

-Organize or go to a contemporary art event.

-Locate any worthless artist whose work you can nonetheless build a solid sales pitch for -the artist is a persecuted minority, or a former junkie, or is 'bravely' championing some deviant sexual agenda, or uses excrements[3] to desecrate religious -preferably christian[4]- relics...
Bonus points if the artist actually masters any technical skill(s).

-Strike a deal with the artist: propose to buy all of their work for a low sum (relatively to you, the tycoon!).

-Agree with the artist to only sell the works to you to simulate scarcity.

B-Meanwhile, build a media buzz about the 'art ist': his/her art works are the first to sell and command huge sums of money, apparently! Any artwork by that artist still 'remaining' in the art gallery, is labeled as 'sold'. This is the development phase of the scam. Hype builds up around the artist, whom, with your connections, is landing prestigious speeches, workshops and 'artschool' teaching/lecturing contracts. Remember that the only criteria for modern art, are shock, irony and price tag. Both con artists,

---

3   See: 'Piss Christ' by andres Serrano.
4   See: 'Holy family' by Juan Davila.

(Modernist artist and their rich patron) are now faithfully applying the shock and irony part.

C-Maturation stage: Buzz has built up sufficiently over a period of 10-15 years; the artist has made enough money through workshops, media coverage, 'art' program lectures and probably a couple of 'publications'. It is now time for you, the tycoon, to organize a few art auctions and sell some of those works you purchased at a trifle, and which you insured for millions.

Now who would actually *buy* those modern 'art' pieces? Quite simply, any gangster who wants to turn dirty money into something which looks much less suspicious, insure it for millions, then burn it and collect the 'clean insurance money'. The gangster could also sell it back to an unsuspecting nouveau riche who wants to look knowledgeable in art. Those simple-minded people see a Basquiat or a Pollock as an 'investment' of sorts. By the time the hype wears off, such works would be recognized for what they really are: blobs of paint and excrement without any artistic or cultural merit. As always in a scam, some people benefit, and some find themselves hoodwinked and looking like fools.

'The Annunciation' (detail), Jan van Eyck, 1435.

Unlike a Monalisa, the subject of this painting is not posing for the artist. He is instead, intensely felt, sourced from beyond tangible reality. The result transcends photography, representational art and reality itself. The composition is planned in its most minute components, with each detail exuding the raging eternal battle that is waged underneath the deceiving calm of the desolate landscape.

Art, science and vision fuse in a work whose idea is simple but powerful: To reflect the paradoxal nature of existence - A king in tattered robes, A storm beneath the calm, Hope in desolation, Power in apparent fragility, Death and Eternity, Heaven and Hell, Temptation and Will...

'Christ In The Wilderness' by Ivan Kramskoi. Oil on Canvas - 1872. 184 cm x 214 cm, Moscow.

Rude Awakening

In an unexpected 'Life imitates Art' twist, humanity finds itself facing an existential challenge in the form of the COVID-19 'pandemic'. We have all seen this scenario play out in horror movies, but never have we thought it would happen in real life, *to us!* – A mysterious illness decimating a divided and panicked humanity. As bands of looters kill each other over the last roll of toilet paper, a dooms-day loon in greasy, torn clothes, screams at the heavens, dirty nails clawing the thin air as he warns of the impend-ing doom awaiting us. People in gas masks hurry, heads down, past the scrawny figure as the government blares its sirens signaling the hour of curfew.

Somewhere, a scientist, or a professor, or just a level-headed adult attempts to control the situation from sliding into total chaos, by organizing their community, drawing plans, imagining scenarios, supervising ration distribution or devising some makeshift defense/safety measure. This lone beacon of sanity is drowned out in the deluge of panic, as the mindless mob is too drunk on mass hysteria to be able to reason or display common sense anymore.

As ideologies of equality and feel-good mentalities crumble in the face of anarchy, it may now be time to sort the good friendships from the fake ones, the grown-up minds from those in arrested development, the reliable from the broken, and reinforce solid friendships and family* ties. Recognize the level-headed leaders and planners among us and form a social nucleus/hierarchy with them.

Governments will seek to take our freedoms un-der the excuse of 'temporary but necessary' or 'emer-gency public health' measures. We should be able to recognize this as probably one of the last real pushes of

*The nuclear family, while essential, is not enough. Sustainable family life is only possible via the extended family, clan or tribe.

Globalism to enslave us under the aegis of 'one benevolent One-World-Government'. One positive aspect of the whole pandemic/market crash/social collapse situation, is the slow but sure public awareness of the non-essential nature of ideologies like social justice, equality, Feminism and assorted Leftist garbage; it's a time for realism, pragmatism and heroism: People are bound to recognize the correct worth of each other, sooner or later.

Times like these (whether orchestrated or completely coincidental, which is doubtful) are the perfect opportunity to establish and consolidate totalitarian, global control. While only mega-corporations can weather and even thrive under prolonged lockdowns, small and medium businesses are killed and bought off cheaply. What better cover for abolishing private property by consolidating it in the hands of the globalist few, than such a manufactured panic? In such times, people are at their most vulnerable; out of their jobs, out of money, out of options. It is the time where we look for guidance and are desperate for help. It is the time where we are ready to relinquish whatever liberties we still enjoy in order to 'stay alive'. In the heat of panic, we are unable to process how someone who advocates for population control is offering us a vaccine so we can survive the 'Pandemic'...

What will our choice be? Complete surrender of will and agency to a so-called benevolent global authority which also happens to be totally anonymous? Or manning up in the presence of danger and defeating it with our determination, discipline, will, responsibility and faith?

CONCLUSION

"Your gut instinct is the purest form of truth that there is [...] doing genius stuff, doing something original will never be built up from things that make logical sense." - James 'Warrior' Hellwig

Despite its finite nature and vulnerability, humanity has two methods to achieve earthly immortality: a physical immortality through reproduction and a spiritual one through knowledge, through creating timeless art, philosophy and culture.

Humans noticed their own fragility in the face of a ruthless nature and learned their place early on. Their intelligence allowed them to devise ingenious technology through which they harnessed the force of the elements and sometimes, in their hubris, they'd think that by shortly using their power, they have conquered them.

The older systems which produced kingdoms, empires, cultures and their subsequent art, science and knowledge, had one common denominator: none of them were egalitarian. All of them were hierarchical. All of them were also religious, whether monotheistic or polytheistic. Their mythology was the cultural expression of their soul. The more they forgot it, the faster their cultures disintegrated. Memory is an essential part of what makes us human. links of memory -otherwise known as traditions- are the essence of what is important to their respective people. Remembering the good and learning from the bad is a basic key to human evolution. Allowing ideologies to undermine the past in the name of 'progress' is an elaborate con job that seduces us with its apparent positivity. It approaches us like a friend and gains our trust.

Hubris is believing that our forefathers were dumb and weak and that we are smarter and abler. Darwinist theory and its 'survival of the fittest' creed helped reinforce the fallacy that the past is bound to be weaker than the current times, giving us a massive morphine shot of narcissism. As this mentality took hold of humanity, it reduced beliefs, traditions and any knowledge predating us to irrelevance and to the level of vain superstition. It is putting Man in the center and measuring everything else with the ruler of the new religion of Man-worship:

Humanism.

By putting Man in the center of the world, humanity is using a standard that is finite, mortal, fallible, and inconsistent, and therefore creating a world of confusion where good and evil are endlessly redefined.

By disconnecting themselves from nature through the blind pursuit of technology for its own sake, people forgot thier initial place as a *part* of nature and not its center. Arrogance made them drift increasingly farther from nature, fabricating crude, unsustainable substitutes for it; confining himself in dull cities and square cubicles, they then estranged themselves from themselves, by declaring war on their own past. This is how Modernity was born; a schism with humanity's own historical, traditional (ie, eternal) past.

The rift did not stop here. In his ideological pursuit for a more 'equal' world, Man further estranged himself from the opposite sex. Feminism and the resulting MGTOW movement are the symptoms of the aggravated condition of humanity: the sexes declaring war on each other! The tools of these ideologies are robbing humanity of its two methods for earthly immortality:
Reproduction and human thought/knowledge to pass on for the generations to come.

Finally, adopting atheistic ideologies, Man is taking the easy choice but a choice nonetheless: to be reduced to one's chemical and mechanistic behaviors and stimuli, completely opposite to the Nietzschean Superman or to the Christian or Hinduist ascetism, where the mind exerts ruthless dictatorship over bodily urges and appetites. Under the banner of 'progress' the people will 'break out' from their theistic shackles. They already fool themselves that this is 'freedom'.

But what inspiring folktales and legends will a god-less society produce and what traditions? What mythology and what heroism? What eternal Art and star-reaching technology can come from a society that touts killing the unborn (the future) as a 'human right' and deliberately neglects the dying old (the past), strictly concerned by its immediate own self? Shaped by utilitarian times and surrounded by convenience, Man is choosing trendy short-term consumables over long-term goals, to his own detriment. The toll on the environment is too great not to notice. The Lord of the Rings' scene of the Ents and Huorns destroying Isengard, is taking an increasingly prophetic mantle. By making the choice to submit to one's impulses and urges rather than be in control of them, Man is relinquishing his capacity to exercise his will. He is giving up all agency by turning away the greatest proof of God: the gift of choice and free will.

END

RETURN TO PHOENICIA

-Dedicated to Guillaume Faye-

The following short fiction is a personal theory and interpretation about the origins of the Phoenician people. Its events initially take place around 20000 BC...

I

Enoch was a loyal servant of Baal, the god of fertility and rebirth. Like his own father and his father before him, Enoch kept the sacred tablets which, according to now distant legends, explained the birth of Enoch's people.

It was Baal who came down to Earth, and resided in that land first. A curious god, he decided to take part in his own creation and, the tablets say, he made of Canaan his home, several millenia before the times of Enoch...

He walked among his people and taught them how to work the earth, grow plants, tame beasts, thrive and prosper. His teachings were handed down to his people on clay tablets, and these tablets were conserved in the temple of Baal by enoch's ancestors.
They contained the secrets to move stones of impossible size and build wondrous citadels, to grow crops, to brew mead, to dye linen, to build sturdy vessels from cedar wood, to communicate in written language and to make music.

Having taught his people as a parent would teach

his children, Baal left the land of Canaan, asking his people to remember his love for them. With this invaluable knowledge, Enoch's people thrived, and were themselves regarded as gods wherever they traveled, because their power was knowledge itself.

Thousands of years passed, and Baal's memory flickered out from the heart of his people. They regarded themselves as gods now and forgot to pay homage to their father, who once walked among them, and taught them how to master the earth's elements. They also forgot the ways of decency, and in their arrogance committed the foulest deeds and rationalized every bit of them. Enoch's faith however, like that of his forefathers, remained pure. As guardian of the temple of Baal, he tended to the temple's needs, kept it in good repair, and offered weekly oblations of bread, mead and a cut of fresh meat from his fattest calf.

One morning, as he was entering the temple, a tall bearded man appeared to him. He did not see him enter and was surprised to find him there. Enoch never saw this man before, but strangely enough, he felt as if he has always known him. His eyes contained the knowledge of aeons. Enoch felt entranced by the presence of this strange man.

-Enoch, he said, I have been waiting for you. Time is short and you have work to do.

Enoch felt his feet giving away and with a mixture of awe and fear, he found out he could not ask the man how he knew his name, as the words died out in his throat.

-Fear not, Enoch, for you are my good son, my beloved, and so I am here to save you and your kin. The rest of my people has gone too far down in their vice. You, however, will start everything anew.

Enoch fell to his knees. My lord, he said. His face kissed the floor, as he understood who was actually with him inside the temple.

-You will now become the vessel of all past knowledge which I once handed down to your forefathers. These clay tablets and the science within, are now embedded in you.

As the bearded figure uttered those words, the clay tablets sitting on the temple's altar crumbled into dust before Enoch's horrified eyes. In that same instant, Enoch felt his entire being submerged with a warm energy, as if every element of nature was transferring the key to its substance into Enoch's consciousness. *'And now you will need to build a strong ship for you and your family, for I will bring a great flood and smother all human life from the face of this earth'.*

The tall figure continued:

The flood will last 49 days, so bring enough food for you and your tribe to last you that long.

'My lord, Enoch uttered, once the 49 days are over, and if all life is smothered from the earth, how will we survive then?

-'You do not need to take more than what I have instructed you to take, as once the 49 days are over, animals will repopulate the earth, but you, your family and their kin, will be the only people left.

Then the tall man added: *'The vessel is to be built upon the roof of your home. The flood will be upon you within 2 moons. Go and gather your children and their kin, Enoch, my son.*

'Lord Baal!'

But the bearded man was no longer in the temple, night has already fallen and Enoch was alone.

It seemed as if the encounter barely lasted a few minutes. Enoch felt an immense knowledge imparted to him, swarming his head and drowning his being. But unlike the suffocating feeling of real drowning, It was a peaceful and protective feeling, as if being in the maternal womb, but completely conscious of it.

Enoch came out of the temple. A dark night enveloped Sur, and no moon or stars shone in the firmament. His meeting with Baal lasted the entire day as incalculable and ancient knowledge was transferred into Enoch's being, by the one who once walked the young earth.

Many mocked Enoch as he started building his vessel on the roof of his stone house upon the hill, and nobody noticed the missing tablets in the temple... He kept working on his task and paying weekly tribute on the day of *shams*, at the temple of Baal.

Then the flood came.

A great crack was heard in the city of Sur and half the sea wall fell into the ocean. Terror filled the hearts as the ground kept shaking for endless minutes, and houses crumbled upon their dwellers. Roads caved in and the streets became a terrible scene of bedlam as shameless looting and acts of madness immediately took place all while helpless people lay dying.

Then all movement stopped as a continuous humming sound was heard. The humming became a rumble, a sonic wave engulfing the city. The people raised their heads to the sky but there were no clouds. No thunder, and yet the rumbling noise was getting louder. Then the people of Sur looked towards the source of the hum...

A great wall of water was racing towards the city of Sur, extanding through the entire horizon. A massive gray line that was growing thicker and taller as the minutes passed. The citizens of Sur were paralyzed with terror as if their feet were nailed to the ground, and their wide eyes remained locked to the inexorably approaching wall of watery death. The rumble became a sustained thunder and the people of Sur had their hands upon their ears, and screaming their horror at the rushing wall coming at them from the sea.

Enoch and his children looked in horror from the deck of their vessel, perched on top of their house, as the ocean engulfed the city of Sur in a matter of minutes...

Enoch counted the days as his ship sailed a rainy sea with no sign of life in any direction.

Then on the morning of the 42nd day, he found himself sailing between two mountains, as if in a great peaceful river. The river meandered like a serpent, as the ship kept its serene voyage, surrounded by verdant mountains from which the song of birds could now be heard.

-'It is as Baal has said: The earth's animals have returned to the forests. We shall not starve!' Then Enoch turned towards his family: 'We will call this the Shuf river. Because after endless days of torment, we finally see the Lord's face shining upon us to show us the way!'

Then on the 49th morning, as Enoch was preparing to give thanks to Baal on the day of *Shams*, his vessel hit the soft wet earth and halted.

Enoch and his tribe exited the boat and gave homage to Baal on dry land for their safe journey: "This land which we have reached, this paradise between the mountains, it will be called Baal-Bek! for Baal is our leader and has guided us to safety", he rejoiced.

Baal-Bek became a prosperous and rich city, as Enoch, with the knowledge given to him at the temple, built a greater temple in tribute to Baal, and a splendid city in his honor. Baal-Bek, a fertile land protected by mountains from both sides, enjoyed an opening to the sea from which Enoch's tribe went forth again to repopulate the Earth.

II

The doorbell rang, jolting the old man from his lonely stupor. He has received no visit for two years now, and was beginning to finally enjoy it. He went groggily to the door and shot the young man standing outside with a malevolent stare through the cracked opening.

-"Dr. Paul Castle?"

"Who is asking?"

-"Are you the Scientist, Dr Castle? Excuse me sir, but it was difficult finding..."

"YES I am the EX-scientist. EX-historian. EX-everything! Now what do you want?", grumbled the professor. The delivery man, apparently told to expect the professor's eccentric demeanor, remained unfazed, handing him an envelope:

-"Uhm, I have here an invitation for you, sir. From Stormcrow Enterprises. Mr. Stormcrow requests the pleasure of your presence and wanted you to receive his invitation.In person. He said he would not take no for an answer. He'd also have a private plane ready for you. It's on Tuesday. In 2 days. 'Scuse the short notice."

Paul Castle's interest was peaked all the way up, but he camouflaged it with a neutral tone while flipping through the invitation; "I've always wondered how Stormcrow did become the instant celebrity he is now... Despite his youth!"

- "Indeed, he's 42, sir", said the messenger enthusiastically, "Well sir, Mr stromcrow is a genius in computer programming. Made his fortune in cryptocurrencies while still in college, then not being one to put his eggs in the same basket, he diversified his investments into everything from ores, to renewables, to agriculture, real estate shipping, art and of course programming, registering 200 patents in computer programming last year *alone. One wonders if this guy ever sleeps at all!"*. He paused to catch his breath.

"Some people are allergic to sleep", Castle absently responded, without taking his eyes off the strange invitation.

III

Dr Paul Castle stood on a busy street outside the Stormcrow Enterprises highrise. At 60, he still traveled light and carried a small backpack. A man in a ball cap appeared as if out of nowhere and gestured him into the building. He was taken into a key-operated private elevator which seemed to go into the depths of the Earth for what seemed like a full minute. The doctor found himself in an immense, well ventilated room where an army of artists were busy making exact replicas of what he quickly recognized to be world renowned art works. He stood next to an Asian painter making a Caravaggio replica that could not be differentiated from the original. In a corner, a large machine with robotic hands and a belt chain wheel system not unlike a tank's, seemed to be sculpting a large block of white marble.

-"*Mr stormcrow will join you shortly,sir*", the ball cap man announced. But Paul Castle was slack-jawed before another Asian sculptor executing a flawless Bernini. He did not notice the tall man appearing next to him two minutes later, startling him:

-"*Dr. Castle! I hope you had a pleasant trip, welcome to my workshop!*"

"Mr Stormcrow', Paul said with a smile, 'I... don't understand... Why would someone like you be making replicas when you could just go and buy the Louvre?" And before the mildly amused stare of his host, he continued, "Especially since everything's up for sale today in Europe. Half the damn thing now belongs to Arab princes.
And why am I here anyway?"

- Please call me John! 'Excellent observations. You don't maneuver and go straight to the point. No bullshit, and I like that! You are here because the world is ending.'

Castle was caught off-guard with the seemingly outlandish response: "Haha, what?"

-"I had to narrow it down but that was maybe too narrowed down. Let me explain:

Of course you have heard of the wave of politically motivated removal and destruction of valuable pieces of historical art. Many instances of the most backwards vandalism have happened here in the US, but mainly in Europe, and elsewhere in the Middle East. Invaluable pieces of knowledge have been forever lost to us due to 'enlightened' mobs of -ironically- college students torching and destroying everything they perceived as 'unequal', 'patriarchal', 'classical', 'aristocratic', 'undemocratic', 'triggering', 'oppressive' or 'fascist', whatever the heck that means to these apes. And the police forces already have too much on their hands in terms of immigrant waves storming their borders to care about a few art pieces torn down or vandalized. Fortunately we have anticipated and prevented several such works from organized vandalism - because let me tell you, those zombies cannot be acting out of their own accord. Someone must be organizing them. Someone who benefits from the world crashing into a mass of controllable drones with absolutely no agency. And so, through our agents strategically placed in many museums and libraries, we have smuggled out as many valuable pieces as we could, had them replicated by human artists or by machines, then returned the replicas to the museums while the originals were hidden and secured from the vandals'.

Stormcrow made a brief pause, *"Last week, when the mobs destroyed the London National museum, 90% of its* contents were already replicas...The Louvre, by the way, is now 75% replicas. Chen, whose Caravaggio you were admiring, achieved the masterful Mona Lisa which has been replacing the original for 8 years now...' Stormcrow was visibly amused by the look of his visitor and was enjoying his own storytelling.

Paul Castle was a living statue, assimilating and processing the hail of information that his host was raining on him. Stormcrow chuckled:

-"What? You think the Salvator Mundi which was sold to the Saudi prince in 2017, is the original? Hah!
Do you smoke?" Stormcrow concluded while proferring a box of cigarillos.

Castle dumbly took a cigarillo and absently lodged it between his lips as Jonathan Stormcrow deftly produced a lighter, "So why am I doing this, you might ask."

And before the inquisitive but captivated stare of the professor, Stormcrow continued; "quite simply, as I stated earlier, because the world is ending. Not in the final, biblical 'floods and volcanoes' sense, but this current cycle is drawing to a close. The world, Dr. Castle - by the way, can I call you Paul?- is -in computer terms- about to reset. And to successfully reset, we need seed knowledge. Or else, the end will effectively turn biblical, which means, final.

-"But why come to me, Mr... Uh, John? i'm a dis-credited historian. A disgraced scientist!"

-"You were persecuted for advancing the theory that Baal-bek, the ancient Phoenician city was a coastal city, while today, it sits in the middle of nowhere, in an arid plain and so your theory produced a tsunami of disbelief in the scientific spheres which quickly degenerated into a gigantic spasm of mockery, followed by violent denial for a heap of political, religious and social reasons. The thing is, I see sense in your the-ory, and based on many researches done about the Baalbek region, everything points out to the fact that this region was the birthplace of the very first agricultural community and civilization.

Stormcrow paused to draw on his cigarillo before continuing, *"I've brought you here to tell you that i want to test your theory -and my faith in it- by financing it. You will be leading an archeological excavation in Baal-bek to find the original city buried under the Jupiter temple and later Roman vestiges, and discover the knowledge which lies underneath, and which holds the secrets to move gigantic stones like the famed trilithon, build terrific palaces, and grow crops when nobody knew how to do that. In short, dear Paul, we're securing whatever knowledge we can save from this dying world, and we're out to unearth the oldest knowledge that the Canaanites used to become the first architects, the first farmers, the first shipwrights and the pioneers of the written word!*

The professor was struggling to keep track of the information Stormcrow was throwing at him and was wondering if this whole encounter was some filmed prank to further humiliate and discredit him. Curiosity getting the best of him, he decided to play along:

- "But even a wealthy philantropist like yourself will need to mobilize huge amounts of liquidity to fund such a -excuse the term, but I mean it as a compliment- crazy venture!"

-*"I appreciate the compliment, prof', and you're right, this project requires massive funding, and the people are providing it"*, Said Stormcrow enigmatically, and under Castle's helplessly questioning gaze, he added: *"Follow me, professor. You'll soon understand"*. Another one-minute elevator trip, then the doors opened on what Paul Castle guessed to be a computer lab; an enormous facility of servers and laptops with flickering screens. Both men wandered amid the forest of screens, then Castle broke the silence: "Unmanned computers?" Then looking closer at the screens, he saw they were invariably social media profiles that automatically updated themselves with new content.

The professor faced John Stormcrow: "So you hack into people's Instagram and Youtube accounts to divert their revenues", he scowled. "OK... Clever". Stormcrow's eyes flickered with a spark of amusement: *"Professor, none of these influencer accounts are real. Every one of them is a hyperrealistic 3-D model, flawlessly textured and impossible to differenciate from real life human models",* And before the professor's round-eyed look, he continued, *"And every beta male and impressionable female is paying premium cash to follow platitude-spewing models who are actually computer-generated".*

Stormcrow briefy paused, with the cigarillo between his exposed teeth. Castle thought he looked like a young Clint Eastwood with shoulder-long hair, a futuristic cowboy standing in a wasteland of computers. *"The genius who made this happen', Stormcrow continued, ' is an old school friend and current partner. He composed the 3-D texture and model library and I wrote the procedural script. We can create perfectly accurate human avatars from the library's unlimited combinational possibilities".* Stormcrow pointed his cigarillo toward a door at the end of the computer lab. A panel on the dark brushed metal door spelled a single name:

"Morpheus".

"You'll get to meet him later, as his skills will be vital to your mission, professor!"

Paul Castle almost forgot the purpose of his presence at the Stormcrow building and stated, with a toneless, drifting voice "The lost keys to civilization"...

-*"The FIRST civilization, Dr. Castle!",* cheerily echoed Stormcrow's voice. Pulling on the last of his smoke then tossing it into a bin, he calmly stared at his visitor- *"Hopefully dear professor, we'll be finding those keys in time. I do believe we have the technology to unlock this still hidden knowledge. What better seed knowledge to reboot Humanity with, than the wisdom of the ancients?"*

-To be continued

Enoch, High priest of Baal

BIBLIOGRAPHY

1-"Whitey on the Moon: Race, Politics, and the death of the U.S. Space Program", 1958 - 1972' -2014- Paul Kersey.

2-"Homosexuality and American Psychiatry: The Politics of Diagnosis" -1981- Ronald Bayer.

3-"The Culture of Critique: An Evolutionary Analysis of Jewish Involvement in Twentieth-Century Intellectual and Political Movements" -2002- Kevin MacDonald.

4-"The Barbarian Bible: The True History of Man Since the Fall of Troy" -2013- Ianto Watt.

5-"Aa-1025: The Memoirs of a Communist's infiltration in to the Church"- 2009 Marie Carré.

6- "The Catholic Church and the Cultural Revolution" -Fidelity Press - 2016- E. Michael. Jones.

7- "The Story of Philosophy" -Simon & Schuster- 1952- Will Durant

8- "Multiculturalism and the Politics of Guilt" -University of Missouri Press -2003- P.E. Gottfried.

9-"The Babylonian Talmud: Tractates Gittin-Abhodah Zarah-Sanhedrin-Yebamoth (English/Hebrew edition) - 1976- Soncino Press- Epstein.

10-"God's Bankers: A History of Money and Power at the Vatican" -Simon & Schuster -2015- Gerald Posner.

11- '"Qabale, Qliphoth et Magie Goétique" -Chronos- 2017- Thomas Karlsson.

12-"A House of Many Mansions" -I B Tauris & Co Ltd - New edition 2005- Kamal Salibi.

13- "Carthage: Fact & Myth"- Sidestone Press -2015- Docter, . Boussoffara, Keurs.

14- "The Mathematical Basis of The Arts" - Philosophical Library; First Edition -1948- J. Schillinger

15- "Beauty, Neuroscience, and Architecture: Timeless Patterns and Their Impact on Our Well-Being" - Fibonacci, LLC -2018- D. Ruggles.

16- "The Decline & Fall of Western Art" - CreateSpace Independent Publishing- 2018- Brendan P. Heard.

17- "Imperium" -Wermod and Wermod Publishing Group; Annotated edition- 2013- F.P. Yockey

18- "The Holy Bible" KJV -Hendrickson Publishers, Inc -2006 edition.

Made in the USA
Las Vegas, NV
25 October 2021